CULTURAL DYNAMICS AND STRATEGIES OF THE INDIAN ÉLITE (1870–1947)

Centre de Sciences Humaines (Centre for Social Sciences and Humanities): Created in New Delhi in 1990 the CSH, is part of the network of research centres of the French Ministry of Foreign Affairs. The Centre's research work in primarily oriented towards the study of issues concerning the contemporary dynamics of development in India and South Asia. The activities of the Centre are focused on four main themes, namely: Economic growth and sustainable development, International and regional relations, Institutional structures and political constructions of identity and Urban dynamics.

Centre de Sciences Humaines, 2, Aurangzeb Roab, New Delhi 110011, India, Tel: (91) 11 3041 00 70, Fax: (91 11) 3041 00 79
E-mail: public@csh-delhi.com
Website: http://www.csh-delhi.com

Institut Français de Pondichéry (French Institute of Pondicherry): Created in 1955, the IFP is a multidisciplinary research and advanced educational institute. Major research works are focusing on Sanskrit and Tamil languages and literatures—in close collaboration with the Ecole Française d'Extrême-Orient—ecosystems, biodiversity and sustainability, dynamics of population and socio-economic development.

(Institut Français de Pondichéry, 11, Saint Louis Street, PB 33
Pondicherry 605001, Tel: (91) 413 2334 168
Fax: (91) 413 2339 534
E-mail: ifpdir@ifpindia.org

Cultural Dynamics and Strategies of the Indian Élite (1870–1947)

Indo-French Relations during the Raj

SAMUEL BERTHET

CENTRE DE SCIENCES HUMAINES
2006

First published 2006

ISBN 81-7304-717-0

Published by
Ajay Kumar Jain *for*
Manohar Publisher & Distributors
4753/23 Ansari road, Daryaganj
New Delhi 110 002

Typeset by
Ajay Art
Delhi-110006

Printed by
Lordson Publishers Pvt. Ltd.
Delhi 110 007

Distributed in South Asia by

FOUNDATION
BOOKS

4381/4, Ansari Road
Daryaganj, New Delhi 110 002
and its branches at Mumbai, Hyderabad,
Bangalore, Chennai, Kolkata

Contents

Acknowledgements

I would like to thank Jacques Weber for his patience and trust. He supervised the extensive PhD thesis that inspired this book. Jacques Pouchepadass has also provided me with valuable support during the writing of this book. Indeed his faith in me has always been a source of encouragement. Pierre Amado and Pierre Singaravelou have also made immense contributions with their perceptive comments.

Joël Ruet and Véronique Dupont must also be thanked for their support, as well as Dominique Girard and Maud Girard-Geslan.

In addition, I have also discovered significant works, largely due to the cooperation of Sylvain Lévi's family. In that regard, a special mention must be made of Catherine Vermeil, as well as of Jacques Cloarec for granting me access to Alain Danielou's papers and archives. I would also like to thank all the archive centres, from where the materials have been gathered and particularly the archive centre of the Ministry of the External Affairs in Nantes, but also in the Quai d'Orsay (Paris), Rabindra Bhavan (Santiniketan), the British Library (London), the Alliance française de Paris, the Société des Missions-Étrangères (Paris), the Jésuites de la Province de France (Vanves), the university library and the municipal library (Rennes).

The ongoing work of Pierre Singaravelou reinforced the fact that I was searching in the right direction, which is always a relief. The scholarly interest of Hari Vasudevan was another considerable boost.

Neela Majumdar and Myriam Rasiwala must also be acknowledged for their wonderful translation of this book. And, of course, Siddharth Chowdhury's professionalism is much appreciated.

Last, but not the least, special thanks are also due to Attreyee Roy Chowdhury for an extremely efficient and classy work, which involves the transformation of manuscripts into actual books.

SAMUEL BERTHET

Introduction

France and India have had an interaction extending over three centuries. Yet relations between the two countries are still marked by mutual ignorance. Indeed, this contradiction constitutes what could be called the 'Franco-Indian paradox'. The reasons behind what Roger-Pol Droit calls *l'oubli de l'Inde* (India's forgotten) from a philosophical point of view which he assesses as being a twentieth-century phenomenon, can be understood through historical analysis: '*Je suis convaincu que si l'on veut voir changer quelque peu la situation, il faut retraverser, autrement, tout un réseau historique. Aller fouiller, longtemps. . . .*'[1] (I am persuaded that if one wants to see any changes in the situation, it will be necessary to go through the entire historical background in a different way—sift through it for a long time. . . .)

The impact of the exchanges between India and France have been instrumental in the making of the mental and institutional framework of both countries. While relations have been well analysed for the period that saw French expansion in India during the seventeenth and the eighteenth centuries, relations between the two countries have almost totally been ignored for the crucial years from the 1870s to Indian independence. This is an odd omission for a period that saw the concept of nationalism gaining momentum both countries. This period also saw a definite shift in French foreign policy and the fate of an important part of the population of the world, i.e. the people under the British Raj, and Princely states taking an equally decisive turn.

The appropriation of French culture by the Indian élite is one of the most astonishing cultural shifts of our modern age. It is also a clear indication of the assimilation of the colonizers' attributes by the Indian élite, by stepping into the colonizers' cultural environment, intruding further than the boundaries that the former established for the latter. In this sense, the history of French culture in India undeniably constitutes an important aspect of the changing relationship between the Indian nationalist élite and Great Britain. In this book, we shall examine briefly only one part of the problematic raised in the context of a study that is much wider in scope.[2] The study focuses on the role of institutions and the complex interplay of multilateral relations that affected cultural relations the world over towards the end of the nineteenth century. Cultural, scientific, and technical relations between these two nations were marked by several turning points through the nineteenth and twentieth centuries. These events have remained largely unknown, even to this day. The analysis offered here supports a vision of an uneven history of colonialism. A study of the role of intermediate actors like France as well as Germany and the United States in the face-to-face colonizer–colonized interaction between Great Britain and India reveals new perspectives and opens up areas for further and more nuanced interpretations.

France and India had been in direct contact with each other since the seventeenth century through trade relations. In the eighteenth century, the French bourgeoisie fell under the spell of Indian textiles, and Indian techniques became a source of inspiration for French manufacturers.[3] The Indian peninsula was described as the 'land of great wealth'.[4] Relations between the two countries were not limited solely to trade, for two different civilizations had come into contact with each other. From the end of the eighteenth century to the middle of the nineteenth century, India occupied a growing space in intellectual debates in France, taking concrete form in the creation of a Sanskrit chair at the Sorbonne in 1814, for instance. India and its cultural heritage were the focus of research, including the origins of languages and religions. The Romantics who put India on a pedestal adopted the country as one of their favourite themes and regarded the Indian subcontinent as the cradle of human culture and civilization.[5]

At the same time, in India, the assimilation of Western culture became a prerequisite for access to an élite social status. Was it through unconscious imitation, or was it an effort to appropriate an instrument of power? Whatever may be the case, Western culture was embraced by an increasing number of the Indian élite thanks to the influence of the British. That is how the Indian élite was introduced to French culture. Toru Dutt, a young Bengali wrote a novel in French as early as the 1870s. In 1886, following the recognition of French in university curricula, Bombay's Parsee students set-up a French Club. These two events were important milestones in India's road to 'Francophonie' (French as a world language) in the subcontinent.

At the same time, a socially well-placed Indian community had settled down in France. In 1907, a few members of this community presented the world with the earliest known versions of the Indian national flag in Paris.[6] On his part, Sylvain Lévi, the leader of French Indology of that time collaborated with Tagore in connection with Santiniketan. There were several such examples that attested to the extent of cultural relations between the two countries. Today, it seems necessary to take a second look at the ups and downs in the history of Franco-Indian cultural relations both in order to understand the contemporary culture of the Indian élite and to try and comprehend the collective unconscious of the French.[7]

The different forms of France's cultural presence in India must be examined through the various initiatives taken—most often by members of the Indian élite themselves. The reasons behind the Indian élite's interest in and desire to promote French culture seem to have nothing to do with the French government's policy decisions. Colette Khan describes the situation in these words:

> Regardless of France's efforts to export its image, language and culture, India inherited its own tradition of French studies from the colonial era, combining indigenous socio-cultural parameters and complex educational objectives in its own way [. . .]. By taking an interest in

French civilisation and, as a corollary, in its language, the subcontinent's inhabitants saw it rather as an evolutionary dimension of their own culture, in keeping with a world vision that the English language had been building for them for a century and a half.[8]

The interest in French culture of a section of the Indian élite and the fact of its presence in an environment dominated by the Anglo-Saxon factor need to be examined, while keeping in mind any possible contradictions between this dynamic and French policies.

The appropriation of French culture by Indian élites had two motives. The first one was part of their endeavour to familiarize themselves with Western customs and the ingredients or elements of modern culture. The second was an integral part of the making of social rituals by new élites seeking to establish their dominance over Indian society according to the modes of enforcement described by Pierre Bourdieu in *Langage et pouvoir symbolique.*[9] This interpretation is supported by the reactions of British authorities to the spread of French language and the exclusiveness they displayed in their French-speakers' association, La Société des Amis de la France dans l'Inde britannique (The Society of Friends of France in British India), based in Simla.

'CULTURE': EVOLUTIONS AND IMPLICATIONS

Culture bears intrinsically these two antagonistic facets: a creative one and a political one. The word 'culture' is borrowed from the Latin 'cultura'. The etymology of the word 'culture' reflects the development of human society itself; 'agriculture' in the sense of 'ploughed field, cultivated and sowed land', 'cult' in the sense of worship, and culture as the 'development of one's intellectual faculties through appropriate exercises', have common origins.[10] It was at the end of the eighteenth century, under Kant's influence, that the notion of 'civilisation envisaged in its intellectual aspects' was integrated into the term 'culture'. The notion of culture was to take on different nuances in meaning from the end of the nineteenth century. In the twentieth century, the term first took on an ethnological and anthropological definition, to indicate 'all acquired forms of behaviour in human societies', particularly through Mauss's influence. In 1907, the adjective 'cultural' was seen to have the meaning of 'relating to religious culture'. In 1927, the word acquired a general meaning. In the 1950s, under the influence of the English language, the meaning 'relating to acquired forms of behaviour' was attributed to it, particularly under Bourdieu's influence. Bourdieu underlined the use of language and culture by various institutions and by the élites as a mechanism for social reproduction, highlighting the importance of sociological factors in patterns of cultural construction. At the same time, post-colonial studies uncovered the complex relationships between the mutual influences involved in the major cultural patterns that developed in the course of the nineteenth and twentieth centuries, such as the notions of East and West. As for postmodern studies, they underline the importance of culture in the complex and polymorphous identity-building strategies of various groups in each society. Thus, the notion of culture in its different forms covers a vast semantic field, with several implications.

The construction of a modern society by Indian élites followed the cultural warp laid by the country's colonial rulers and they appropriated it. The development of French culture was both the product of and an active element in this process of assimilation/emancipation. The appropriation of French culture undoubtedly included an element of unconscious imitation, highlighted both by Colette Khan with regard to the Indian élite and French culture. Furthermore, French culture also played a role in constructing social customs and rituals and institutions for the social reproduction of a new, élite emerging on the social scene. However, there are certain specificities in the history of French culture in India in the nineteenth and twentieth centuries that make it difficult to confine it to established theoretical frameworks. Indeed, French culture enjoyed an autonomous existence in relation to British colonial power—at least, it existed outside the Raj—and was not an indispensable factor in the upward social mobility of India's modern élite. The development of a certain affinity with French culture among the Indian élite was part of an empowering strategy *vis-à-vis* a political and economic power that was establishing its dominance through the control and spread of culture—an objective that was formulated clearly in Macaulay's famous 'Minutes'. The interest in French culture formed part of the process of appropriating a narrative capacity, which—as Edward Said demonstrates—was closely linked to that of nation building.[11] Indeed, the development of Francophilia and Francophonie in India was part of this very movement for the acquisition of narrative power, which in turn was related to the process of building the Indian nation. This explains the very harsh response of the Raj to the spread of French language and culture in India and the virulence of Anglo-Indian Gallophobic propaganda. The fact that the Indian élite assimilated Anglo-Saxon language and culture to such a degree that in the nineteenth century it produced English literature of the highest quality—which was even recognized internationally as early as 1913 by a Nobel Prize—was evidence of the defiance by Indians living under the Raj, against their rulers. The fact that the same élite proved itself capable of appropriating the attributes of Western élites—for whom French language and culture constituted a sign of distinction at the time—is highly revealing of the degree of empowerment that was then taking place.

'CULTURE' AND 'CIVILIZATION'

The formalization of the notion of culture by power centres was only strengthened further if they harboured imperialistic designs. When that happened, this kind of formalization could take the form of large-scale projects that could sometimes even take on a messianic guise, under the cover of universalism. Such was the case with Great Britain in India in the nineteenth century and the first half of the twentieth century. This was also the case with France, with reference to which Salon rightly speaks of its cultural messianism. Indeed, France expressed its imperialistic designs through universalist ideals. Its imperial ambitions were supported by military, administrative, economic, and cultural actions. However, for obvious reasons of power relationships, these actions were limited to specific areas of the world from which India was excluded. Apart from the five French trading posts in India, it was essentially the universalist values of French culture that came to the attention of the Indian élite. These were more often than not expressed through French books translated into English, but also at times in their original versions, by the nineteenth century. Although the importance of the role played by the few direct contacts between representatives of French culture and the Indian élite—whether Tagore or R.D. Tata—also has to be considered, the appropriation of French culture by the Indian élite essentially took place through indirect contacts, on the basis of a voluntary and autonomous approach with regard to France's cultural actions. Furthermore, the appropriation of French culture placed a special emphasis on the values of freedom and liberation emanating from the country's revolutionary tradition, and against the French colonial policies being implemented at the time. Indeed, that may well constitute one of the reasons for the warm relations between France and India, through the images that they had built of each other and to which they clung, rather than through the development of relations based on any real mutual understanding. Nonetheless, there is at least one occurrence of direct conflict between the two 'messianic cultures', through their most prominent representatives, Rabindranath Tagore and Sylvain Lévi. This controversy underlined the difficulties arising from the semantic proximity of the notions of *culture* and *civilization*. Albert Salon observes in his study on France's cultural actions in the world:

> It is not surprising that certain concepts, such as those of 'culture' and 'civilisation', which affect the very essence of collective personalities and identities, have triggered controversies—even full-fledged philosophical disputes.

Indeed, the importance of this remark can clearly be seen in the context of the Franco-Indian dialogue, as the content ascribed to the terms 'civilization' and 'culture' has been both the subject of fruitful dialogue and deep misunderstanding. On the one hand, the collaboration between the élites of the two countries through the concept of *Grande Inde* (Greater India), in which the two personalities played an instrumental role, was used to reassess the French messianic cultural message and, on the other hand, it contributed in turn to the building of an Indian cultural message. But apart from the areas of common interest, conflicting interpretations were inevitable, especially for two deeply committed intellectuals. Moreover, the *cultural* and *civilizational* debate could not be separated from the political context.

NOTES

1. R.-P. Droit, *L'Oubli de l'Inde*, Paris: PUF, 1989, p. 204. He wrote elsewhere: 'This history is long muddled, made [up] of encounters and side steps'.
2. S. Berthet, 'La culture française en Inde de 1870 à 1962: présences et actions. Dynamiques indiennes et politique française', thesis under the direction of Prof. Jacques Weber, Nantes University, 2002.
3. G. Deleury, *Les Indes florissantes: anthologie des voyageurs français, 1750–1820*, S.E. Idris Hassan Latif (préf.), Paris: Laffont, 1991.
4. P. Haudrere, G. le Bouedec, *Les Compagnies des Indes*, Rennes: ed. Ouest France, 1999.
5. A. Okada, *L'Inde du 19ème siècle, voyage aux sources de l'imaginaire*, Marseille: AGEP, 1991; J. Assayag, 'Aurore et crépuscule de l'Eve indienne: l'imaginaire de la danseuse de temple entre Théophile Gautier et Pierre Loti', in D. Lombard (ed.), *Rêver l'Asie*, Paris: EHESS, 1993, pp. 251–67.
6. S.C. Sarkar (1955), *Hindustan Handbook*, Calcutta: M.C Sarkar & Son, p. 139.
7. Roger-Pol Droit also wrote: 'le cas de la France constitue un exemple sigulier. Il accentue les paradoxes de cet oubli (de l'Inde)', (The case of France is a very particular one. It brings out the paradoxes of this neglect) R.-P. Droit (1989), *L'Oubli de l'Inde*, p. 20.
8. C. Khan, *État et développement des études françaises dans the monde indien: l'exemple de la province musulmane du Bengale*, Thèse de littérature et civilisation française de doctorat de 3ème cycle, sous la direction L. de Versini, Université de Nancy II, 1984, p. 1.

9. P. Bourdieu, *Langage et pouvoir symbolique*, Paris: Seuil, 2001.
10. A. Rey (dir.), *Robert, Dictionnaire historique de la langue française*, vol. II, Paris: Robert, 1998, pp. 974–5.
11. Edward Said, *Culture and Imperialism*, London: Vintage, 1993, pp. xii–xiii.

CHAPTER 1

The British in India and French Culture

The stand taken by British society in India may seem somewhat contradictory. From the public point of view, anti-French propaganda was deployed constantly, in particular through the press, but also through educational institutions. This is not surprising as the opposition to Catholic France had been and was still by the second half of the nineteenth century a constitutive element of British identity and assertion as a nation.[1] However, in private, the British did not hesitate to display their love for French language and culture, even turning it into an attribute, as long as Indians were excluded, as was practically always the case. For instance, this is seen clearly functioning of in Simla, in the La Société des Amis de la France dans l'Inde britannique (The Society of Friends of France in British India). But was that really a contradiction? Indeed, it had more to do with the strategy of excluding the means of narration referred to by Said—more specifically, the means of narrating modernity, for which French culture was a vehicle at the time, with all its emancipatary potential. The British stand *vis-à-vis* French culture sheds light on the difference between the positions taken by the colonizers in their own country and in their colony, the difference between the perceptions of their own interests (teaching French was considered useful in Great Britain) and those of the people they governed in their empire (teaching French was considered pointless and even dangerous in India).

ANTI-FRENCH PROPAGANDA: FEAR, HATRED, OR STRATEGY?

In the last quarter of the nineteenth century, the effects of the progress made by the press in India were also contradictory.

More than ever before, newspapers had become a tool of propaganda for the British authorities, who used them in order to strengthen their rule over India by controlling the flow of information both domestically and with the outside world. They also worked together to forge a national opinion that weighed more and more heavily on India's political life. Apart from the main press establishments that were in the hands of the British authorities, the latter also controlled Reuters, the only news agency in India. Thus, François Bérard remarked on the impact of the press as early as the beginning of the 1880s, even before the Indian National Congress[2] was founded. The use of the press was also central to the activities of the Maratha nationalist, Bal Gangadhar Tilak. It was in this framework that the British authorities launched their propaganda—if not their rhetoric—against France, essentially in order to assert their power in the eyes of Indians. Their extremely virulent Gallophobic propaganda was aimed at discrediting the power of France in the world, especially when the latter relaunched its expansionist policy, in particular in Asia.

In November 1898, the Consul General of France in Calcutta noticed the following in a newspaper: 'Had England not been so excessively complacent towards France in West Africa, the extent of French possessions there would have been much less.

During the Fashoda dispute, the Anglo-Indian press raised a public outcry. With reference to the Upper Nile issue, the Consul at the time noted a: '. . . particularly violent and aggressive tone that can be heard daily in the assessments made by the British press in India on the subject of the occupation of Fashoda by Commander Marchand.

He quoted an extract from an article:

> In fact, Egypt is presently under a protectorate of Great Britain and will remain so despite protests from an envious and powerless nation. We will surely be victorious; all we need now is to want that victory. There are no doubts as to the outcome of a war. After losing Alsace and Lorraine, this time France will lose its colonies, beginning with Pondicherry and Chandernagore, which the Government of India need only stretch its hand to pluck.

According to him, the attacks by the Anglo-Indian press were a means used by the British authorities to assert their supremacy over the Indian people:

All this bragging is essentially aimed at impressing the Indian people, in whose eyes England had, until now, been able to project a certain predominance with regard to other European powers. We cannot be sure that the Indian people have allowed themselves to be bamboozled by these rantings, which are without any doubt too loud not to seem presumptuous and not to hide—behind a certain audacity—the fear of complications from which Great Britain (because of its multiple responsibilities that call for action in various parts of the world) would have more to lose than gain.

Where necessary, the press did not hesitate to use deliberate falsehoods: 'For a long time now, the British have been spreading the ridiculous story among the Burmese that the reason why no more French ships are coming is that the British have taken them all from us.'

Statements of this kind confirm that the Anglo-Indian authorities, through their attacks against France in the press, were trying to convince the Indians that there was no alternative to their domination in a world where the British Crown was the only reigning power.

Moreover, impelled by political developments in the country and the fear of a Russian invasion—fomented by the British authorities, Anglo-Indian opinion not only expressed its desire to control all of Indian territory more openly, but also to eliminate foreign enclaves that offered refuge to all those who revolted against British authority.[3] Thus, the *Englishman* published an article on 12 November 1898 entitled 'The capture of Chandernagore: A thrilling episode', which described the taking over of the trading post and the triumphant entry of the British forces before the submissive French authorities: 'It was a bloodless victory. A triumphant entry of the allied forces, the raising of the Union Jack.'[4]

While the Fashoda episode had exacerbated feelings on all sides and provoked malicious comments, the Consul—disappointed that the settlement of the issue had not put a stop to the acerbic criticism printed in newspapers like the *Pioneer* and the *Englishman*—made the following observation, detecting a 'generally highly malicious tone' and a

... regrettable trend—which I have often pointed out to the Department over the last almost three years that I have been here—that has increased following the Fashoda incident, and that does not seem to have lost any of its animosity at the news of our troops fleeing the area they had occupied. It is with great emphasis (which is in very bad taste) that the newspapers—which, one must say, are, in fact, only expressing the feelings of the manifestly Gallophobic British public in India—have commented on the evacuation of Fashoda: '. . . Great Britain has indicated what it wants: it has made it clear that we must conform, and that it owes nothing in return.'[5]

Once again, the Consul explained these attacks as having been instigated by the 'desire to make an impression on the "native"'. He noted, however, certain 'signs of a rather curious state of mind that does not seem limited solely to the least cultured and least reasonable segment of British society in India'.[6]

Were the British in India really afraid that the French would recover their power, or were they simply using that as an excuse? One may well wonder, especially if one reads the reactions of the Anglo-Indian press in 1901, faced with the establishment of French colonial ports in Dakar, Fort de France, Diego Suarez in Madagascar, and in Saigon. The establishment of these ports was interpreted as having been instigated by the desire to:

seal off the west of the Mediterranean, neutralise British positions in Gibraltar and Malta, and control the routes leading to the Cape of Good Hope [. . .]. It is up to Great Britain to pay greater attention than ever before to the organisation and defence of its own colonies and to make fresh sacrifices in order to avoid any unpleasant surprises, which are always possible.

An article published at around the same time in the paper, the *Engineer*, entitled 'The French domination of the seas' reinforced the fear of the expansion of France's maritime power in order to call for greater military investment by London. Thus, the old 'Napoleonic' fears were once again revived. Were these fears real or just a red flag being waved in order to promote a greater commitment by London to the defence of its colony? As it was France's policy, largely dictated by colonial solidarity and its respect for Britain's prerogatives in its empire—as manifested a few years earlier in Burma, for instance this hatred of the French appears as an additional, imaginary element in Anglo-Indian minds in response to very specific colonial prerogatives.

In 1904, with the Entente Cordiale and the first official acts of rapprochement between France and England, the Consul General entertained the hope that his country would be treated kindly. In the same year, an increase in nationalistic fervour was noted, a worrying trend in the eyes of the British authorities.[7] On 19 March 1904, the Consul noted with great satisfaction, the Indian press had welcomed the Franco-British Entente Cordiale and was therefore able to write on 15 July 1904:

> *The Times of India*, the Presidency's primary newspaper and a semi-official publication, expressed a cordiality to which we were hitherto unaccustomed. This proved that something had changed in the relations between the two nations, to the immense benefit of our material and moral interests with regard to British India.

However, the change in attitude proved to be short-lived and, in the spring of 1906, during the incidents marked by Franco-German rivalry in Morocco, several articles appeared vehemently criticizing the French stand. One of them, published in the *Pioneer*, questioned France's weakness *vis-à-vis* Germany, and provoked the following comment from the Consul General:

> But this paper's opinions have evidently had less of an impact in this instance, despite the highly placed colonial officials and officers whose views it reflects, because the people in these offices seem to be totally incapable of thinking in the same way that the majority of the British voters think today. . . . Indeed, France's greatest misfortune—and that of Europe—would be the realization of the only too obvious wishes of British *jingoïsme*, which only dreams of seeing France and Germany fight over the wretched issue of Morocco one day, as I myself have discovered.

Indeed, note must be taken of the difference—underlined several times by the Consul—between Anglo-Indian opinion (especially that held by the highest officials in India) and public opinion in England. This confirms how France was made part of the colonial Anglo-Indian imagery.

A distinction also has to be made between the public behaviour of the British in India and their behaviour in private. Thus, in the small town of Simla, far away from the big peninsular cities and away from the eyes of the Indians, intellectual, cultural, and political activities were solely and always the prerogative of the representatives of British power. At the initiative of the British residents, an association was formed in 1911. The Alliance Française committee was established. It basically brought together senior members of the British Indian administration, the people close to them, as well as a few members of foreign delegations. The committee was initiated by Mrs Harcourt Butler, the wife of a member of the Viceroy's Executive Council in charge of education. She had to face the suspicions that this initiative raised in official circles. The association called itself La Société des Amis de la France dans l'Inde britannique. Mrs Butler was its chairman, while Sir Henry MacMahon, Director of Foreign Affairs and a member of the Viceroy's Legislative Council, was its vice-president. To begin with, it had over sixty members. The society's history reveals the ambiguity of the relations between British society in India and French culture:

> For anyone who knows about Anglo-Indian society, which was so exclusive and even hostile to everything foreign, this was, indeed, a remarkable result. The credit goes to its chairperson and founder, Mrs Harcourt Butler, the wife of a Member of the Viceroy's Executive Council for Education. Refusing to be discouraged by the prejudices she came up against even in her family, with her own brother-in-law opposing her the most vehemently, she succeeded in garnering the necessary support, with the tacit but effective approval of her husband, who agreed to remain an ordinary member of the committee, and—thanks again to his influence—it was quite possible that once the Society took shape and grew, the Viceroy himself could extend his patronage.

The La Société des Amis de la France dans l'Inde britannique presented itself as a socialite club that enlivened balmy evenings in the government's summer capital. During its meetings, the most brilliant stars of British society in India would gather to exchange 'futile comments' (*propos futiles*) in French. The minutes of the first meeting, held on 17 September 1911, offer us a glimpse of the proceedings:

> In honour of this French reception, Mrs Harcourt Butler had delicately chosen to wear the most exquisite of the dresses that she must have received from Paris recently, and around her smiling grace was all that was the most elegant and refined that Simla—the most elegant retreat of India—could offer. Almost the full complement of the Supreme Council of India was there. For the sole Frenchman in Simla, it was better than a flattering sign of friendliness towards his country. It was really touching that men who were in charge of administering an Empire of 300 million inhabitants had agreed to forget the grave concerns and responsibilities of their posts, to gather together and exchange futile comments between Britishers, in a language that was not their own, no matter how familiar it may have been.

Anglo-Indian society was able to indulge itself fully in its Francophile inclinations in this hill station, within a circle closed to all Indian elements. Indeed, in spite of the success of these socialite meetings, a journalist from the *Statesman* expressed a certain perplexity regarding the association's ability of developing real links between France and India. Furthermore, despite the creation of this Francophile group that aimed at bringing together the most well-placed British representatives, a Franco-British rapprochement appeared to be far from imminent in India.

Hence, it was a private society that had no Indian members, apart from the Maharaja of Kapurthala.[8] The association reveals the contradictory attitude of the British authorities *vis-à-vis* French culture in India. Among themselves, in a strictly private context, inaccessible to Indians, they accepted it and acknowledged its prestige. When contacts between the Indian people and French culture increased, as was the case in the last quarter of the nineteenth century, following the growth in the teaching of French, the British authorities made every effort to suppress this close interaction.

THE CONTINENTAL ALLIANCE AND COLONIAL OVERSEAS RIVALRY

The distinctly Gallophobic nature of the Anglo-Indian press was reaffirmed during and after First World War:

> Our agents in British India have pointed out the hostile attitude of the Indian press towards France several times, for a long time, and have expressed their amazement at the fact that the most virulent in their attitude towards us are English language newspapers of an unofficial character, such as *The Times of India* (Bombay) and *The Statesman* (Calcutta). The tone of these papers—even during the war—was such that our Consuls deemed it necessary to intervene personally several times.[9]

German propaganda, which was also far from favourable to France, added to the influence of the English language press and the Reuters news agency. In 1923, the Consul in Bombay once again warned the Quai d'Orsay about the different kinds of propaganda being spread against France:

> The Francophobic campaign is being nourished by the usual theses of Germanophile propaganda, to which are added the far from friendly echoes of the Gallophobic Turkish press.
>
> It is inevitable that the campaign directed against France by this paper and by other nationalistic Indian bodies, such as *Moslem Outlook*, *Servant of India*, *Modern Review*, etc., will have some effects in the long term. It is very ably supported by the Anglo-Indian press, which, after being somewhat troubled by the sympathy expressed towards us by the Islamic world, secretly hopes to see the undoubted prestige France still enjoys among Hindu circles and, above all, the Muslims in India, damaged.[10]

Two years later, the Anglo-Indian press launched a fresh Gallophobic campaign. During the insurrections in the Riff and in Syria, it condemned the unfair treatment meted out by the French authorities to the Muslims in its various colonies:

> The plotting has started again with renewed vigour, following the incidents in Syria. The most tendentious telegrammes are given the highest priority, and are further highlighted by the most violent comments. The most visible space is selected for inserting sensational titles for unbelievable reports from so-called correspondents, and the

treatment meted out by France against its Muslim subjects in all its possessions in Africa and Asia is condemned; it is being called upon to give up its mandate as soon as possible, in response to the clearly expressed will of the Syrian people.

These perfidious comments are slowly gaining ground, which is why Muslims have recently established a league—both in Bombay and Calcutta—to boycott French goods. Our commercial attaché has spoken on behalf of our traders and expressed their concerns, while warning us about the possible consequences of this movement, which constitutes an immediate threat to our moral and material interests in India and, consequently, the entire Islamic world.[11]

In fact, even more than being against its interests in India, the anti-French propaganda being spread by the British authorities through the press was perceived by France as a threat to its Muslim colonies and protectorates—indeed, to its colonies the world over.[12]

Apart from the incidents in the Riff and Syria in 1926, France's colonial policy with regard to its Muslim subjects remained the target of the Anglo-Indian press during this entire period. Thus, in 1935, for instance, the Governor of Pondicherry quoted these comments from an article entitled 'Around the Muslim World' in the *Star of India*: 'It is an undoubted fact that the French government has very little regard for the religious beliefs of the countries that are subject to it.[13]

During the liberation, the Calcutta and Bombay consulates remained very attentive to the ways in which French issues were dealt with in the Indian press. As early as September 1944, some dispatches reveal the ways in which France's position was perceived.[14] On 14 September, a dispatch from the Consul in Bombay underlined a renewed respect for France following the role played by the French army in the country's liberation. In this regard, the presence in Bombay and Calcutta of a comité de la France Libre (Free France Committee) must be pointed out.[15] Inspired by a romantic image in which depictions of a revolutionary France still played a major role, the Indian élite compared the events leading to the liberation of Paris with those of the Commune.[16] In response, British authorities exerted their influence on the press by emphasizing the role of the Allies and General de Gaulle's problems.

The report on the Indian press in the second half of September stressed another issue that soon became of primary importance—that of the colonies. The issue was initially described quite favourably:

> The emancipation of Syria and Lebanon from French domination is like an invitation to Hindu nationalists to win their independence.
>
> The immediate acknowledgement that the United States of America granted to the new State also received favourable comments, but the vested interests of the Americans in the Near East have caused some misgivings.[17]

The way in which France was treated in the press, therefore, depended on the way in which the situation was developing in India, as well as on the influence of the British, as noted by the Consul in Bombay:

> The attitude towards France and its government remains rather erratic. From time to time the press accepts my suggestions and allows friendly articles to be published, but at times it pulls itself together and publishes articles that are sometimes very violent. On the whole, there is very little sympathy for us. What annoys the British is that too often, Indian nationalists profess to believe that General de Gaulle is not only the representative of France's freedom, but also that of all people, including India and, for some, the French Indies.[18]

The British authorities acted quickly in taking effective measures against the popularity of General de Gaulle among Indian nationalists. Thus, the Consul in Bombay sent several press cuttings on the subject, which were: '. . . typical of the kinds of attacks directed against General de Gaulle in the 'Letters from London' in *The Times of India*.[19]

THE NATIONALIST MOVEMENT AND FRENCH CULTURE: THE REVOLUTIONARY THREAT

French Influence on the Indian Revolutionary Movement

While it was only at the end of the nineteenth century and particularly the beginning of the twentieth century that Indian revolutionaries began to use French revolutionary ideology for their own nationalistic ends,[20] the assimilation of French philosophical thinking began early in the nineteenth century. Rammohun Roy and his followers had read Voltaire in the original French. Roy even visited France in 1831.[21] In the mid-nineteenth century, positivism flourished in Calcutta, where a large number of societies were established. The reform of Hinduism, with which the latter remained associated, was marked by the influence of eighteenth-century French deism.[22] Several translations of French philosophical works were published under the pen of Francophile Bengalis, such as *Les Aventures de Télémaque* by Fénélon, as well as the works of Comte, Voltaire, Rousseau, etc. Along with these translations into English, Bengali translations of French authors were also published. The authors of these translations were among the greatest writers of Indian literature in English such as Michael Madhusudan Dutt and Bengali writers, such as Bankim Chandra Chatterji. Apart from the works of Rousseau and Comte, those of B.C. Chatterji—a writer whose works dealt with Indian nationalism—also bore the imprint of the influence of Hugo and Renan.[23] Among the élite of the Raj, the intellectual influence of French thinking spread rapidly. French culture, therefore, contributed to ideological developments in India and hence to the development of Indian nationalistic culture that was then taking place.

Due to the disappointment following the disillusion regarding British liberalism, the Indian élite became increasingly attracted to French philosophy and thinking. It was against this revolutionary background that the appropriation of France's culture and history of ideas by Indians could have represented a certain threat to the Raj.[24] One instance of the appropriation of French culture in India had already taken place during the French Revolution, to which some Indian sovereigns in the south of the peninsula, such as Tipu Sultan, gave a nationalistic, anti-British interpretation.[25] However, the phenomenon was still limited and marginal. It was in the context of the Swaraj movement that this appropriation would take on a greater scope. Indeed, during the Swaraj movement, direct references to French revolutionary ideology were made far more frequently. For instance, in 1909, in Bengal, the main hub of revolutionary ideology, Aurobindo Ghose, the great Indian nationalist, called for an uprising in a nationalist Indian newspaper, *Bengali*, reiterating the French revolutionary motto: 'There are three words that have the power to pull governments down: liberty, equality, fraternity. The divine fiat has been announced, calling upon India to live: Unite! Be free! Be great!'[26]

The mid-twentieth century was marked by the publishing of critical articles in France about the British administration in papers like *Le Temps* that appeared to reflect the thinking of the Third Republic's governing élite. The French press's renewed interest in Indian issues found an echo in India. The Consul General was able to appreciate the enthusiasm generated in India by the expression of a critical view of Indian affairs:

> In August, an article in *Le Temps* on the partition of Bengal created a sensation in India, as I informed the Department twice.
>
> This time, the objectivity of the point of view expressed and the sympathetic acuity of the inspiration were worthy of this admirably informed newspaper [. . .]. Here, in the main bodies of the Conservative Party that agreed on so many points with the admen of *Le Temps*, there was great astonishment, mixed with disappointment.
>
> On the Indian side, there was unalloyed satisfaction, along with a feeling of something unexpected, unhoped for. An impartial France with no ulterior motives, France—England's friend, the real France, the France of yore, with its great love for justice, freedom and human progress—had lent an attentive ear to a defamed Bengal, to an India that remained loyalist but firm in defending its rights [. . .]. And this soon translated into an upswing in trade relations, whose signals I gathered from the Consulate. Good politics, that! Emotions don't always harm business. And another article published in *Le Temps* on 31 December last had just as powerful an effect, but this shows, only too happily, that the circumstances—and, with them, the appraisal of our stand—are no longer the same, and have changed for the better. The Indian cause has made great progress since then. Indeed, we have witnessed some extraordinary changes over the last few weeks.

However, such a critical analysis was more of an exception, and France soon went back to supporting its neighbour across the Channel.

Nonetheless, Indian opposition to the British administration continued to increase, particularly on French soil. Chandernagore became a hub of violent action launched by Bengali nationalists. The Charu Chandra Roy case—he was the deputy director of Dupleix College in Chandernagore—then took up most of the space in French diplomatic correspondence on Franco-Indian relations in 1909. Charu Chandra Roy was suspected of being involved directly in terrorist-type nationalistic activities, but was acquitted in January 1909. The *Statesman* accused France of supporting Bengali nationalists. Charu Chandra Roy was also known for his translations of French articles in Indian newspapers. While Bengal and Chandernagore were the main hubs of the terrorist movement, it also affected French trading posts in other regions of India.[27] For instance, in 1911, the MEA referred to the Ministry of the Colonies regarding a request emanating from the English Embassy in Paris of the plans of French authorities 'to repress swadeshi attempts' in their settlements. Earlier another affair had provoked what may be considered a major turning point in French history—the 'Savarkar affair'. By the beginning of the twentieth century, seeking the support of the government of France against the Indian nationalist movement had become a vital matter for the survival of the Raj. Despite the fact that the Indian nationalist movement had no ramifications for the French colonial empire, the British authorities cleverly cloaked what was their national interest in the garb of a general bid for colonial power, and more widely as a confrontation between East and West. Indian nationalists did not hold any negative feelings against France, and indeed most of the Indian élite were inclined towards seeking a collaboration with France to assert the way in which they had made Western culture their own, and, of course, also to counterbalance the unilateralism of their relationship with the British.

NOTES

1. Linda Colley, *Britons: Forging the Nation, 1707–1837*, New Haven: Yale University Press, 1992.
2. M. Bérard (de), 'Voyage à Muury, Himalaya du Nord, et Voyage dans the Nord de l'Inde, excursion à Attok sur l'Indus', *Tour du Monde*, pp. 113–44, 2ème semestre, 1880.

3. K. Misra-Besnard, the *mouvement nationaliste en Inde, the cas de Chandernagore: the premier maillon de la décolonisation (1905–1952)*, dirigé par Jacques Weber, Université de Nantes, 1998.
4. The article ends with these words: 'Reader, it was but a dream'. The capture of Chandernagor. A Thrilling Episode: '*This was a bloodless victory. The triumphal entry of the combined forces, the hosting of the Union Jack. Reader, it was but a dream.*'
5. AMAE/P – Correspondence politique et commerciale-Nouvelle série Inde no. 31, Relation avec la France (ff. 32–40), Calcutta, 02.06.1899.
6. Ibid.
7. R.J. Popplewell, *Intelligence and Imperial Defence*', p. 1.
8. The association did not oppose First World War, most probably because of the strengthened cooperation between the British and the French police and authorities occasioned by the extraordinary circumstances.
9. AMAE/P – AO 1918–1940, PB no. 36, AE à Ambassadeur de France à Londres, 07.01.1926.
10. AMAE/P – AO 1918–1940, PB no. 42, consul to AE, 19.05.1923.
11. AMAE/P – AO 1918–1940, PB no. 36- AE à Ambassadeur de France à Londres, 07.01.1926.
12. 'In January, on the ferry on my way to my post, while reading the newspaper made available to the passengers by the Peninsular and Oriental Company between Aden and Bombay, I had the opportunity to notice the aggressive tone, when it was not violent attacks, from the English press leaders against our country. English newspapers converge in a furious unison against France. This campaign had been restarted by the Bombay *Times of India*, precisely when the campaign of our ambassador was logically supposed to bear its fruits.'

    'Sur the paquebot qui me menait à mon poste en janvier, j'avais eu l'occasion de constater, par la lecture des journaux mis à la disposition des passagers de la Peninsular & Oriental entre Aden et Bombay, the ton agressif, - quand ce n'était pas des attaques violentes, - des leaders de la presse anglaise des Indes contre notre pays. Les journaux anglais s'accordent dans un furibond unisson contre la France [. . .]. Cette campagne a précisément recommencé dans the *Times of India* de Bombay, au moment où la démarche de notre ambassadeur aurait dû logiquement porter ses fruits.' AMAE/P – AO 1918–1940, PB no. 36, consul à Bombay to AE, 21.04.1926.

The reviews of the English newspapers published in India by the Consul General in Calcutta were also sent to the French authorities in Indochina.

13. AMAE/P – AO 1918–1940, PB no. 36, Pondichéry to AE, 09.12.1935.
14. AMAE/P – AO 1944–1955, Inde 77, Report on the India press from 15–30 November 1944.
15. AMAE/P – AO 1944–1955, Inde 105, A.M. Massigli, Commissaire to AE (Alger), 30.03.1944 and AMAE/P – AO 1944–1955, Inde 105–106 (ff. 8-10) Direction politique Asie, Afrique, Océanie, Note de M. Massigli.
16. AMAE/P – AO 1944–1955, Inde 77, Consulate (Bombay) to AE, 14.09.1944.
17. Id., Report on the India press from 15 to 30 September 1944.
18. Id., Consul of France in Bombay, 'Note sur l'attitude à l'égard de la France', 17.11.1944.
19. Ibid.
20. Yallam Palli Vaikuntham, 'The French Revolution and the Late 18th Century Colonial South India', p. 257.
21. S. Sarkar, 'Calcutta and the "Bengal Renaissance"', p. 101, in S. Chaudhuri (ed.), *Calcutta, The Living City, the Past*, vol. I, Calcutta: Oxford University Press, 1995.
22. C. Khan, *État et développement des études françaises dans the monde indien: l'exemple de la province musulmane du Bengale*, pp. 75–6.
23. Notably his two books dealing with religious thought, for instance *Life of Krishna*. Ibid.
24. The French political experiment in its settlements does not seem to have played any decisive role in the making of Indian national political life. See J. Weber, 'Les institutions représentatives en Inde au 19e siècle', in *Les Cahiers du SAHIB*, no. 3, Rennes: PUR, pp. 135–67.
25. Y.P. Vaikuntham, 'The French Revolution and the Late 18th Century Colonial South India', in C. Wanquet, B. Jullien (Dir.), *Révolution française et Océan indien, prémices, paroxysmes, héritages et déviances*, pp. 249–57.
26. A French newspaper, *Les Nouvelles*, published an article entitled 'Révolte de l'Asie'. This article referred to the 5 July 1909 declaration made by Aurobindo Ghose.
27. AMAE/P.

CHAPTER 2

The Roots of Francophilia among the Indian Élite

In India, French culture spread from the centres of dissemination of British culture. In Bengal, the spread of French culture fell in line with the region's tradition of erudite culture and a progressive approach associated with building a national ideology. In Bombay, it was based on the social dynamism of the people—essentially the Parsee élite—as French studies on Zoroastrianism had kindled a greater interest in the French language within this community. Other Francophile and even French-speaking centres developed in some of the princely states such as Baroda, Kapurthala, and Hyderabad.

THE BENGALI RENAISSANCE

Around the turn of the nineteenth century, the metropolis of Calcutta had become a hub of the Bengali middle class, and attracted students from different parts of the Presidency.[1] Very soon, the British authorities drew attention to the emergence of this Bengali élite: 'People everywhere are speaking of Bengali babus with disdain—the most numerous and educated category, along with being native opponents.'[2]

The Bengali élite was at the forefront of a cultural renaissance that began well before relations with the British authorities became tense. It was one of the most interesting cultural phenomena in contemporary history. It was an encounter between the representatives of a rich and original culture and Western culture. Concerned about not limiting themselves exclusively to the influence of the British, Bengali intellectuals were curious about what the rest of Europe could offer. French culture, therefore, found a place in several areas of the Bengali cultural movement: literature, philosophy, Indology, and, later, painting.

In the nineteenth century, the Bengalis started evincing a much greater interest in French culture, particularly through the major reformist thinkers of the times, such as Rammohun Roy and his disciples, and French culture played a distinct role in the lines of thought that emerged in Bengal. B.C. Chatterji claimed to follow Auguste Comte's philosophy, and the poet, Michael Madhusudan Dutt, who had spent some time in France, described it as a paradise on earth. In 1839, a Frenchman, Hermann Geoffroy, at the request of Gourmohan Adhya, came to manage the Oriental Seminary, considered the most important institution for higher education after Hindu College. The three pillars on which Franco–Bengali friendship was built could be found here—science, philosophy, and political science—the arts in other words, in all the meanings of the term, particularly the art of living.

Dwarkanath Tagore, on returning from his second journey to England, also visited Paris. He was granted an audience there by King Louis-Philippe. He met Eugène Burnouf, a great Indologist in the French capital, as well as one of his students, Max Müller. The Prince gave a concert of vocal music and his generous distribution of shawls to many would long remain in people's memories. On his return to India, Dwarkanath Tagore contributed to a reaffirmation of the prestige of French culture among Bengal's élite and, above all, within his own highly important family: 'He sowed the seeds of a dogged worship of the French language and arts among his huge family.'[3]

French culture played a role in Bengal's cultural renaissance in the sense that Anglicized Hindus would endeavour to read everything that a cultured nineteenth-century Englishman would read. While much of the reading of French works was done in their English version, some of the works were read in the original French. The French works chosen to this end depended on the interests, preferences, and curiosity of individual members of Bengal's élite, contributing to the development of a modern and original culture. A special penchant for reformist thinkers such as Comte and Renan, can be identified, along with an appreciation for provocative and innovative writers like Baudelaire and Maupassant.

The Bengali élite's capacity to learn was such that as of the mid-nineteenth century it was able to play a role in spreading French culture in the world. Thus, two young poetesses from Bengal's business circles, Toru and Aru Dutt, published *A Sheaf Gleaned in French Fields*, an anthology of French poetry, in London, in 1876. Despite her early death in 1877, at the age of twenty-one, Toru Dutt was able to witness the anthology's success as a second edition was published during her lifetime. On her death, Toru Dutt left behind a French novel in the drawers of her desk, *Le Journal de Mademoiselle d'Arvers*.[4] The two sisters also gave India its first translation of *Fleurs du Mal*. This work by Baudelaire was remarkably popular in India. It was translated several times into Bengali, as well as into other major Indian languages.

Jyotindranath Tagore, the elder brother of the Nobel laureate, translated the works of Molière, Racine, Gautier, Cousin, Loti, Balzac, Hugo, Copée, and Maupassant from the French into Bengali. Maupassant's influence on Bengali literature is well recognized. Jyotindranath Tagore's studies of his works led the Bengalis to explore this new literary genre. For instance, Rabindranath Tagore himself was influenced by the author of the *Contes de la Bécasse*, which can easily be seen in his works.[5] Rabindranath Tagore also claimed to have been influenced by Victor Hugo. Indeed, the two men were often compared for their remarkably prolific artistic genius, expressed in all the various literary genres, from poetry to novels, and also encompassing theatre and the plastic arts.

Moreover, through his translations of Molière's works—particularly the *Bourgeois Gentilhomme*—Jyotindranath Tagore contributed to the birth of a theatrical genre in the Bengali repertoire which could be described as a farce with a social edge. From 1789 to 1924, sixteen different translators produced Bengali editions of Molière's works, some of them based on the English versions. Dumas, Zola, Verne, and Hugo were also translated from the English versions into Bengali, and became popular authors.

Several anthologies of poetry too were written and published in French. Those by the Dutt sisters have already been mentioned. Others were published in Calcutta itself, such as, for instance, the one by Indira Devi Chaudhuri, Rabindranath Tagore's niece, who had earned a B.A. degree in French in the 1890s. Her husband, Pramatha Chaudhuri, was himself the author of sonnets influenced by French literature, playing an active role in popularizing the latter. Apart from literature and the arts, it must also be noted that the catholic mission in Bengal was attached to the Belgian institution of the Compagnie de Jésus. Indeed, the Belgian Jesuits played a dominant role in Calcutta's well-known Saint Xavier's College. Established in 1835, it was the primary Jesuit university college in Asia, after the order was revived in 1814. Having moved to Calcutta's famous Park Street in the 1850s, the college was set-up in a former public theatre, which bore a French name, Le Sans-Souci. In 1862, it became affiliated to Calcutta University. From 1865 to 1908, it was governed by a shining light among the intellectuals—Father Lafont, well known for all that he had done in the name of scientific progress and honoured with the title of Officer of the Academy by the French government in 1902. There is no doubt that, at the turn of the nineteenth century, against the background of several decades of exchanges in book-learning and matters intellectual, Franco–Indian exchanges played a substantial role in enlivening Calcutta's cultural landscape.

THE CERCLE FRANCAIS IN CALCUTTA

The first French school in India mentioned in the Quai d'Orsay's records was established in the early 1890s by Le Faucheur, a clerk in the consulate general in Calcutta. Other French professors were able to spread the teaching of French through English schools or by giving private lessons, but there was no school devoted exclusively to the teaching of French. In 1893, there were around six to twelve students in Le Faucheur's school. The support he received from the Alliance Française enabled him to increase enrolments. Le Faucheur also taught French in the City College. There was a small French cultural club in the

Bengali capital. A French artist, Jean-Jacques Belnos, had a studio there, in the Kasaitola district, where he sold his miniatures and gave lessons in painting for Rs. 20 per month. The violinist, Phillipe Sandré, became the first director of Calcutta's conservatory of classical music.

In 1913, an association that set itself the aim of spreading French culture and arts was set up. It called itself the Cercle français de Calcutta. It was going to be a new section of an existing association called the Society for Propagating Literatures. Phillipe Sandré's influence could be felt in this association, as it was founded 'under the auspices of the Calcutta Conservatory of Music, whose sponsoring committee was composed of several VIPs'. On 16 November 1916, the Cercle français took the name of Société Artistique et Littéraire.[6] The group's activities were essentially directed at propagating the French language and arts. The Société Artistique et Littéraire was located at a well-known address, 2, Park Mansions, the future address of the Alliance Française and the Cultural Centre of Calcutta.

Among other French personalities in Calcutta were Suzanne and Andrée Karpelès. Of French nationality, though of Greek origin, they had spent several years of their childhood in Calcutta, which gave them the opportunity to learn Bengali. They grew up in the atmosphere of cultural ferment that pervaded the city at the time, and it is likely that they came to know the Tagore family then. They played a role in promoting Tagore's work in France, perhaps even before Alexandra David-Néel and Saint John Perse. In 1914, they took part in organizing an exhibition in Paris of paintings by Bengali artists collected by Abanindranath Tagore. They were to play a very important role in Franco–Indian relations in the period between the two wars.

The Tagore family was a point of convergence for foreign visitors. In 1912, Alexandra David-Néel was introduced into the bosom of the family and its entourage. Faced with a great talent that was already firmly established in Bengal, she immediately informed French literary circles—particularly the famous publishing house, Mercure de France—about Rabindranath Tagore's genius. Alexandra David-Néel refers to her meeting with the poet in a letter to her husband. In it, she writes that she had been invited to the home of a rich Hindu family, the Tagores.[7] She later gives her impressions of the evening in one of her letters to a member of Paris's literary circles: 'An atmosphere of art, intellectuality, high spirituality—all the delicious impressions I had on crossing the threshold of his family's aristocratic home. . . .'[8]

Thus, even before he gained international renown, Tagore's work was introduced to French literary circles, which explains how Gide's translation, begun in 1912, was published as early as 1913, the very year that Tagore was awarded the Nobel Prize. But it must also be pointed out that Gide's translation of Tagore's work was not the first, and that two other translations had already been done. It was on the initiative and with the active support of Saint John Perse, who met the poet in London in 1912, that Gide was granted exclusive rights to translate Tagore's work, which would soon be recognized by the Swedish Academy.[9]

In Calcutta, Alexandra David-Néel also met 'a young chemist who had earned his degrees in Paris—a friend of Sylvain Lévi'.[10]

Sylvain Lévi attracted a number of students to Paris at the end of the nineteenth century, and himself visited Calcutta for the first time during his travels in India in 1898.[11] His work became so famous that in 1913 the Calcutta University granted him a doctorate *honoris causa* at the same time as Rabindranath Tagore.[12] Due to the war, the Sorbonne University professor was unable to come and receive his degree. But Tagore's invitation to take part in the establishment of the Visva Bharati University in 1921 gave him the opportunity to do so. In the second half of December, he was ceremoniously handed over his *honoris causa* doctorate degree.[13] When he returned in January 1922 for an Orientalists' Congress, he was unanimously elected to the following post:

On the first day itself, Mr. Sylvain Lévi was nominated as the Chairman. [. . .]

Scholars in the field of ancient and modern Indian literature, philology, art, sculpture and numismatics had gathered from all around India. During his stay in Calcutta, Mr. Sylvain Lévi was the guest of the Governor and received the most flattering attention in European and native intellectual circles.

Professor Sylvain Lévi plans to visit Dhaka University (Bengal), where he has been invited to deliver a series of lectures.[14]

During weekends, many of Calcutta's scholars went to Santiniketan especially to attend Professor Lévi's classes.[15]

27 November. Lecture by S. on Buddhist writings. About twenty members of the audience had come all the way from Calcutta, and three of them stayed on for a longer visit.[16]

Various projects were planned at the time, as noted by his wife: 'Several students have already asked for his guidance, and for work meetings.'[17] One of them was Prabodh Bagchi, a student who had until then followed a particularly interesting career path. After graduating from Calcutta University, he became a Chinese and Japanese language specialist, as well as an expert in Jain studies. Ashutosh Mukherjee sent him on a research assignment to Visva Bharati, to work under Lévi's guidance. The latter proposed that Bagchi should accompany him on an assignment in Nepal. The Bengali scholar was then granted the University's Ghosh travel scholarship, for research under Lévi in Indochina, Japan, and finally, France, where he went in 1923. He remained there until 1926, when he obtained his doctorate in humanities for his work on Indian civilization.[18] He then joined the Department of Ancient Indian History and Culture at Calcutta University and also became the secretary of the Royal Asiatic Society.[19] Bagchi was not the only Calcutta University scholar to do his research under Sylvain Lévi. Some of the others were Kalidas Nag, Subodh Mukherjee, and Niranjan Prasad Chakravarty. In the words of Georges Coedès, inspired by Lévi's work, these scholars went on to do a series of studies that marked 'a new era in the history of Hindu Indology.'[20] That was how the concept of India as a civilizing country—put forward by Lévi—was strengthened.[21] The concept developed the idea of Indian colonization through culture, mainly in South-East Asia, where several vestiges of Hindu civilization could be found. Indeed, French archaeological expeditions helped in bringing many of these vestiges to light.[22]

Thus, fairly strong links were built between Indian and French Indologist schools on the basis of the concept of *Grande Inde* (Greater India). Santiniketan and Tagore gave it further impetus, and Calcutta's intellectuals went on to support and further strengthen it.[23] The Greater India Society was founded in Calcutta in 1926. Several articles written by Efeo members were published in its magazine. In Paris, Sénart established the Institut de civilisation indienne in 1927. It was the first institute on Indology in France, and Lévi was to be its director.[24]

Calcutta often received many prestigious visitors on their way to Santiniketan. Among them, the most important was obviously Sylvain Lévi. In 1932, the Consul General in Calcutta drew the Quai d'Orsay's attention to the circles of affinity that Indian professors had formed around French culture on returning from their studies in France: 'Those who have studied in France generally gather together and form "cells" in the centres they live in, which it would be a mistake not to use to expand our intellectual influence.'[25]

Another symbolic personage among French-speaking and Francophile Bengali intellectuals was Kalidas Nag. A friend of Tagore, Lévi, and Romain Rolland, among others, he was one of the pillars of the humanist intellectual movement in India.[26] The principal of Mahindra College in Colombo, he joined the Sorbonne in 1922 for research on the *Arthashastra* and diplomacy in ancient India, under Lévi's guidance. He obtained his doctorate in 1923 and returned to India. Meanwhile, he had met Rolland, with whom he formed a friendship and with whom he exchanged letters for a long time. On returning to Calcutta, he taught ancient Indian history at the university. He married Shanta Devi, a writer and the daughter of Ramananda Chatterjee.[27] In 1926, Nag published his works under the title, *Greater India*,[28] thereby supporting the Greater India notion. In 1928, he set-up a Francophile circle at Calcutta University, the Société Indo-Latine.[29] Along with teaching the history of Indian civilization, Nag also taught French. The noted writer, Nirad C. Chaudhuri, was one of his students. On this subject, he once wrote to Romain Rolland: 'Many of my pupils at the university can now read French books and we have founded a regular Société Indo-Latine where I shall have to discuss some of your works.'[30]

In 1932, he started publishing the magazine, *Indian and the World*, with the support of the Indian Bureau, which described itself as 'an organ of internationalism and cultural federation'. Whenever he got the opportunity he gave French culture as much space as he could in the magazine.

In another letter to Rolland, Nag described the heated debates taking place in the French-speaking Bengali community. His translation of one of the works that received the French Nobel Prize drew criticism from some members of this community:

> . . . now our neo-Parisian compatriots attempted to ridicule me and to lower my hero [Romain Rolland] whom they dubbed as more or less 'un-French' [. . .]. I feel keenly, Master, that your autobiography should be continued by all means, just to open the eyes of these 'Indian Parisians'![31]

A few years earlier, the Lévis had already been able to take the measure of the degree of knowledge of French culture among some members of the Bengali élite. In the poet's family home, where they were staying, they got on well with the Tagore family and their friends, including Sir J.C. Bose. They were invited by a number of well-known personalities. When they visited the Chaudhuris,[32] the wife of the great Indologist was really impressed by the erudition of this couple:

> Both of them know French, and the knowledge the gentleman has of our literature—the feeling he has for it, from Villon to Jean-Richard Bloch, is truly astonishing. His library stocks almost all of our best literature. He was able to understand the doubts expressed in our language—which are not really a negation, but arise out of the need for clarity that our language expresses so well. And for several years, he has helped those around him to also appreciate French.[33]

His wife, Désirée Lévi, described how French was spreading among the Bengali élite:

> During these too short days, our hosts introduced us to their family and friends. Unforgettable meetings, those! No country could have

more beautiful faces, with their wonderful eyes, noble posture, so much grace and dignity, and opulent, shimmering clothes—truly a feast for the eyes. Almost all had visited the West—i.e. England, some of the women had studied in our country and knew French, even spoke it, and organised French literary circles at their homes.[34]

No visit by any other French personalities had the kind of the impact that the visit of the philologist and his wife had on Calcutta Society. Nevertheless, some of the others do deserve to be mentioned, such as the several visits by Alain Daniélou and Raymond Burnier from 1932 onwards. These two soon found like-minded people among the city's élite. Prior to their first visit to India, Daniélou had met the Bengali dancer, Uday Shankar, and his impresario, Haren Ghosh, in Paris. Uday Shankar had made history in the world of theatre in India. During his first visit to Calcutta, the two Frenchmen met with Haren Ghosh and then were soon included in the Tagores' circle. During their various trips to India, they took part in the country's cultural and intellectual life and themselves played a role in the renaissance of Indian art. As a result of their explorations, Daniélou went on to publish several articles on iconography, temple architecture, sculpture, etc., in the magazine published by the Indian Society of Oriental Art in Calcutta. Burnier contributed his photographs to these works, along with those of other eminent specialists such as Alice Boner and Stella Kramrisch. Thus, whether it was in the case of Lévi's career or that of Daniélou, Santiniketan and Tagore played a central role.

Santiniketan, a Laboratory for the Coming Together of Indian Identity and French Culture

'. . . The East and the West found themselves fraternally united in my person. Thus it was that I was called upon to realize the meaning of my name in my own life.'[35] In 1903, the first foreign student joined Santiniketan, Hori San, a Japanese who went there to study Sanskrit.[36] Tagore's various trips around the world had planted the seeds of an idea in his mind—that of setting up a centre of cooperation with the rest of Asia. First World War, the result of the exacerbation of nationalist sentiments, gave an even greater impetus and urgency to the idea of setting up a centre open not only to Asia, but also to the entire world. In 1916, during a visit to Japan, the idea of establishing an international university took root in the poet's mind. Among those who encouraged him in his endeavours were Sylvain Lévi, Romain Rolland, and Paul Richard.[37] In the troubled times that followed the War, and witnessed a rising discontent in the colonies, Tagore seemed to be someone who could bring the East and the West together. In 1918, he started working on setting up an international university, Visva Bharati, and between the two Wars, his institutions found a place in the sun. What initially looked like a rudimentary refectory lost in the midst of rice fields soon became a centre with a number of establishments: an agronomical institute, crafts centres, a school, a high school, and, in 1921, a prestigious university—Visva Bharati. A number of Indian intellectuals and artists of all ages gathered there. These institutions claimed to be Indian, that is, distinct from the Raj's educational system, which was based on the British model. They were also spurred by the ambition of bringing about social reforms and the will to be of service to multiple cultural influences.

During his travels in Asia, America and Europe, Tagore had invited the most important professors he met to visit Santiniketan and Visva Bharati and to lend a hand. And they did, in large numbers, making Santiniketan an international melting pot of cultures.[38] Santiniketan also served as a centre of initiation into Indian life (*école de l'Inde*) for several French personalities. In this connection, Daniélou, who went there several times in the period 1932–45, wrote:

> Santiniketan was the only place in India where Europeans could meet Indians on the same footing, in an Indian climate, even if the atmosphere wasn't truly traditional, as the poet belonged to the Brahmo Samaj, a reformist sect [. . .] and rejected all the taboos that made contacts with Hindus difficult. The visitors were many: poets, writers, artists, philosophers and scientists. The best-known Oxford professors spent time in Santiniketan. It was from this nursery that several of those who played a key role in independent India came, including Indira Gandhi.[39]

The institutions set-up by the poet were aimed at empowering the Indian élite. In one of his dispatches, the French Consul General explained Tagore's approach in these words:

> The aim of the institute is to train an intellectual élite whose influence would be felt not only in India but beyond. The poet insists that his students have a perfect knowledge of European literature, sciences and philosophical theories and make the most of them, in order to be able to compare them with the methods used in India at the time and in times past.[40]

This description helps us in understanding the support given to an initiative that would have aroused the suspicion of the Quai d'Orsay's agents had it been launched by any one other than Tagore. The poet's personality, basking in the glow of his international celebrity, freed him from the prejudices and suspicions that generally prevailed, at least partly. In 1922, Désirée Lévi had already started talking about the 'uninterrupted flow of visitors from both worlds'.[41] Moreover, India's greatest professors lent a hand in the poet's work. Among them, she noted the presence of those who had returned from abroad. Together, they formed in Santiniketan what Désirée Lévi called '. . . (a) sort of smiling, indulgent and happy Port-Royal . . .'[42] and a 'tropical Sorbonne'.[43]

Sylvain Lévi and Tagore: An Intellectual Journey

The first meeting between Professor Sylvain Lévi and Rabindranath Tagore took place in 1920.[44] The poet was enthused by Lévi's personality, an enthusiasm that was only enhanced by the disappointments and criticism he had met with during his stay in England, before reaching France.[45] Some references to these feelings can be found in Kalidas Nag's journal, in which he describes a certain euphoria that existed among French and Indian intellectuals in the early 1920s:

> So my Paris 'dig' was humming with life and we managed to develop an 'Indian centre' as it were, whence responsible French professors, publicists, author and artists could get reliable information about developments in India in those critical years (1920–21) when Mahatma Gandhi took the lead in national politics and Dr. Tagore began

sounding his clarion call of prophecy. His Visva Bharati would soon be inaugurated and Professor Sylvain Lévi will be the first of the Western savants to collaborate with Tagore. I began sending my articles on Lévi and French Indology, on Rodin and Nataraja, and Indian iconography. All Indians of Paris were invited by us to the farewell tea party for Professor Lévi at the Café Voltaire. Professor Paranjape wrote a Prashati in Sanskrit which was translated into French by Professor Jules Bloch. The *Vandé Mataram* was sung and Miss Naoroji presented some of her Gujarati, Hindi and Kutchchi songs. I felicitated Professor Lévi on behalf of the Santiniketan group, and Professor Lévi gave an inspiring address on France and India on cultural collaboration, thanking the Indians of Paris for the warm send-off to India. The function was a real success and we parted with high hopes.[46]

In April 1921, the two men met in Strasbourg University.[47] The university had decided to sponsor and subsidize the future Visva Bharati University, described even before its official inauguration as a 'sister university'. Everything seemed to point towards a cooperation based both on scientific values and those of friendship. Thus, the Nobel laureate invited the philologist to lend a hand in building his university by coming to teach there as a visiting professor.[48] Although he had received a similar invitation from Harvard University, Lévi agreed.[49] With the help of Calcutta University, which had also planned to invite him, the poet obtained the funds necessary to cover the Sorbonne professor's travel costs and the expenses for his stay in Bengal. During their Indian sojourn of twelve months and one week, Sylvain Lévi and his wife also visited Nepal, Mysore, and Bombay.[50] On their arrival in Calcutta on 7 November, the Tagores offered them their hospitality in their family home, Jorasanko, in the heart of the city's Indian district. On 9 November, they finally reached Santiniketan. Five days later, a welcome ceremony was organized in honour of the Sorbonne University professor. He was paid tribute for having agreed to contribute to the university's activities:

On behalf of the students of Viswa Bharati, we offer to you our heartfelt gratitude for the trouble you have taken in coming over to our Ashram, setting aside for a time claims of others who are nearer your home.

Master, before we begin to receive our lessons from your hands, allow us to take this opportunity to assure you of our reverence for your personality which has blended in itself the love of truth with a wide human interest which is needed for the production of an ideal teacher.

We welcome you in this land of our fathers to which you have dedicated your life for the purpose of exploring its past; and we are proud to feel that you will help us who are seeking its bosom for that sacrificial fire of wisdom which must find its own place in the eternal festival of light in human culture.

We remain,
Sir,
Yours obediently,
Students of Viswa Bharati.[51]

Sylvain Lévi made several contributions to the university's activities. He taught Sanskrit, Pali, Chinese, Tibetan, and Buddhist literature.[52] At the time, Visva Bharati was the only university in India that taught Tibetan.[53] He also held classes on India's relations with Western civilization. Among his students were many great scholars, including Haricharan Bandhopadhyaya, Sinhalese Buddhists—and Tagore himself. Tagore attended classes and taught Lévi Bengali in return.

Interest in French culture grew among the institution's professors and students. Désirée Lévi took charge of teaching French literature, thereby improving upon the classes already being taught at the same time by Morris, the professor in-charge of French classes at the university.[54] A significant increase in the number of BA French students was observed, including in French language and literature classes, being offered since 1919.[55] Désirée Lévi also took part in the discussion circles organized by the women. In them, she spoke about the role of women in Europe during the War. During their stay in Santiniketan, links between France and India were formed and strengthened through the Lévis. On Friday, 23 December 1921, the couple attended the official inauguration of the 'international university' in the presence of the philosopher, Seal.[56] Thus, Lévi was both Visva Bharati's first visiting professor and one of its founding members. In spite of the intellectual and political wrangling that later took place between the Indologist and the poet, Désirée Lévi continued to correspond with Tagore. Lévi and Tagore met again in Calcutta, in 1928, during the Frenchman's last visit to India. The philologist had come to bid farewell to Santiniketan.

During Lévi's stay, the Consul General visited Santiniketan on 29–30 November 1921. It was the first time that a representative of the Quai d'Orsay was able to get a clear idea of the interest in French culture and influence prevailing at the University, and to support an Indian initiative, although the said initiative was inspired by the aim of the cultural, intellectual, and finally, political emancipation of India.[57] The Consul General was not the only one to ignore the normal precautions taken by French representatives in these matters. The admiring and warm tone of Champion's remarks addressed to Tagore must also be stressed (he was the Governor of Chandernagore), for instance in this letter written on the occasion of the poet's seventieth birthday:

> I wish you a long and happy life that will enable you to continue your admirable work for humanity and *universal brotherhood* and also wish sincerely that your latest message, '*Vandé Mataram*' is understood by all as it should be.[58]

Thus, in 1930, the Governor of a French colony hailed the message sent out by the representative of a colonized country—a message that, seventeen years later, on the country's independence, would become India's national anthem.

Other Visitors and French Residents

Apart from the Lévis, other Francophone personalities also spent time in the poet's school. Their visits made it possible to have some French cultural presence there. In one way or the other, almost all these visitors were supporters of a dialogue between India and France—or, more broadly speaking, the East and the West. It would be interesting to take a look at some of them. There was another Indologist who was definitely the first French visitor—Albert Foucher. He sent a letter to Tagore from Calcutta on 7 January 1920, expressing his joy at having been able to visit the poet's school, although his stay there had unfortunately been very brief.[59] We know that during his stay there in January 1921, Paul Richard, the former Consul of France in Japan and the husband of Mira Richard, also taught French for a few weeks, along with Professor Morris.[60] In May 1922, it was Fernand Benoît's turn to help Morris out. A linguist, of German–Swiss origin, he also taught German at the same time. He remained in Santiniketan until 1925.[61] He translated a work by Tagore into French and also contributed to the *Visva Bharati Quarterly*, publishing several articles between 1923 and 1929.[62] Benoît seems to have been an active member of the group of intellectuals associated with Tagore, Kalidas Nag, and Romain Rolland.

Patrick Geddes, the famous Scottish intellectual, sociologist, and educationist, met Tagore in Paris in 1921. The poet invited him to join his university, which Geddes did for a few weeks some months later. In 1926, Patrick Geddes was put in charge of Montpellier University's centre for foreign students. He established an Indian college there. Arthur Geddes, his son, an assistant professor of sociology at Bombay University, joined Sriniketan in 1922. In the part of the university devoted to agronomic studies, he undertook an ethnological study of Bengal's villages for a doctoral thesis submitted to Montpellier University in 1923.[63] In 1922, the French painter, Andrée Karpelès, who had spent several years of his childhood in Calcutta, joined Kala Bhavan as a professor. Under the leadership of Abanindranath Tagore, Mukul Dey, and Nandalal Bose, Santiniketan's Fine Arts Department was considered an *avantgarde* centre of contemporary art in India. Thanks to Karpelès, an admirer of the post-Impressionists, students were able to familiarize themselves with the most contemporary artistic currents sweeping through Europe. She also initiated the teaching of pottery. On her side, she learnt the technique of engraving wood from the poet's elder brother. After her departure in 1923, she continued to remain an active, and effective interface between India—especially Bengal—and France.[64]

A very important visit took place in end 1932—that of two young travellers returning from an exploratory trip in Afghanistan. They were Raymond Burnier, a Swiss photographer, and Alain Daniélou, an artist who was also a scholar in multi-purpose engineering. The latter worked actively, practising choreography and doing research in musicology, notably along with the composer, Max d'Ollone' and the engineer, Maurice Marthenot. The first visit by these two young explorers marked the start of a long series of visits and regular collaboration with Tagore and his university. The two men first made a plan with Tagore to set-up a network of sister schools of Santiniketan in Europe. Then, in order for the poet to collect funds for his institution from his friends, the former put them in charge of setting up an association that would take the name of the Friends of Tagore Association. In India, Burnier and Daniélou criss-crossed the peninsula in a mobile van and gathered one of the first ever collections of art photographs devoted to medieval Hindu sculpture and architecture.[65] In Santiniketan, Raymond Burnier also prepared a historical series of photographs of different places and Tagore's portraits.

Thanks to his artistic and especially his musical activities, Alain Daniélou began his long years of cooperation with Sangit Bhavan, the university's music department, which was also responsible for distributing the poet's songs. Tagore entrusted the department to the young man from Brittany, before other projects led the two companions to Benares in 1938.[66] Although he was based in Benares, he remained in touch with Calcutta and Santiniketan. His work soon came to be considered an authoritative work in the field of Indian classical music. He occupied the post of joint director in Benares Hindu University's music department, which he set-up along with the great musician, Omkarnath Thakur. In 1947, Ratindranath Tagore, the poet's son, entrusted Daniélou with the orchestration of the national anthem, *Jana Gana Mana*, composed by his father, and a national song, *Vandé Mataram*, by B.C. Chatterjee, set to music by his father.[67] Daniélou did the work in France, with the help of the composer, Max d'Ollonne. He also sometimes took part in events at which Bengalis and French people gathered together, giving musical recitals.[68] In 1950, he was nominated as the chairperson of the All Music Conference in

Calcutta, which brought together India's greatest musicians once a year. He continued his collaboration with Santiniketan, as he continued publishing articles in the university's magazine up to 1949, and even made several visits.

Christine Bossennec's visit to Santiniketan would mark a new phase in the history of Tagore's school and would also have repercussions on cultural relations between France and India. Tagore wrote to Daniélou and Burnier in 1934 seeking to recruit a woman to head the women's section of the institution that he had set-up in 1930.[69] In 1935, the two men organized and funded Bossennec's trip to India and her stay there. She was a specialist in Greek and Roman literature and a professor at the Sainte-Marie School in Neuilly. She soon became known for her thoroughness as well as her kindness and intelligence. She reorganized and transformed the women's section.[70] Having learnt Bengali, she was soon adopted by Tagore and his entourage. She also took charge of French lessons. In 1940, Bossennec left Santiniketan for Darjeeling, where she continued to teach French. Nevertheless, she remained in touch with the university. When she left Santiniketan, *Visva-Bharati News* announced her departure in these words: 'We regret to inform you of the departure of Christiane[71] Bossennec [. . .]. She leaves behind her uniformly brilliant academic departments and will be very difficult to replace.'[72]

The same year, Bossennec accompanied the old and ailing poet to Kalimpong, where he dictated his memoirs before friends who had gathered around him.[73]

AN INDO-FRENCH CENTRE IN CALCUTTA

In March 1939, the Alliance Française sent a representative charged with setting up a committee for the association and a French language chair at the Calcutta University.[74] During his stay in India, which ended in May 1939, the said representative took several steps towards his goal, particularly with Tagore's help. The Alliance Française de Calcutta was set-up on 1 March 1940.[75] Colette Khan speaks of '*des érudits et des penseurs du comité initial*' (the scholars and thinkers of the initial committee),[76] thereby presenting the founders of this Alliance as a circle of intellectuals. The documents relating to the association's twentieth anniversary also mention '*les personnalités si bien connues du premier comité*' (the well-known members of the first committee), also without taking any names.[77] In 1945, Professor Lacombe's testimony painted a picture of a very active Alliance Française.[78]

The presence of Bossennec in Calcutta, side by side with the cultural attaché, as early as 1945, proved to be a valuable asset for cementing relations between the two countries.[79] In this regard, Lacombe wrote: '. . . a professor at Tagore's university for several years, Bossennec enjoys a reputation in local intellectual circles that could be of great benefit to our prestige.[80] He later wrote: 'Her intimate knowledge of Bengal's cultured society would be of great help to me.'[81]

In 1947, France set-up a Cultural Centre in Calcutta. It shared the same premises as the Alliance—a building on the prestigious Park Street, the same premises that housed the Société Artistique et Littéraire. Thus, in 1947, Bossennec became the director of both institutions. Managed by the former director of Santiniketan's women's section, the Alliance Française became a meeting point for the intellectual, artistic, and scientific élite of the city. André Ross, the chancellor at the Consulate, described it all as follows: 'Thanks to her, I was soon included in a circle of like-minded friends, gathering around Ranu Mukherjee.'[82] The film-maker, Jean Renoir, who made several trips to Bengal between 1949 and 1950, wrote about the people he had met at the Alliance Française and who had accompanied him during his shooting:

> The group was the personification of India's enlightened bourgeoisie. It included professors, lawyers, doctors, government officials, and independent professionals. There were several women from Santiniketan University.[83]

The Franco–Indian friendship built around Santiniketan and Tagore could also be found around one of the poet's muses, Lady Ranu Mukherjee who later became the chairperson of the Alliance Française in the early 1950s and was one of the luminaries of the art world.

We find the same opinions echoed in a testimonial by Jean Batbedat, an embassy trainee of the Orient section:

> While writing these lines, I can see the musical evenings at Rajeshwari and Sudhin Datta's house unfurl before my eyes, where we also discussed Bengali and French poetry. Also visits to the home of the great scholar, Bose, and his wife Nalini.[84]

Among members of the Bengali élite, the feeling was of having found an interlocutor who was able to appreciate their cultural values, an interlocutor that had been frustrated not to have found so far.[85]

The success of the Alliance Française de Calcutta also marked the success of French teaching. In 1948, the Alliance Française had just one class of forty students. From 1948 to 1950, four new beginners' classes were introduced. In 1949, the Consul made an observation about 'the advances made by France's cultural influence in Bengal'.[86] In the month of September that year—a month marking the end of the monsoon and the beginning of the artistic season in Calcutta—an exhibition of reproductions of canvases by French painters was held, sponsored by the Society of Fine Arts, India's biggest art association.[87] The exhibition attracted over a hundred visitors per day and drew high praise from the press, which described it as the most important cultural event since the war.[88] On his part, the Consul General recommended the organization of an exhibition of paintings by Indian artists. As for the rest, Indian artists—particularly Bengalis—made several trips to and fro, which found an echo in the works done by the Calcutta artists.[89] Indeed, the former capital of British India liked to compare itself to Paris. One of the features shared by the two cities was the institution of the *adda*[90] that gathered in coffee shops, where artists, intellectuals, students, and others met to discuss and debate ideas in a friendly atmosphere. The *addas* were often compared to the discussions held in Paris cafés.

Another event also helped make the years 1949–1950 a remarkable period in Franco-Indian cultural relations—the shooting of Renoir's film, after his American period and before his return to France. Renoir decided to adapt Rumer Godden's Anglo–Indian novel, *The River*, for his first Technicolor film. Assisted by his nephew, Claude, and accompanied by an Indian crew, he shot the film that he liked best amongst all his work.[91]

In early 1949, during location shooting, and from end 1949 to May 1950, the shooting of Renoir's film led to several gatherings. Bossennec's help once again proved invaluable in organizing a film crew and in arranging meetings between the film-maker and the people. Alain Daniélou helped on the artistic side and set-up a meeting between Renoir and the dancer, Radha, the daughter of the chairperson of the Theosophical Society. In his memoirs, Renoir recalled these events thus:

> It was in Benaras, the holy city, that we made the acquaintance of Radha, the dancer. We had met her future husband, Raymond Burnier, through the French Cultural Attaché in Calcutta, Christine Bossennec, who had asked me to give a lecture to the students of the school. He invited us to spend the Christmas holidays in his palace in Benaras [. . .]. It was there that I met Alain Daniélou, the musicologist who knows India so well. Radha taught me about the dance form called 'Kathakali'.[92]

Radha's personality led to changes in the script, with the dancer's role being expanded. Daniélou collaborated in arranging the musical portions, which also had to be extended. The shooting also led to a meeting between two great film-makers—Renoir and Satyajit Ray, then an unknown young man. The latter, the son of the famous writer, humorist, and cartoonist, Sukumar Ray, was a former student of the Fine Arts Department in Santiniketan.[93] In 1947, he set-up the Calcutta Film Society with Chidananda Dasgupta.[94] The future film-maker, employed at the time in an advertising agency, was given permission by Renoir to visit the sets or locations whenever he liked, Satyajit visited whenever his work permitted him to do so. Along with other Bengali personalities, he too participated in the *addas* that Renoir attended. The erudition and warmth of the French film-maker were appreciated by one and all. Indeed, the feeling of respect was reciprocal, as Renoir wrote, during his location shooting:

I shot test runs with a Hindu cameraman and an Indian crew. I edited them with an Indian chief editor. They are all competent and have the kind of respect for our trade that I would like to see in white technicians too. We met young people, students, and they are fascinating.[95]

The shooting would lead to indelible memories for the French director, who was to refer to it very often in the future.[96] He left just as many memories behind him with his Indian partners. This experience also influenced Ray's choices. However, the influence was not of the kind that one would think. Indeed, the young Indian director did not seem to have been influenced stylistically by the director of *La Règle du Jeu* (The Rules of the Game). On the other hand, through their various meetings, Ray was able to exchange his viewpoints about cinema with the French director. During these discussions, Renoir tried to convince Ray to choose an Indian story for his first film and to let his own style bloom, rather than following the Hollywood model with which the young Bengali was highly impressed at the time.[97] Renoir's advice, as well as the discovery of Italian neo-realism, particularly in De Sica's *Le Voleur de Bicyclette* (The Bicycle Thief), decided Ray's selection of script for his first film—*Pather Panchali*—which turned out to be a happy choice, as we all know. In 1956, the happy epilogue of this meeting—which marked a turning point in the cultural history of the two countries—led to an award for best 'Human Document' at Cannes for the adaptation of the novel by Bibhuti Bhushan Bandopadhyaya. As for *Le Fleuve* (The River), it won the first prize at the Venice Biennale. It is a rather strange work, halfway between a documentary and an example of 'existentialist' thinking. The action is relegated to a secondary place and the protagonists, against a luxurious setting, seem to be mere pawns in a game played by a destiny they cannot control. The line between the 'Indian world' and the 'European world' seems to fade while the director uncovers layer after layer of half-philosophical, half-humorous thoughts, punctuated by scenes that border on a documentary style.

In 1950, the chargé d'affaires[98] described the foundations of the Alliance Française and the Cultural Centre as being strong, their customers 'always on the rise',[99] and the public increasingly interested in the various events being organized. He concluded, 'As of now, these activities have given our cultural organisation in Calcutta a place in the city's intellectual life.'[100] Regarding the importance of the former capital, the Cultural Counsellor added, 'Calcutta's importance as a major hub in this part of the world has far from diminished, despite the fact that the seat of the central government has shifted to New Delhi.'[101]

In Bombay, as in Calcutta, the interest of Bombay's élite in French culture was part of the modernization and emancipation wave in India. The movement led to the organization of the Cercle Littéraire or Literary Circle, which functioned like a cultural centre.

THE CERCLE LITTÉRAIRE IN BOMBAY

Since the last quarter of the nineteenth century, Bombay, another hub of British influence, had also turned into a centre for French culture. The Cercle Littéraire, set-up in 1886, was a further illustration of its place in the strategies of emancipation in which the Westernized Indian élite were engaged. As the Orientalist, James Darmesteter,[102] noted, the establishment of the Cercle Littéraire was not only a milestone in the history of French culture in India, but was also one in the most remarkable episodes of the history of French culture in the world:

> The establishment of this circle, which goes back to 1886, is one of the most creditable episodes in the history of French influence abroad; it was a spontaneous tribute to our civilisation, without having been prompted or inspired by a French intervention—official or unofficial.[103]

When the Ministry of External Affairs sent a circular to the Consulate in Bombay on the activities of an association for the propagation of the French language that had recently been created—the Alliance Française—the Consul was able to reply to the Quai d'Orsay by giving them surprising news about the establishment by Bombayites—mostly Parsees—of an association based on the aim of propagating French culture and language. The links between French culture and the Parsee community began with Anquetil Duperron, towards the end of the eighteenth century, the latter began an in-depth study of the *Zend Avesta*. Sometimes considered the father of French Indology. During his stay, he started searching for the manuscript, in order to work on the first full translation based on the original text. The interest of French Indologists in Parsee traditions continued after Anquetil Duperron.[104] During the great movement of translations and comparative language studies that swept France in the nineteenth century, Burnouf and Darmesteter continued with the research conducted on the Zend language. The large number of Parsees enrolled in Bombay University soon started showing greater interest in this particular language, which gave them access to scientific studies that were devoted to their culture and origins. All the more so since they had gradually lost Zend and had adopted Gujarati as their mother tongue after one thousand years in India. From the mid-nineteenth century, while trying to revive their culture and language, they showed great interest in these studies. One of them, K.R. Cama, during a visit to London while accompanying Dadabhai Naoroji on a mission to establish the first Indian trading house in 1857, travelled on to Erlangen and Paris. There he inquired about European investigative methods with regard to studies on Zoroastrian culture. On his return to India, he gave a fresh impetus to studies on the *Avesta*.

The Parsee community has been mentioned in almost all French books and articles devoted to India. A reference can be found as early as 1857 in an article from *L'Illustration*, and obviously also in the two major travelogues on India written by Alfred Grandidier and Louis Rousselet in the 1870s for the famous travel magazine, *Le Tour du Monde*. In 1913, Captain Claude Lafontaine gave the following description of the country in his travelogue, *A travers l'Inde*:

> There are 94,000 Parsees in India (1901 census), most of whom live in Bombay; they are traders, bankers, almost all very rich and philanthropic, and although they are not so numerous, they are highly placed due to their prosperity; they are educated, open to progress of all kinds and share more than a few characteristics with Europeans. One of them, Mr. Tata, recently married a Parisian.[105] Not only do they have a good head for business, but they also have a good head

for politics; they were able to please the British, in spite of their wealth, by offering large donations, building hospitals, and so on. One of them, Dinshaw Petit, the founder of a Home, was knighted by Queen Victoria, while another founded the School of Fine Arts.[106]

This quotation gives us a summary of the main characteristics of the Parsee community—their economic power, political role, and sponsorship of educational activities and institutions. The two men referred to by Lafontaine, among the wealthiest representatives of the Parsee community, took part in the activities of the Cercle Littéraire and were therefore associated with the propagation of French culture.

A factor the Parsees had in common with the Bengalis was the role that they had played in developing the educational system under the Raj. In this regard, the role played by Parsee women deserves a special mention. Albert Métin, a professor at the colonial higher institute of commerce, wrote about them:

Parsee women rival Englishwomen in the use of bicycles or in playing tennis [. . .]. In Bombay, the teachers are Parsees, unless they are European and, in the Presidency, the Parsees are almost the only women who have entered the educational field. In Poona, the main military town in the Deccan and the former Maratha capital, the female teachers in secondary schools for girls are Parsees. In Baroda, the capital of a native State, the superintendent in charge of organizing and managing the Teacher's Training College is a Parsee lady.[107]

Indeed, it was the perseverance of Ratnabai and Mihirbai Ardeshir, two Parsee women students, that helped the inclusion of French in a larger number of university curricula. In 1897, on the death of Ratnabai, who had become a teacher at Wilson College, a scholarship was created in her name, awarded once a year to a student of French. As for her sister, she had studied at the Faculty of Medicine in Paris as early as 1891.

The Birth of a Franco–Parsee Association

The Cercle Littéraire, first christened the Cercle Franco–Parsee or the Franco–Parsee Circle, was inaugurated in November 1886, six months after its establishment. Donations from wealthy representatives of the Parsee community, most notably from Sir Dinshaw Petit, made it possible to set-up this association, which became a centre for the promotion and spread of French culture. The creation of the Cercle Littéraire was described by Noti and Davar—two of its most active members—as the direct result of the admission of French among the second languages authorized for university examinations, the upward social mobility of the Indian élite, and, more generally, as the result of the development of direct contacts with Europe:

Prior to 1886, French was not recognized as one of the second languages in the higher Arts Examinations of the Bombay University. It was included only in the course prescribed for the Entrance or Matriculation Examination. This fact, however, in itself, as well as the growing intercourse between India and Europe since the early seventies, the great influx into England of Indian students for persuing their studies for the services and the learned professions, and the increasing number of native gentlemen and ladies who have taken to studying French served effectively to open the eyes both of students and parents and tutors to the immense advantage of studying the French language as a medium of high culture and professional success.[108]

On his part, Darmesteter describes developments in India in his *Lettres sur l'Inde* (Letters on India):

22 November. By a happy coincidence, I reached just in time to attend a most unexpected French festival, which was all the more important because it was not a French initiative and because France's genius was the sole reason behind it. This evening, the Cercle Littéraire will be inaugurated, founded by Parsee students for the study of French language and literature. The story behind it deserves to be told.

Three years ago, two young Parsee women, Mihirbai and Ratnabai, the daughters of the solicitor, Ardeshir, came forward and asked to submit a French exam. They were refused and told, 'Take one of the six classical languages: Latin, Greek, Sanskrit, Arabic, Hebrew or Persian.' The father submitted a petition to the University's Senate for French to be introduced as a seventh classical language. The petition was rejected; a fresh petition was submitted, supported by a strong wave of opinion among the Parsees and defended very energetically in the Senate by a Spaniard, Professor Pedraza, the true creator of the French movement.[109]

Then, in an article on the Cercle Littéraire:

> While French entered only through the cracks in University and official curricula, it penetrated private society with no opposition. A few young lovers of French met and set-up a French club and a French library. A sort of scientific and religious recognition had first attracted the young Parsee élite to the study of French. Literary curiosity then completed the work that had been started by religious gratitude.[110]

It was the recognition of the French language by the university in 1886 that triggered a wave of enthusiasm among the Parsee students and made them decide to form a group:

> . . . following the admission of our language by Bombay University, around fifty young people, almost all Parsis, met under the chairmanship of a language professor, in order to form an association, which they first wished to name the 'Club français' (French Club), before changing it to the 'Cercle littéraire'.
>
> The association will undoubtedly meet with several difficulties, but they will not be insurmountable and, thanks to the persevering nature of the Parsis, as well as the help they are likely to get from other members of the Mahomedan and Hindu communities and, lastly, from the few French people living in Bombay, there is reason to believe that they will achieve positive results.[111]

The Cercle Littéraire was formed on 23 June 1886 under the chairmanship of Pedraza, a professor of French of Spanish origin and was inaugurated six months later, on 20 November 1886.

> On 20 November 1886, the Cercle Littéraire was inaugurated in Bombay by Mr. Henri Follet, the French Consul. It was founded six months earlier by French language students. The ceremony took place in the premises of the 'Cercle' at Church Gate Street. In the audience could be seen, next to Mr. Follet, Mr. Henri Moet, the Vice-Consul of France, His Excellency, Mirza Hussein Kulikhan, the Consul General of Persia, the Honorable Mr. F.F. Adam, Professors Darmesteter, Woodworth and Pedraza from Bombay University, the Honorable Supreme Court Judges, Mr. West and Mr. Jardine; Doctors J. Gerson de Cunha, J.A. de Gama, Cowasjee, Pestonjee, etc. The only language used during the entire session was French [. . .].
>
> Mr. J.E. Davar read a report on the origins and foundation of the society. (On its establishment) it had just 35 members; the number has risen since, and it has 70 members today, not counting the 25 honorary

members. Membership fees stand at Rs. 6,000 (almost 45,000 French Francs).[112]

It must be pointed out that a donation of Rs. 4,000[113] was made by Dinshaw Petit, to be used for the foundation of a library bearing his name, and donations of Rs. 500 respectively by Jehangir Nusserwanjee Mody and Jamsetjee Nusserwanjee Petit. Thanks to its generous donors, the Cercle Littéraire was able to purchase the works of classical and modern authors, as well as scientific studies, magazines and illustrated periodicals. In the 1890s, the library had 1,836 works of a wide variety. It managed to increase its stocks thanks to its 'skilful eclectism', guided by a certain curiosity both for the arts as well as for the sciences. Thus, works by the following authors could be found in its catalogue: Rimbaud, Renan, Lavisse, Faguet, Simon, Taine, and even Maspéro. It was undoubtedly the first exclusively French library under the Raj. It was a place of contact with France and its current events.[114] Finally, the Cercle Littéraire awarded students who got the best marks in the French examinations—without doubt amongst the first awards granted to students of French in British India, if not the first. With regard to Sir Dinshaw Petit, who also bore the nickname of the 'Parsee Rothschild', it is interesting to note that despite his French surname—Petit—he did not know French. It was with great pride that he kept on the surname that was given at the beginning of the century by French sailors to his grandfather, a mercantile broker in Surat. Although he did not speak French, Dinshaw Petit was determined to be associated with the Cercle Littéraire through his sponsorship, by giving the library his name. Indications of the advances made by French in the highest circles of Bombay's business élite could be seen in the fact that Jehangir Petit, his son, who was also a member of the Cercle Littéraire, did speak French.

The Cercle Littéraire did not take long to grow, and in 1891 it already had around 200 members. It also opened its doors to members of other communities. So along with the few French people in Bombay, the British, the Portuguese, the Hindus, the Jews, and the Muslims also became members. However, half the membership remained Parsee. Davar, the association's secretary, and Pedraza, its founder, were awarded the title of Officer of the Academy in 1892 for their efforts at promoting the teaching of French. The members of the Cercle Littéraire became fervent defenders of French *vis-à-vis* a British administration that was troubled by the development of links between the Indian élite and French culture. The Cercle Littéraire also became a place where visiting French nationals stopped by, as confirmed by a French traveller:

> That is where the few French people passing through are hosted and where those who have done something for literature or science are celebrated—it's an exotic corner of France, a spiritual colony born of a spontaneous generation.

At the start of the century, in 1903, it was in the Cercle Littéraire—in the person of one of its eminent representatives, J.S. Noti—that Fontainieu, a member of the EFEO, found a devoted assistant to complete the collection of Sanskrit books of the French Institute of Indologist Studies.[115] Prestigious names were then listed among the honorary members of the Cercle, such as Prince Henri of Orleans, the linguist Michel Bréal, the Orientalist Emile Sénart,[116] a member of the Institute, and the Count of Potier. In 1902–3, nine of its members lived in Paris and one in Toulouse.

The visit of President Clémenceau and Professor Lévi were historic moments in the relations between Bombay's élite and France. During the long tours that he was just undertaking after losing the elections in 1920, President Clémenceau visited India and came to Bombay. It was the first ever visit by a President of France to India. However, he came as a tourist. At Mount Petit, he gave a speech that would remain in the memories of the members of the Cercle Littéraire gathered there. In 1922, the Lévi couple visited Bombay in Tagore's company. On reaching the station, they found a welcome committee composed of eminent intellectuals and fervent Francophiles.

> We reached the station in Bombay; from a distance, I could see my student from Santiniketan, Professor Morris, who taught French, and was waiting for us [. . .], and with him was our host, Mr. R.D. Tata, the banker who was also Parsee, as well as Nariman, the journalist,

who accompanied him and, with them, Rao, this one a Hindu, the same man who had sent us a simple card on 12 September 1914 on which was written: 'le jour de gloire est arrivé' (the day of glory is here).[117]

Thus, apart from R.D. Tata and Morris, a French professor at Santiniketan, there was an eminent intellectual, Nariman,[118] and Rao, one of the country's most important journalists.[119] As mentioned in a letter from Désirée Lévi, many were looking forward to Professor Lévi's visit: '. . . receptions, meetings, visitors to receive or people to visit, not to speak of the daily lecture, to the extent that I don't really know where I am'.[120]

In Parsee society, the Lévis were able to appreciate the widespread use of French:

> We are in France here; any conversation that starts in English because of Tagore always ends in our dialect, due to a natural, irresistible tendency. The young woman who greeted us in her mother's absence [. . .] has a way of saying, 'C'est fantastique!' that reminds me of all my nieces. Her brother will be doing his military service soon—a duty to be fulfilled all the more joyfully because it means an eighteen-month stay in France where his two children were born, where they were raised, and where their three brothers and sisters can be found now, as they are studying there. It's really a unique community, this Parsee society, so alien to India, so indifferent to it, about which it knows nothing, and about which it really does not bother to learn anything, so completely Westernised is it. Miss T. and her brother have seen nothing of India apart from Bombay and its surroundings. Every time they have even a few holidays or some free time, they spend the time in Europe [. . .]. With the Parsees, we're in the West—they all know France, particularly Paris, its shops and fashions [. . .] and the Parsees are fully aware of our touches of elegance.[121]

A text printed in Bombay, found among the archives of the philologist's descendant, also recalls how grateful people in the city were to the great Indologist. More generally the text pays tribute to the French Indologists who had spent time in India:

> In this meeting of the friends of Oriental Learning (i.e. B.B. Royal Asiatic Society) we offer our most hearty welcome to Dr Sylvain Lévi who is also versed in the Lore of the East [. . .].
>
> At one time India (the land of Bharat) was glorious; and great and

glorious was her literature; our glory has now become an object of remembrance, but one thing we have not forgotten, and it is hospitality to our guests [. . .].

The sons of India, the land of Bharat, whose language was well cultured and whose culture and civilization were adopted by other nations, have now become helpless and disrespected. Why should this be?

I remember a friend of mine who had been your countryman. He was well versed in Oriental Languages, and his name was James Darmesteter. He was an Ocean of Sympathy toward us Indians. May you be pleased to follow his example![122]

Lévi felt a greater affinity with the famous linguist, Modi:

A very well-known scholar, who knows France perfectly well himself—its scholars and their works, he has a way of saying 'le grand Burnouf' that goes straight to the heart of my Indologist—reading French with him, we are truly in the company of a citizen of the world.[123]

In 1925, Professor Modi was honoured with a Chevalier of the Légion d'honneur, while E.J. Davar, the son of the former secretary of the Cercle,[124] was awarded the title of Officer of the Academy. From the end of the 1920s, Father Caïus was chairman of the association. The Cercle Littéraire's library then had over 3,000 works.[125] In an indication of the spread of French, in 1929, the Consul announced that French professors could come and work in India, particularly by giving private lessons in French, as well as a few lessons in European institutes or university colleges.[126]

The Cercle's library continued to add works purchased in Paris to its collection. Along with works by Orientalists, readers were offered a vast and diverse choice:

For those who love the stark beauty of the classics, there are the majestic pages of Corneille or Boileau, for the romantics, there is the passionate poetry of Musset and Lamartine, while readers of novels would always find almost all the books that have contributed to the development of the French novel—the novels of Flaubert, de Goncourt, Balzac, Zola, Paul Bourget, Pierre Loti and, among the contemporaries, François Mauriac, André Maurois and André Gide, among others.

The library also has sections devoted to poetry, literature, essays and the belles-lettres, history, science, biography and so on.[127]

A book committee was set-up, in order to examine proposals from the Cercle's members for the selection of books to be ordered. The circulating library proposed a diverse panel of French magazines and newspapers, including, in particular, *L'Illustration*, *Les Annales*, *Journal des Débats*, *Le Monde Illustré*, *La Revue des Deux mondes*, *La Nouvelle Revue*, *La Revue Bleue*, *La Revue Musicale*, *Commerce*, *Pour Vous*, etc.[128] In 1938, the number of works collected rose to 5,400.

In 1937, the Cercle celebrated its fiftieth anniversary.[129] The same year, Yves Petit-Dutaillis, an interior decorator settled in the city since the early 1930s and a member of the Cercle Littéraire, was granted the title of Delegate of the Alliance Française.[130] Along with Father Caïus, he conducted the Cercle's meetings, henceforth held twice a week, on Tuesdays and Wednesdays. They were fairly popular: 'The weekly meetings of the Cercle Littéraire are increasingly growing into a meeting point for the city's intellectual élite.'[131]

The following year, Dutaillis established the Alliance Française de Bombay.[132]

FRENCH CULTURE, THE PRINCES, AND THE PENINSULAR MARGINS

Some Indian princes also had certain things in common with the Parsee and the Bengali élite. Like them, they too were in direct touch with the British and played an active role in the administration of the Indian peninsula, through the administration of their own states, which was sometimes better developed than that of the Raj. Indeed, few princes asked for foreign cooperation for infrastructural development in their states, especially the ruler of Mysore. Their support for the modernization of India was not limited to the territories under their jurisdiction. Institutions such as Santiniketan, for instance, received financial backing several times from these princes, in particular the Maharaja of Tripura, who also funded the work of Sir J.C. Bose.[133] Rabindranath Tagore's work was also supported by several princes throughout his life. Other examples were the ruler of Baroda, who became involved in the students' movement abroad, and at certain instances the Nizam of Hyderabad. Finally, an élite composed of bank managers, directors of educational institutions, etc., gravitated towards the most important sovereigns. This élite followed in the wake of its sovereigns—several of whom had homes in France[134]—travelling and sometimes even studying in Europe.[135]

From the second half of the eighteenth century to the beginning of the nineteenth century, the links between several Indian sovereigns and the French adventurers who were placed at their service were well known. Throughout the nineteenth century and up to the beginning of the twentieth century, the memories of some of these adventurers remained alive, particularly those of General Raymond in Hyderabad, as shown by several memories and recollections. The Bourbons of Bhopal, or *Firingis*, constitute another example of Indo–French friendship as a legacy of the adventures of the French in India in the modern era. Louis Rousselet presents a vivid description of the Princely states in his account written in the early 1870s.[136] At the turn of the nineteenth century, a new power struggle broke out between the Indian sovereigns, who were looking to retain their autonomy, and the British authorities, who wished to hold on to their sovereignty and control all initiatives made within their empire. Thus, for some Indian sovereigns, cultural co-operation with France was welcome in order to counterbalance British control. The actions taken by the Burmese and the Nepalese rulers also followed the same lines. This trend continued in Burma until the mid-1880s, while in Nepal it continued until Second World War.

Hyderabad was one of those states that historically had special relations with France, which sometimes extended into the contemporary era, i.e. the nineteenth and twentieth centuries. In 1900, a group of Alliance Française members visited Secunderabad. The group, affiliated to the Alliance Française, would last several years. The Nizam of Hyderabad and members of his court visited France regularly. The state of Hyderabad was to play a decisive role in the establishment of the first Pasteur Institute in India. In the princely states of Baroda, Patiala, and Kapurthala, French culture was given a place in the sun. The Gaekwad of Baroda, who ruled over a small kingdom surrounded by the Bombay Presidency, stood out at the end of the nineteenth century on account of his progressive actions in the fields of education and economic development.[137] In 1910, Filippi, a delegate of the Alliance Française, was nominated as a professor to Baroda College, where he set-up an action committee for the Alliance Française. R.D. Tata was one of its honorary members.

The princely state of Kapurthala in Punjab had 21,721 inhabitants in 1879. According to the 1911 census, there were 51 French residents living in the Punjab region. Maharaja Jagatjit Singh stood out as a member of the Cercle Littéraire and the Société des Amis de la France in British India. In 1911, the Consul described him as being 'well known in Paris', a claim that was also confirmed in the society columns in the paper, *L'Illustration*. Maharaja Jagatjit Singh, a dedicated Francophile and Francophone, had spent a part of his childhood in France and owned a house in the Boulogne Woods in Paris.[138] He was a well-known figure in the capital's high society circles. He kept a diary, which he wrote in French, and sometimes used Molière's language with the British residents deputed to his state, using the services of an interpreter, although he was himself perfectly capable of expressing himself in English.[139] He even took the help of French architects for the construction of his palace, built along the lines of the Château de Versailles.[140] Princess Brinda Mathi, the first wife of the reigning prince of Kapurthala, was also brought up in Paris. She had spent ten years of her childhood with the Hachette family, which was associated with the publishing house of the same name.[141]

France was also present in Mysore through its missionaries. In 1916, the Yuvaraja founded a university in his capital. Brajendranath Seal, the philosopher who also played a role in setting up Santiniketan, became its chancellor. In 1920, there were more than 10,000 schools in the state. The king maintained a level of education and hygiene in his kingdom that was lauded by foreign visitors like Désirée Lévi.[142] The Lévis were welcomed warmly to the kingdom. Professor Lévi's abilities as a great teacher were also called upon while on a visit to Mysore in

Tagore's company.[143] The Yuvaraja knew Paris well as he had pursued a part of his studies at the Sorbonne.[144] In 1920, during one of his visits, he had even met with the President of the Republic.

Among the king's entourage, everyone unhesitatingly displayed their patriotism, as well as their feelings for France. As a long-standing rival of Great Britain, France continued to evoke warm feelings among Indians as mentioned by Lévi's guide:

> From the top of the hill where the Maharaja has built himself a bungalow, the plain, the city and its ponds spread out like a map. In the background, you can see a large water storage dam—the second largest in the world, according to the Mysorian. He is just as proud of his small country as of the greatest, which has given the world so many of its philosophers, while the West had only 'Spencer, Bergson, and a few French philosophers'. However, for any electrical work, don't engineers, machines and projects also come from America, and can't England's hand be seen everywhere? 'Yes,' sighed our guide, 'Mysore was once a great empire, a friend of the French; I will show you a book with letters from Napoleon to Tipu Sahib and—oh yes!—Mr. Clémenceau.' Our nation's Tiger made a very good and very strong impression everywhere here; his words are quoted, his deeds and actions lauded; in some other age, he could have become a legend.[145]

Among the Indian princes who were decorated with a Légion d'honneur were the Maharaja of Patiala, well known for his love of France as well as his contribution to the war effort (he had sent troops to the French front). The Consul in Bombay recalled that '. . . his feelings were expressed very effectively during the war and he occupies a very important position in India right now'.[146]

During this period, relations between the great Indian princes and the British authorities remained contentious, with the latter attempting to stifle any desire for political action on the part of these sovereigns.[147] Some dispossessed princes continued to see France as a possible recourse. After taking refuge in Pondicherry from 1911 to 1916, Prince Sudarshan, mentioned earlier, wrote several times to the Consul General between 1919 and 1924. He appealed for France's help in defending his rights to the land that had been taken away from him.[148] He was not the first Indian aristocrat to have taken refuge in France's primary trading post in India, since Dilip Singh, son of Ranjit Singh—the founder of the Sikh kingdom of Punjab—had opened the way in 1887, when he was trying to escape from the British authorities.[149]

In 1932 and 1934, Raja Ram Baijal of Suraj Kund, while in Allahabad, made desperate appeals to the President of the French Republic, written in French, on behalf of all the aristocratic families of India and their subjects, while also condemning the British regime.[150]

The strong and notable presence of French culture in several parts of princely India was the result of the changing ideas of the sovereigns, thanks to their interaction with Western culture. Until 1948, and even after they had been incorporated into the Indian Union, several princely capitals continued to operate as hubs for the spread of French culture, in particular Kapurthala, Hyderabad, and Baroda.

NOTES

1. S. Sarkar, 'L'entrée dans the siècle: la première révolte', in J.-L. Racine (dir.), *Calcutta 1905–1971, au cœur des création et des révoltes du siècle*, Paris, 1997, p. 28.
2. A. Métin, *L'Inde aujourd'hui, Etude sociale*, A. Colin, Paris, 1903; p. 218.
3. C. Khan, *État et développement des études françaises dans the monde indien: l'exemple de la province musulmane du Bengale*, Laurent Versini (dir.), Université de Nancy II, 1984, pp. 75–6.
4. T. Dutt, *Journal de Mademoiselle d'Arvers*, Didier, Paris: Didier, 1879.
5. See, for instance, the short story *Jibito o Mrito*. K. Roy, *Rabindranath Tagore*, New Delhi: National Gallery of Modern Art, 1988, p. 47.
6. Private archives of R. Palchoudury, *Discours prononcé à l'Alliance française pour the bicentenaire de la révolution française*, 1989, p. 2. AMAE/P – nouvelle Série, Inde no. 33, (f. 167) – CG to AE, 20.12.16.

7. A. David-Néel, *Correspondence avec son mari, édition intégrale 1904–1941*, Paris: Plon, 2000, p. 119 (letter dated 16 January 1912). Archives of Rabindra Bhavan in Santiniketan - Correspondence Tagore - Alexandra David-Néel.
8. Archives of Rabindra Bhavan in Santiniketan - Correspondence Tagore - Alexandra David-Néel.
9. In 1932, Gide wrote about his discovery of Tagore's work: 'By then, the readers of Tagore were very few, even in England, when in 1912 I translated his *Gitanjali*.'
10. A. David-Néel, *Correspondence avec son mari, édition intégrale 1904–1941*, op. cit., pp. 138 and 771. Letter of 16 January 1912. The first visit of Alexandra David-Néel to Calcutta, in 1912, had been noticed both by the British authorities and the press. Coming back from her long and famous journey in Tibet, she stayed for more than two month in Darjeeling, from June to August 1924, and then in Calcutta until the beginning of 1925.
11. S. Lévi, *Népal, étude historique d'un royaume hindou*, pp. 37–8, M. Gaborieau and G. Toffin (préf.), Paris: Kailash, 1985, 2 vols., pp. 394–408.
12. N. Dé, *Madam Lévir Dyari*, Kolkata: Ananda Publishers, pp. 141–6.
13. D. Lévi, *Dans l'Inde*, op. cit., p. 53.
14. AMAE/P - AO 1918–1940, PB no. 22, CG to AE, 04.02.1922.
15. The weekend in Santiniketan begins on Tuesday afternoon and ends on Wednesday evening.
16. D. Lévi, *Dans l'Inde*, op. cit., p. 33.
17. Ibid., p. 43.
18. Prabodh Bagchi published, among other works, *India and China: A thousand years of cultural relations*. He was also the translator of *Pre-Aryan and pre-Dravidian in India*, translated from a collection of works by Sylvain Lévi, Jean Przyluski, and Jules Bloch, and also compiled a Sanskrit–Chinese dictionary.
19. In 1945, he joined Visva Bharati as the research director, holding the chair of Indology and the post of the principal of Vidyabhavan. In 1948, he was appointed as honorary member by the Efeo.
20. P. Singaravélou, 'Les Indologistes français et the *Greater India*', op. cit.
21. S. Lévi, *L'Inde civilisatrice*, Paris: A. Maisonneuve (Publications de l'Institut de civilisation indienne), 1938.
22. G. Coedes, *Les Etats hindouisés d'Indochine et d'Indonésie*, Paris: Les éditions du Broccard, 1948.

23. Singaravélou, 'Les Indologistes français et the *Greater India*', op. cit.
24. It is directly associated with the *Société asiatique*, Sylvain Lévi's students (Alfred Foucher, Louis Renou, Jean Filliozat . . .) will take over.
25. AMAE/P – AO 1918–1940, PB no. 71, CG to AE, 30.12.1932.
26. K. Nag, R. Rolland, *Correspondence, The Tower and the Sea*, pp. 293–8, op. cit.
27. Foremost intellectual, editor of *Prabasi* and *The Modern Review.*
28. Also author of *Pre-historic Japan*, and *India and the Pacific World*.
29. Chinmoy Guha (ed.), Romain Rolland, Kalidas Nag Correspondence, *The Tower and the Sea*, p. 245, op. cit.
30. Id., p. 245.
31. Id., pp. 242–3.
32. The husband, Pramatha Chaudhuri, went to France during his studies in England, and his brother also visited France during the War.
33. D. Lévi, *Dans l'Inde*, op. cit., p. 50. The individuals mentioned by Désirée Lévi are Indira Devi Chaudhuri and his brothers, Pramatha and Asutosh Chaudhuri. N. Dé, *Madame Lévir Diary*, op. cit., p. 45.
34. D. Lévi, *Dans l'Inde*, op. cit., pp. 53–4.
35. R. Tagore, *Souvenirs d'enfance*, p. 160, C. Bossennec and R. Datta (trad.), Paris: Gallimard, 1964.
36. U. Gupta, 'Santiniketan and Sriniketan, a historical introduction', in *Visva-Bharati Quarterly*, vol. 41, no. 1/4, Calcutta, May 1975–April 1976, 1977, pp. 270-325.
37. Ibid.
38. In addition to the Indian personalities and the Tibetan pandits who came there to teach in those institutions in the Bengal countryside, many foreign scholars, artists, and other visitors came to Santiniketan. The list of the countries from where these foreign personalities came is impressive. From Japan to the USA, from China and Palestine, and from almost all the European countries. To the already known list, my work permit to add the names of the great Swiss specialist on Indian architecture, Alice Boner, the French Indologist, Alfred Foucher, and the Romanian scholar Mircea Eliade. To know the other foreign personalities who visited Santiniketan: P. Debonath, *Rabirtithé Bidéshi* (Bengali): Calcutta, Mitra & Ghosh Publishers, nouvelle édition, 2000, 117p.

39. A. Daniélou, *Chemin du Labyrinthe*, Monaco: Rocher, 1993, pp. 105–6.
40. AMAE/P – AO 1918–1940, PB no. 22, CG to AE, 07.12.1921.
41. D. Lévi, *Dans l'Inde*, op. cit., pp. 83–4.
42. Id., pp. 27–8.
43. Id., p. 41.
44. N. Dé, *Madam Lévir Dyari*, op. cit., p. 1.
45. K. Dutta, A. Robinson, *Rabindranath Tagore: The Myriad-minded Man*, New Delhi: Rupa & Co., p. 228.
46. K. Nag, *Memoirs*, Calcutta: Writers Workshop, 1994, p. 9.
47. After the reintegration of Alsace and Lorraine into French territory, the French government sent some of the greatest scholars to Strasbourg University.
48. N. Dé, *Madame Lévir Diary*, op. cit., *Bhumika* (introduction).
49. Ibid.
50. D. Lévi, *Dans l'Inde*, op. cit., p. 53.
51. Private archives – *M. et Mme Vermeil.*
52. D. Lévi, *Dans l'Inde*, op. cit., pp. 39 and 83.
53. N. Dé, *Madam Lévir Dyari*, op. cit., *Bhumika*.
54. D. Lévi, *Dans l'Inde*, op. cit., p. 20.
55. N. Dé, *Madam Lévir Dyari*, op. cit., p. 9.
56. Id., p. 59.
57. S. Sarkar, 'L'entrée dans the siècle, la première révolte', J. Racine (dir.), *Calcutta 1905–1971*, op. cit., p. 39.
58. Id. Letter of 11.05.1930 from M. Champion.
59. Archives of Rabindra Bhavan-Santiniketan-Correspondance Tagore-France-Foucher to Tagore, 7.01.1920.
60. P. Debonath, *Rabirtithé Bidéshi*, pp. 14–15.
61. See also au sujet de Fernand Benoît, R. Rolland, *Rabindranath Tagore et Romain Rolland, Lettres et autres écrits*, op. cit.

    P. Debonath, *Rabirtithé Bidéshi*, pp. 26–7. According to the study, Fernand Benoît, married to a Bengali, left Santiniketan for Varanasi in 1925. There, he joined the Benares Hindu University and died in 1961. Fernand Benoît also translated one drama: R. Tagore, *La Machine*, F. Benoît and A.C. Chakravarty (trad.), Rieder, Paris, .1929.
62. P. Debonath, *Rabirtithé Bidéshi*, pp. 107–8.
63. A. Geddes, *La Civilisation rurale du Bengale Occidental et les facteurs démographiques*, A. Demangeon (préf.), Paris: Armand Colin, 1923.
64. P. Debonath, *Rabirtithé Bidéshi*, op. cit., pp. 33–5.

65. R. Chanda, *Shob Hoté Apan*, Calcutta: Visva Bharati, 1995 (2nd edn.), pp. 110–12.
66. R. Chanda, *Shob Hoté Apan*, op. cit., pp. 110–12. See also A. Daniélou, *Les Chemins du Labyrinthe*, op. cit., pp. 108–9.

    In Varanasi, integrated in the orthodox circles of the city, Daniélou carried out research works on music, translated Hindi and Sanskrit texts, and collected old manuscripts. Those manuscripts are now housed in the Cini Foundation.
67. B. Chattopadhyaya, R. Tagore, *Vandé Mataram*, adaptation and orchestration by Alain Daniélou, N.C. Mitra, Calcutta: Visva Bharati, 1947.

    R. Tagore, *Jana Gana Mana*, adaptation and orchestration by Alain Daniélou, N.C. Mitra, Calcutta: Visva Bharati, 1947.
68. Private interviews with Chidananda Dasgupta and Jean Batbedat.
69. Archives of Rabindra Bhavan à Santiniketan, *Visva-Bharati News*.

    Private Archives – Mr and Mrs Youenou: S. Liné (ed.), *Hommage à Christine Bossennec*.
70. Ibid. See also: R. Chanda, *Shob Hoté Apan*, op. cit.
71. Her real name was Christiane.
72. P. Debonath, *Rabirtithé Bidésh*, op. cit., pp. 92–3. Christine Bossennec kept in touch with Santiniketan for many years. P. Debonath concludes: 'Many students and inhabitants of Santiniketan keep memories of this foreigner'.
73. See post-face de R. Tagore, op. cit., *Souvenirs d'Enfance*.

    Christine Bossennec also translated for the same collection *Vagabond et Autres Nouvelles*.

    R. Tagore, *Vagabond et Autres Nouvelles*, C. Bossennec, K. Bhattacharya (trad.), Paris: Gallimard, 1962.
74. Archives of Rabindra Bhavan à Santiniketan-Correspondance Tagore-France – A. Lehuvaux to Anil Chanda, 30.03.1939.
75. Private archives – Henry Bourgeot: *XXe anniversaire de l'Alliance française de Calcutta*.
76. K. Colette, *État et développement des études françaises dans the monde indien: l'exemple de la province musulmane du Bengale*, op. cit., p. 81.
77. Private Archives – Henry Bourgeot: *XXe anniversaire de l'Alliance française de Calcutta*.
78. Private Archives – M and Mrs Youenou: S. Liné (ed.): *Hommage à Christine Bossennec*.
79. Ibid.
80. AMAE/P – AO 1944–1955 - Inde-100 - direction Asie-Océanie

– *Note pour la direction générale des Relations culturelles*, 06.08.1945.

81. O. Lacombe, 'J'ai fait la connaissance de Christine', in S. Liné, *Témoignage des amis de Christine*, recueil inédit (Private archives).
82. A. Ross, 'Il y a un an j'apprenais par Alain Daniélou . . .', in S. Liné, *Témoignage des amis de Christine*, op. cit.
83. J. Renoir, *Ma vie mes films*, Paris: Flammarion, 1974, p. 236.
84. J. Batbedat, 'Je voudrais évoquer Christine à Calcutta . . .', in S. Liné, *Témoignage des amis de Christine*, op. cit.
85. Private interview with Chidananda Dasgupta, 17.06.2000.
86. AMAE/P – AO 1944–1955, Inde 100, Consulat général (Calcutta) to embassy in Delhi, 27.09.1949.
87. Ibid.
88. Ibid.
89. P. Sen, 'Painting', pp. 72–8, in M. Vatin (ed.), *Calcutta*, 1994, Singapore.
90. Collective talks.
91. J. Renoir, *Correspondence 1913–1978*, D. Thompson, L. Lobianco, Plon, Paris, 1998, p. 227.
92. J. Renoir, *Ma vie et mes films*, op. cit., p. 237.
93. Satyajit Ray (1921–92).
94. Cineaste, companion of Satyajit Ray from their teenage years, Chidananda Dasgupta is a prominent cinema critic.
95. J. Renoir, *Correspondence 1913–1978*, op. cit., p. 227.
96. 'India and Indians helped me to wipe out the last traces of my nationalism. I spent in India two unforgettable years. As soon as we arrived in Dum Dum, at Calcutta airport, Dido and me were surrounded by around twenty young people who welcomed us with a touching warmth'.

    J. Renoir, *Ma vie mes films*, op. cit., p. 260.
97. C. Dasgupta, 'Quelques souvenirs du passage de Jean Renoir à Calcutta', pp. 4–7, in *La Lettre des Critiques*, no. 7, Paris, March 1998.
98. Christian Belle, chargé d'affaires de France assumed office during the transition between the departure of Daniel Lévi and the arrival of Stanislas Ostrorog.
99. AMAE/P – AO 1944–1955, Inde 100, ambassader de Delhi to AE, 02.10.1950.
100. Ibid.
101. AMAE/P – Relations culturelles 1944–1959, no. 95 (5-Diffusion

presse), attaché culturel to Consulat général (Calcutta), 20.08.1948.

102. Student of Michel Bréal, specialist on ancient Iran, and professor at the Collège de France. He was secretary of the Société asiatique from 1884 until his death in 1894.

103. AMAE/N – Consulate Bombay no. 12, the Cercle Littéraire: J. Darmesteter, 'Le Cercle Franco-Parsee de Bombay', pp. i–iii, *journal des débats*, 2.11.1891, and Archives of the Alliance française in Paris, *Bulletin de l'Alliance française*, no. 38, 10.12.1991, pp. 132–3.

104. Among the French studies on Parsees: *Vendidad Sade, l'un des textes de Zoroastre d'après the manuscrit zend de la bibliothèque du Roi, avec un commentaire, une traduction nouvelle et un mémoire sur la langue zende considérée dans ses rapports avec the sanscrit et les anciens idiomes de l'Europe*, Paris, 1829–32.

Etudes sur la langue et les textes zends, par Eugène Burnouf, Tome 1, 1850.

Abrégé de la grammaire zend, par Ignace Pietraszewski, 1861.

Etudes de grammaire comparée. Les composés syntactiques en grec, en latin, en latin, et subsidiairement en zend et en indien, par Francis Meunier, 1872.

Grammaire de la langue zend, par Abel Hovelaque, 1869, 2nd edn. 1878.

Manuel de la langue de l'Avesta, par C. de Harlez.

Les observations de James Damesteter sur the Vendidad, par C. de Harlez, 1883.

Un réformateur Parsee dans l'histoire contemporaine de l'Inde, Behramji M. Malabari, trad de l'anglais d'après M. Darayam Gida, par D. Menant, 1898.

Une voyageuse au pays des Parsis, par E. Delauney, 1894.

105. He is, of course, R.D. Tata, who married Suzanne Brière in 1902. She was thereafter named Soonu Tata.

106. Sir Jam Jeejeebhoy. C. Lafontaine, *A Travers l'Inde*, Plon, Paris, 1913, pp. 22–3.

107. A. Metin, *L'Inde aujourd'hui*, pp. 21–2.

108. S.J.S. Noti and J.E. Davar, *A Letter from the Bombay Cercle Littéraire Français, Bibliothèque Dinhaw Petit. On the subject of the exclusion of the French language from the University course as recommended by the Indian Universities Commission*, p. 3, 20 October 1902, Bombay.

109. James Darmesteter, *Lettres sur l'Inde, À la Frontière Afghane*, Alphonse Lemerre, Paris, 1888, p. 338.
110. J. Darmesteter, 'Le Cercle Franco-Parsee de Bombay', *journal des débats*, 2.11.1891, pp. i–iii.
111. Archives in the Alliance française in Paris, *Bulletin de l'Alliance française*, nos. 13-14 (01.09–01.11.1886), Paris.
112. Ibid., nos. 15-16 (01.01–01.03.1887).
113. Around 9,000 Francs of that time.
114. The Minutes of the trial of Dreyfus were followed with great attention.
115. In 1904, the consul in Bombay asked the Palmes d'académiques for R.P. Noti, professor of French language and literature in Saint Xavier College as a reward for his help to prof. Fontainieu (Ecole Française d' Extrême Orient) French School of Far East for the help given to Fontainieu of the Efeo.
116. Indologist, president of the Société asiatique from 1908 until his death in 1928.
117. D Lévi, *Dans l'Inde*, op. cit., p. 217.
118. Khurshed Framji Nariman (1883–1948).
    N. Dé, *Madame Lévir Diary*, op. cit., pp. 190–1.
119. Rama K. Rao (1896–1961), ibid.
120. D. Lévi, *Dans l'Inde*, p. 224.
121. Ibid., p. 228. It is the Tata family.
122. Private Archives - Mr and Mrs Vermeil, Bombay: Lok Seva Press.
123. Sir Jivanji Modi (1854–1933). N. Dé, *Madame Lévir Diary*, op. cit., pp. 199–200.
124. J.E. Davar, officier de l'Instruction Publique, in 1906, honorary secretary of the Cercle since its founding until his death on 29 July 1919. He was succeeded by his son, E.J. Davar.
125. Ibid.
126. AMAE/N – Consulate Bombay no. 12, CG to AE, 28.05.1929.
127. Ibid., no. 12: Cercle Littéraire, undated, end of the 1920s or early 1930s.
128. Ibid.
129. AMAE/N – Consulate Bombay no. 12: Cercle Littéraire, *Bombay Sentinel*, 22.07.1937, *Bombay Chronicle* 23.07.1937 documents attachés à la dépêche du consul 27.07.1937.
130. AMAE/N – Consulate Bombay no.12: Cercle Littéraire - Consul to AE, 27.07.1937.
131. Ibid.

132. A. Marquer, *Alliances 2000*, Paris: Alliance française de Paris, pp. 111–12.
133. K. Dutta, A. Robinson, *Rabindranath Tagore, the Myriad-minded Man*, New Delhi: Rupa, 2000, pp. 78–9 and 129–30.
134. A. Morrow, *The Maharajas of India*, Delhi: Shrishti Publishers & Distributors, 1998.
135. B. Latif, *L'Inde où vécut ma mère*, Eon-Frémont (trad.), J. Auboyer (préf.), Paris: Des Femmes, 1987.
   See also: S.M. Khan, *Royaume des Bégums*, Paris: Fayard, 2001.
137. The Gaekward is known for his active participation in industrial conferences and his actions to support the movement for the studies of Indians abroad. AMAE/P, Correspondence consulaire et commerciale – Calcutta no. 12 (ff. 2-5), 06.03.1907.
138. A. Garde, S. Raulet, *Salon Indien*, Paris: Hazan, 1996, pp. 56–7.
139. A. Metin, *L'Inde aujourd'hui, Etude sociale*, op. cit., p. 163.
140. 'Un palais français aux Indes', 11.07.1908, A. Okada (préf.), *L'Inde – Les Dossiers de l'Illustration*, pp. 92–3, Bagneux: Livre de Paris, 1987.
141. A. Morrow, *The Maharajas of India*, op. cit., p. 62.
142. D. Lévi, *Dans l'Inde*, op. cit., pp. 229–38.
143. Id., pp. 229 and 236.
144. A. Morrow, *The Maharajas of India*, op. cit., p. 62.
145. D. Lévi, *Dans l'Inde*, op. cit., p. 233.
146. AMAE/P – AO 1918–1940, PB no. 53, CG to AE (f. 152).
147. The archives mention various attempts to destabilize the princely states.
148. AMAE/N – Consulate Calcutta no. 4: États princiers. See also: *The Humble Memorial of Prince Sudarshan Shrimanth Rajah Bhageeradi Krishna Govind Raj Sudarshan*, Delhi, 21.11.1917, copie attestée 09.08.1919.
149. R.J. Popplewell, *Intelligence and Imperial Defence*, op. cit., pp. 24–5.
150. AMAE/P – AO 1918–1940, PB no. 73, Allahabad, 20.04.1932 and 5.05.1934.

CHAPTER 3

The Birth and Growth of the French Language in India

The ability to speak French and the teaching of French were phenomena that existed in British India even before 1875, not only among the British but also among a very limited number of the Indian élite, especially in Bengal. In 1875, two students sat for the French examination for their Matriculation. We are able to follow the path taken by French teaching in university curricula in British India from that point on, up to the MA degree. While French had been taken up earlier by Bengal's erudite circles, it spread to the area around Bombay in the 1870s. This dynamism accompanied the commercial boom in the city. Pedraza, a Spanish professor, played a decisive role[1] in the introduction of French and its teaching first in high schools, and then in Bombay University, most likely in the 1870s.

In 1886, during their journey, French travellers reported with some surprise the increasing use of French in Bombay among members of the Alliance Française:

> The knowledge of our language has, in fact, spread far wider among the higher classes in India than one would have believed. In the government hotel and while strolling in public areas, you always meet a number of Indians—Parsees or Mahomedans—who have visited our country and are happy to have the opportunity to speak French.

The presence of the French language in India was due both to the considerable increase in communications with Europe and the spread of French in the educational system of British India.

French language teaching spread so rapidly that soon the British authorities sought to marginalize it or even wipe it out.

THE INTRODUCTION OF FRENCH IN BOMBAY UNIVERSITY (1875–1894)

In 1875, two students of the Scottish High School—a Scottish school reserved for Europeans and persons of mixed race—submitted a French paper for the Matriculation examination of Bombay University. That was the first instance of students giving this examination in French in India. It was the wave in favour of France, supported by Pedraza's teaching, that led Bombay University's Arts Faculty to submit a proposal aimed at registering French as a new 'second language' for post-admission examinations. The proposal was supported by the University's Board. It was only in April 1886, after two meetings, that the University Senate adopted the proposal with a wide majority. Among the members of the Senate was Phirozshah Mehta, one of the founder members of the Indian National Congress, and the great Sanskrit scholar, J.K. Trimbak Telag.[2] The Bombay government in turn approved of the proposal and adopted it through Resolution no. 1073 on 12 July. The resolution, which emphasized the advantages of teaching French, especially to women, finally renounced any such discrimination. A wave in favour of French language teaching built up, developing further in the university curricula under the Raj, and increasing its target audience in secondary establishments too, as the Consul observed:

> Until now, Elphinstone College, which is without doubt the most important Government institution and which is considered the Presidency's model school, had not agreed to start a French course. But very recently, it broke with the old tradition and decided that as of 1st July this year, a French professor would be recruited to start classes. As you can see, our language is spreading even further and it is probable that it will continue to do so.[3]

The growth in the teaching of French in the Bombay Presidency did not, however, take place without difficulties in the institutions of British India. Once again, according to the Consul, in Anglo-

Indian teaching circles, the teaching of French did not necessarily mean Francophilia:

> We cannot conceal the fact that in Anglo-Indian schools, French is studied more out of duty than for pleasure. This is all the more easy to understand because the teachers—all British or deeply imbued with British ideas—cannot afford to be suspected of any sympathies for France; they do not fail to use every opportunity to diminish our prestige or our virtues and, particularly, to make us look like a licentious people in the eyes of the students, with a literature that is revolting in its debauchery and immorality, while our poets are incomparably inferior to theirs [. . .]. I won't hide the fact that opinions like these can have a considerable impact on the youth, who are always ready to accept any disrespectful or uncompromising opinions of their teachers.

The Indian élite, on the other hand, far from seeing the teaching of French as a threat to their own culture, saw it rather as an opportunity. Indeed, they were the main people to defend its spread:

> We should not lose sight of the fact that in Anglo-Indian schools, French is the second living language to be taught (after English, of course). But the case is not the same in Parsee schools, where French is optional, along with Persian. However, despite the formidable competition offered by Persian, firstly because it is taught free of cost—which is not the case for French—and then because it is a tradition to which all Parsees are attached, we still see a number of young people taking French classes with unequalled application and enthusiasm—that too for four hours a week, for four years.

In 1886, French was incorporated into the post-admission curriculum of Bombay University. This was probably also done simultaneously in Calcutta University, as it was one of the subjects in the 1893 BA examinations. In Madras too, it was certainly incorporated around the same time or shortly after, as it was a subject in the 1902 BA examinations. French was, therefore, included in the curricula of Indian universities. However, while it was recognized for classes, the same did not hold true for post-admission examinations, which was evidence of reluctance on the part of the British authorities to accept the spread of French among the Indian élite.

French for BA Examinations, Two Parsee Ladies against the Senate

In 1891, while the Bombay University authorities had not yet agreed to register French as a classical language in the university's BA examination curriculum, the efforts of Pedraza and Ratnabai and Mihirbai Ardeshir persuaded them to agree to do so:

> They [the Parsees] are asking for French to be considered as a classical subject in the University curriculum. The Senate was against it for a long time, but finally gave way before the impetuousness of the attack launched by a Spaniard, Señor Pedraza, and two young women, Misses Ratnabai and Mihirbai, the daughters of the solicitor, Ardeshir. (Pedraza), a French professor, had trained a number of students in whom he had infused his enthusiasm for our language and our literature, among whom were the Ardeshir girls. Once they had mastered the language, these young women sat for the Bachelor of Arts (BA) exam. They were asked which classical language they had chosen, and answered, 'French'.
>
> The Senate remarked that French was not a valid classical subject for the BA; they answered that it was the curriculum that was wrong, that French was accepted for the Matriculation exams and that logically, it should also be acceptable for the BA exams. The answer they were given was that logic was one thing, and the curriculum another. They replied that logic had to have the last word. And, what a woman wants, a woman gets. So they won in the end, after a three-year-long struggle.[4]

Finally, French was accepted three years later in the BA examinations by Bombay University. Hence, it was accepted as a classical subject. Thus, until 1902, following the amazing campaign of the Ardeshir sisters, Bombay University's examination curriculum as far as languages were concerned was as follows:

- The Matriculation examinations covered the following subjects: English, a second language depending on the student's choice, arithmetic and algebra, geometry, history and geography, as well as elementary science. The second language could be Sanskrit, Hebrew, Persian, French, Portuguese, Marathi, Gujarati, Kannada, Hindustani or Sindhi.
- For the Intermediate examinations, the optional languages were reduced to seven, including French.

- For the BA and BSc exams, the optional languages were reduced to five, still including French.
- For the Masters (MA) exams, nine languages were admissible, including French and German.

According to the Consulate in Calcutta, there was a practical explanation for the number of women among students of French:

> Two languages (one living, one dead, Latin and French) were optional during the degree examinations and since Latin was more important for government jobs in particular, the boys preferred to learn Latin.

At the same time that these developments were taking place in university curricula, the enrolment for French courses continued to grow.

In 1893, Calcutta University offered French classes, which were structured as follows:

1. Entrance or Matriculation exam. The Consul pointed out in 1893, 'A minimal quantity of French is required for this exam for girls and boys.'[5]
2. First Examination in Arts. After this exam, the Faculty of Arts was divided into Literature and Sciences. French was compulsory for girls and boys.
3. Bachelor of Arts. French was compulsory only for girls.
4. Master of Arts. French was no longer compulsory for either boys or girls, but was an optional subject.[6]

It may be noted that for BA examinations, French was compulsory only for girls. French could also be taught in high schools and in optional Diploma examinations.

FRENCH LANGUAGE IN INDIA: A QUANTITATIVE APPROACH FOR THE YEAR 1893

On 26 May 1893, at the initiative of the Alliance Française, a ministerial circular was sent to the French consulates seeking to assess the extent to which the teaching of French had spread. The various answers sent in response to the circular, despite their lacunae, enable us to trace the birth and development of the teaching of French in the educational institutions of the Raj.

A. Tables Relating to the Teaching of French in the Consular District of Calcutta[7]

As far as the vast consular district of Calcutta was concerned, we have a variety of statements reported here in tabular form, basically relating to the capital of Bengal. They are merely of an indicative, rather than exhaustive, nature. Apart from the humble school of the Consulate General's clerk, French was taught in Calcutta only in 'English medium' establishments.

TEACHING OF FRENCH IN BOMBAY IN 1893 AND ITS GROWTH SINCE THE 1870

There were 12 institutions of higher studies, high schools and university colleges in Bombay that offered French classes.[8] No information is available for the rest of the consular district. French was also being taught in Ahmedabad, Pune, and Karachi. To facilitate comparison and gain an overall idea of the situation in India, we have also chosen to analyse the replies of the Consul in Bombay, regarding the status of the teaching of French in his district, in the form of a table listing the various establishments concerned. The first of these was the Scottish High School, which sent the first students who sat for the French examination for their Matriculation in 1875 in the Bombay district. There may have been some precedents in Calcutta or Madras, but, in any case, this was the first established case in India as a whole. In addition, it may be noted that, according to the Consul, French started to be taught formally in the Presidency's capital in the 1870s:

> In 1870, French was not being taught in any school in the Bombay Presidency. But now, it may be said that it is an inherent part of the teaching curriculum in all Anglo-Indian High Schools, with the two biggest Parsee High Schools themselves having almost 2,000 students, along with it being taught in the Wilson and Elphinstone Colleges.

The Consul added that French was also taught in Ahmedabad, Pune, and Karachi. A fifth of the students sitting for the Matriculation French examination came from these cities. Based on this information, we may, therefore estimate the number of students learning French in these cities to be around 50.

TABLE 3.1: TEACHING OF FRENCH IN CALCUTTA

French Schools

Designation of schools	*Number of students in these schools*	*Observations*
1. Le Faucheur	5	This school was held in Mr. Le Faucheur's home [...]. In addition, Mr. Le Faucheur had 12 more students in the city (private tuitions).

Foreign schools in which French was taught

Designation of schools	*Number of students*	*Students learning French*	
1. Saint Xavier College Subsidized Belgian Jesuits (boys)	800	14	
2. La Martinière School Lay foundation (boys & girls)	B: 159 G: 84	Nil 30	
3. Loreto Convent Catholic, subsidized (girls)	162	69	
4. Doveton Institution Protestant, subsidized (boys and girls)	177	25	
5. Saint Theresa's Convent Catholic, subsidized (girls)	60	2	
6. Free School Municipal, subsidized (boys & girls)	B: 225 G: 200	Nil 23	
7. City College Free school set-up by a society	1,200	28	French classes were taught by Mr. Le Faucheur for an hour, eight times a week. Mr. Le Faucheur received no remuneration from the College as a professor; he was paid by the 28 students, who gave him Rs. 4 a month.
Total	2,842	191	
Total per cent of students learning French in these schools	6.72 per cent		

TABLE 3.2: TEACHING OF FRENCH IN THE CALCUTTA AND MADRAS PRESIDENCIES

	Number of French schools	*Number of students in French schools*	*Number of foreign schools in which French was taught*		
			No. of such schools	*Total no. of their students*	*No. of students learning French*
Chittagong	–	–	–	–	–
Cocanada	–	–	–	–	–
Colombo[9]	–	–	12	2,300	150
Madras	–	–	–	–	–
Calcutta	1	5	7	2,842	191
Total	1	5	19	5,142	341

TABLE 3.3: TEACHING OF FRENCH IN THE FIVE PROVINCES FALLING DIRECTLY UNDER THE VICEROY[10]

Provinces	*Number of foreign schools in which French was taught*			*Observations*
	No. of French schools	*Total no. of their students*	*No. of students learning French*	
Assam	–	–	–	
Bengal	15	1,655	353 (21.33%)	The states did not provide the breakup between male and female students
Central Provinces	3	394	70 (17.76%)	Idem.
North-West Frontier Province	10	921	222 (24.10%)	11 boys and 211 girls
Punjab	6	278	129 (46.40%)	Only girls
Total	34	3,248	774	
Total average students learning French in schools in which it was taught (%)			23.83%	

TABLE 3.4: BOMBAY (AND GENERAL REMARKS ABOUT THE TEACHING OF FRENCH IN AHMEDABAD, KARACHI, AND PUNE)

Institutions (Girls and Boys)	*-Introduction -Teachers*	*Classes offered and number of students learning French*	*Observations*
1. Scottish High School – co-educational school	Not specified. Teaching at least since the early 1870s	- Not specified - About 50 students of both sexes	The first institution to include French in its curriculum
2. Cathedral High School Girls' school	Teaching introduced in 1876	- Three years, 2 hours/week - About 50	
3. Free Fletcher High School Girls' school	- 1879 - Pedraza	- Three years, 2 hours/week - About 20	'Europeans, people of mixed blood (Eurasians) and Europeanised Israelites' went to establishments nos. 1 to 4.
4. Saint Peter High School Girls' school	- 1880 - Pedraza, helped by nuns	- Three years, 1 hour/week - 28	
5. Parsee School/ Fort High School Boys' school	- 1884 - Pedraza, helped by a former student of his (M.J. Salmon)	- Four years, 4 hours/week - About 60 - Four years, 4 hours/week - 'Very few'	'The Principal is reputed to love our language passionately.'
6. New High School Boys' school	- Not specified (founded in 1891) - A former student of Pedraza		

(contd.)

TABLE 3.4 (*contd.*)

Institutions (Girls and Boys)	*-Introduction -Teachers*	*Classes offered and number of students learning French*	*Observations*
7. Empress - Girls High - School Girls school (Parsees)	1889 - Mrs. Winckler - a former student of Pedraza	Not specified About 20	
8. The Parsees - High School - Ecole de filles Girls School	1887 - Mrs. Mary de Ga, a former - student of Pedraza	Four years, 4 hours/week About 30	
9. Wilson - College - (not mentioned)	Not specified - Mrs. Vakil, Parsee, a - former student of Pedraza	'Lectures and preparatory classes for BA, MA Humanities exams' Around 20	
10. Elphinstone - College - (not - mentioned)	Not specified - Pedraza	Tuitions in French literature to prepare for BA exams 15	
11. Elphinstone - High School - Boys' and Girls' school	1893 - Not specified	Not specified (first year when the teaching of French was introduced)	
12. Alexandra - Native Girls, - Institution School for Indian girls	Not specified - Two degree holders – a Parsee and an Irish national	Not specified	
Evaluation of total number of students learning French as mentioned by the Consul[11]		238[12]	

Interpretation of Tables on the Status of French Teaching in India in 1893

The total number of students that appears at the bottom of the tables corresponds to the total number of students recorded in the concerned regions, and not the total number of students learning French. While the figures for Calcutta and Bombay, may be considered more or less reliable they are very approximate for the other regions of the subcontinent. Thus, south India was totally ignored by the French consular services. While sending the table on the teaching of French in the five Provinces directly under the control of the Viceroy, the French Consul General in Calcutta did clarify:

> I have begun an enquiry that will probably take a long time on the schools in other big towns in the interior where French may be taught. I can only say that, as of now, according to the information furnished by the Department of Public Instruction, there is no school that can be classified as a French school in any of these towns, which could later receive grants from the Alliance Française, but only Government schools, heavily subsidised, that teach French, especially to girls.

It must be noted that the information conveyed by the Consul was provided by the British authorities, which had little interest in promoting French education. Several conclusions may be drawn from this, bearing in mind the reservations expressed with regard to the data provided by the two consulates. On the one hand, French was being taught almost entirely throughout the educational system established by the British. On the other hand, institutions under Indian management took on an increasing share in its teaching, as could be seen in Bombay, especially in the case of the Parsees. Another feature was the high percentage of women students.

The North-West Frontier Province, the Central Provinces, and Punjab were included in the Calcutta consular district. Yet, geographically they belonged to separate regions far away from Bengal. The survey of French students in these provinces showed that French was indeed being taught in the subcontinent's northern region and the Central Provinces. The statistics concerning the North-West Frontier Province indicated 222 students were taught French, but with no details on the geographical location and the nature of the institutions where it was taught. As for the northern part of the subcontinent, there are very few details available. As for Bengal, there were 191 students in Calcutta and 353 students in the entire Presidency. The conclusion that could be drawn was that French teaching had taken root outside Calcutta in the Bengal region. The percentage of students learning French was 54 per cent for Calcutta and 46 per cent for the rest of the Presidency. As for the 46 per cent of students studying French in institutions outside Calcutta, there is no information on whether they were in Dhaka, Darjeeling, or elsewhere.

The figures for Calcutta are higher than those for Bombay, which is logical given the fact that the Bengali capital had a higher number of educational institutions. On the other hand, these figures are not as high as they appear to be if the figures for the entire Bengal region are compared to the figures for the Bombay Presidency and adjoining regions. In fact, French teaching in nearby centres such as Poona and Ahmedabad has to be taken into account. These were well-known centres for French education. However, the Consul did not send any accurate information about them. Baroda too should be added, as French also started being taught here at the turn of the century, particularly under the influence of the Tata family, and the north-west region of the British Indian empire, especially the princely states of Patiala and Kapurthala.

As for Bombay, private classes outside the formal system also have to be considered. They had to do with a socially important section of the population, as indicated by the consul:

> As for the students trained by the private courses offered by Mr. Pedraza (1873), there are quite a few and one can meet them almost everywhere, either as school or college teachers, or in the bar, the judiciary, the faculty of medicine, the administration or major business houses.

No figures concerning the students enrolled in private courses are available.

Most probably, French took root earlier in the Calcutta Presidency through the good offices of Bengali scholars than it did in the Bombay Presidency. However, beginning the last quarter of the nineteenth century it seems that the teaching of French was carried out more dynamically in the Bombay Presidency.

The Spanish professor, Pedraza, was not the only representative of the Iberian peninsula to have worked towards spreading French in India. At the periphery of the Raj was Portuguese India, which constituted another centre for the diffusion of French. As was the case in the Portuguese kingdom, French was the second language in the official education policy. The Alliance Française's bulletin specifically corroborates this fact. Ascanio Sebastiao dos Remedios e Costa, an advocate at the royal court of Goa, drew the attention of one of the association's members to the existence of four chairs for French studies, for which the incumbents were paid by the government. These chairs or were they already established in the secondary school in Panjim, the Governor-General's residence, the secondary school in Margao, the capital of Salsette province, the third at the seminary in Salsette, and the fourth in the secondary school in Mapura, the capital of the Bordes province. These four French chairs in Portuguese India made it one of the most important centres for the spread of the French language in the subcontinent. Apart from this, the cognizance of the membership of the Cercle Littéraire must be taken, which included nine persons of Portuguese descent for the year 1900–1.

One of the most astonishing features was the total absence of efforts to survey French teaching in the southern part of the subcontinent. We have the testimony of the great art collector, Emile Guimet, after his voyage in south India, in 1894, in the Alliance Française's bulletin. He referred to Brahmins who were Francophiles and who even spoke French. There is very little doubt that a hub of Francophilia or even a French-speaking community existed in the subcontinent without the knowledge of the Quai d'Orsay (France's Ministry of Foreign Affairs), and the fact that they paid little attention to this. However, there is a lack of specific data to corroborate

Guimet's observations. Gallois-Montbrun also highlighted—again in the Alliance Française bulletin—that many members of the Madras Presidency's high society were members of the association aimed at propagating the French language throughout the world. In 1894, it was noted that several students from Madras and other trading posts opted for French as their second language instead of Sanskrit in the middle school examinations:

> Let us refer to a more consoling fact, which is not devoid of importance. Many students from schools in French India appeared for the entrance examination to Calcutta University with French as their second language (instead of Sanskrit). The same holds true for the English examinations in the Middle School in Madras.[13]

In a 1902 report on Indian universities, French was mentioned as an optional subject for students of both sexes. It is, therefore, possible that French was taught in the University of Madras in the 1890s. However, the reference in the report described a situation in which the learning of French was prized much less by students in Madras than by students at Bombay University.

The Alliance Française bulletins also mention certain initiatives for the establishment of schools and an Alliance Française Committee. In its general assembly on 18 September 1897, the Pondicherry Action Committee announced that one of its objectives was to establish and develop the teaching of French in six private schools, of which two would be in Madras. However, no further communication on the functioning of these six schools was sent later. However, it may be noted that in 1900 the Alliance Française gave a grant to a school in Madras, called the Radjassamy School.

In 1913, bulletin no. 133 mentioned the creation of an Alliance Française Committee in Madras. The next bulletin specified that the committee was formed by 'Mr. Tamby, a "Hindu", an "alumnus of the Colonial College", and brought together a small group of members.' The functioning of the committee was confirmed in 1914. The first meeting was held under very favourable conditions, for it took place at Pachiappa's College, under the chairmanship of S. Srinivasa Iyengar, a high court advocate and Senator of the University of Madras. The outbreak of First World War seems to have put an end to this initiative.

The presence of France in south India was truly paradoxical. It was far more widely present there than in any other part of the subcontinent, for its missionary work, which formed a major part of the French colony of Pondicherry, was concentrated there. However, France had no consular post in south India. Was the absence of the teaching of French as indicated in the 1893 figures linked to the real absence of such teaching in south India or was it due simply to a lack of information? The teaching of French was certainly developed in this region between the last quarter of the nineteenth century and the beginning of the twentieth century.

In conclusion, based on information compiled by the Bombay and Calcutta Consuls, it may be noted that the total number of students registered as learning French was 1,012 in 1893. These figures, although incomplete, are nonetheless quite high, as French was only introduced fairly recently in the syllabus at the secondary level in universities. They help to establish the presence of French teaching among India's Westernized élite. An analysis of the factors that were responsible for the development of French teaching in British India would lead to a better understanding and interpretation of this figure. Since the 1870s, French had taken root and had developed in the educational system established in India by the British, but it had yet to acquire official recognition. In this regard, the largest number of references come from Bombay, through the Cercle Littéraire, which constituted a very active lobby for the promotion and defence of French language teaching.

THE PERIOD OF RAPID GROWTH: 1894–1902

The spread of French teaching in India at the turn of the nineteenth century is attested to by certain figures conveyed by the Consul in Bombay to the Ministry of Foreign Affairs in 1901. According to these figures, at the New High School that had more than a thousand Hindu, Muslim, and Parsee students on its rolls, 350 of them had one hour of French classes a day under the guidance of Pedraza, whereas in 1893 it was said that there were 'very few' students. At Wilson College, there were about 60 students from the Bachelor of Arts and Science (BA and BSc), and MA courses, as against 20 students eight years earlier. Again, in 1901, at Saint Xavier's College, an establishment run by German Jesuits who continued to refuse to include French in their syllabus in 1893, 75 opted for French. Finally, in the prestigious and 'highly popular' Fort and Proprietary High School, about 150 students were registered for French classes. Thus, in these four institutions alone, more than 635 students learning French were recorded. The Consul's forecasts about the rise in the number of students learning French in 1893 were confirmed. The movement to spread the language was entirely endogenous.

The requirements for the examination were found to be of an entirely satisfactory level—even 'difficult', according to the Alliance Française bulletin. In spite of this, French language studies gained in popularity in Bombay's schools and colleges.

> . . . every passing year saw a growing number of candidates for the special examinations. Last year, 46 young people passed a French matriculation examination that opened the doors to university colleges. At the start of the current academic year, there were 13 more.

A survey carried out in 1902 as a supplement to the 1901 survey put the number of French students at 675. The students of the four institutions already mentioned were joined by those of Alexandra Native Girls Institution, with a Parsee principal, which had about 25 students in the French class. A class of about 20 French students was also registered in Empress High School, a free school for young Parsee girls established in 1889. Finally, the bulletin noted that the Sir Jamsetjee Jijeebhoy Institution was in the process of starting a French class. In 1902, the number of registered French students at these six institutions alone crossed 675, as against 238 students in 12 establishments in 1893, which represented an increase of more than 183 per cent for a survey restricted to a clearly smaller base. The establishment for which enrolment figures are available showed an increase of more than 575 per cent in the strength of French classes between 1893 and 1901–2. Finally, the number of students learning French in the two university colleges for which data are available was more than 135.

TABLE 3.5: COMPARATIVE FIGURES PERTAINING TO THE INCREASE IN STUDENT STRENGTH OF FRENCH CLASSES BETWEEN 1893 AND 1902 IN TWO SECONDARY SCHOOLS AND TWO UNIVERSITY COLLEGES IN BOMBAY

Institution	*Number of students learning French in 1893*	*Number of students learning French in 1902*
New High School	'Negligible'	350
Fort and Proprietary High School	About 60 (Fort High School)	150
Wilson College	About 20	About 60
St. Xavier's College	No French courses	75
Total	Less than 100	More than 635

Based on the figures available for educational institutions in Bombay, it may be concluded that an absolute craze for French had been triggered by the inclusion of French courses in the Bombay University syllabus. However, this craze was soon to provoke a reaction from the British authorities.

OFFENSIVES AGAINST THE TEACHING OF FRENCH: 1902–14

In 1902, the Consul wrote to the Ministry of Foreign Affairs about the decision of the Commission on Educational Reforms in Indian Universities with regard to the teaching of French in Indian universities: 'As for French, the report simply stated the following on page 65: "French should not, except for female students, be accepted as an alternative for a classical language." '

That year, a commission was set-up in British India. One of its aims was to study the functioning of universities in India, and eventually transform them into full-time teaching institutions.[14] It also gave the British authorities the opportunity to discontinue the teaching of certain subjects in which the progress made by the Indian students was deemed as undermining their authority. Therefore, it was decided to limit access to the study of French by excluding the subject from the examinations taken by male students.

In the original report referred to by the Consul, an additional detail may be noted on page 20, in a paragraph on modern European languages:

> In Bombay French, and in Madras French or German, is included as an alternative second language in the BA course. In the former case, owing, it is said, to the comparative easiness of the examination, French is taken up by a number of students to the detriment of the study of the classical languages of the Province. This result is to be deplored, and measures should be taken to prevent students from neglecting the study of classical languages in order to secure an easier examination. We deprecate the substitution of a modern for a classical language; but we would allow female candidates to offer French, as is now the rule at Calcutta.

A study of the testimony of different players in the field of university education in India, on which the commission was supposed to have based its report, bore out the claim that French language teaching was mentioned by only three people—all three British, working for the University of Bombay: MacMillan, the principal of Elphinstone College, W.H. Sharp, a professor of philosophy at Elphinstone College, and P. Giles, the director of Public Instruction in Bombay. Among them, only the second gentleman called openly for measures for the discontinuance of French:

> Some change is badly wanted. . . . At present a man may get High honours without being able to write a line correctly, because of the number of marks assigned to composition is very small.
>
> For the last two years, French has become a very popular subject among students on account of it being regarded as easy. It is a pity that French has attained such prominence. It cannot be called a classical language, and it is undesirable that the Indian classical language should be discouraged in its favour. It is possible to extend

study of an easy subject so as to make it difficult to pass in it as in other subjects, but does not appear to have been done in this case. French was introduced in the University curriculum because lady candidates found it difficult to pass in classical languages.

On reading the figures given by MacMillan, which were reproduced in the same report and on which Sharp had based his analysis, one can only wonder at the latter's version of the facts. With regard to the success rate in second language examinations provided by MacMillan—who mentioned the 'extinction' of Greek classes and a considerable reduction in the number of students opting for Latin since the introduction of French—the statistics were as follows:

Previous examination – English: 25%, Sanskrit: 15%, Latin: 26%, Arabic: 12%, French: 23%, Persian: 20%, Avesta and Pahlavi: 10%.

Intermediate examination – English: 25%, Sanskrit: 25%, Latin: 20%, Arabic: 23%, French: 20%, Persian: 18%.

BA examination – English: 25%, Sanskrit: 13%, Latin: 20%, Arabic: 14%, French: 17%, Persian: 20%, Avesta and Pahlavi: 12%.

Besides, MacMillan mentioned a detail that seemed to indicate a higher level of difficulty of the French examinations compared to other languages, as he wrote:

Dans les sujets au choix, aucune note n'est assignée aux examens pour l'épreuve de rédaction ou de composition concernant l'anglais, le sanscrit, l'avesta et le pahlavi, et seulement 5% pour le français.

In the voluntary subject no marks are ascribed to essay or composition in English, Sanskrit, Latin, Avesta, Pahlavi, and only 5 per cent in French.

Moreover, the question papers for MA, BA, Intermediate Arts Examination, Previous Examination, and Matriculation for 1900–1 reveal a highly literary content and very strict requirements.

Finally, no unfavourable opinion was noted about French language teaching among Indian professors teaching other classical Indian languages in universities who, according to Sharp's version of the facts, ought to have been the first to be alarmed. That did not prevent Bombay's Director of Public Instruction from stating:

It is becoming a serious thing, this extraordinary way in which people are taking up French to the neglect of their own classical languages. The only reason is that the French examination is easier than that in Sanskrit. Sometime ago it was easier to pass in Persian than Sanskrit, and then everybody went in for Persian. Now all have gone round to French. That shows that there is something wrong in the standard. There may be a few persons, especially businessmen, to whom French may be useful, but it is inconceivable that French is of any use to the majority of Hindu, Mahomedan, and Parsee students.

Before deciding to restrict French to lady candidates for whom it was originally intended, it would be well to take the advice of the Chamber of Commerce, because it says that French is becoming more and more useful for business purposes. . . . An approximate equalization of the standards would probably put a stop to this abnormal development of French.

The great interest evinced by the British authorities in classical languages may be viewed with a certain astonishment, as it was contradictory to Macaulay's Minute, which had served as a frame of reference since the dispute first broke out between the Orientalists and the Anglicists.

In spite of the alternatives offered, the decision taken by the administration of Lord Curzon the Viceroy, which was engaged in an offensive against the emancipation of the Indian élite in the economic and cultural fields, was to exclude French from the university syllabus for male candidates.[15]

For the Consul in Bombay, the reasons behind the measures taken by the British authorities were self-explanatory. Just like the other subjects that the commission set-up by the Viceroy was trying to discontinue—such as history and political economy—French too was helping in the process of liberation in which Indians were engaged:

The Commission for educational reforms in India, set up by Lord Curzon, fearing the enormous progress made by the natives in all branches of human knowledge, and the harsh criticism besieging his administration, has simply broken up the former mechanism that produced results that were too good, closed down a large number of secondary schools, and made access to University education so difficult, that only a few of the élite—the sons of absolutely loyal natives, could alone enter University portals [. . .].

It is against this ostracism that the Cercle Littéraire's Board is protesting. I am afraid that their protest will be in vain: the issue is not culture, but politics. French ideas are dangerous.

In any case, the fallacious reasoning on which the Commission based its decision was criticized by the members of the Cercle Littéraire. Their representatives rebelled against the findings of the Commission on University Educational Reforms regarding French language teaching, and they brought their action to public notice. While the Consul was sceptical about the outcome of the campaign, given the reasons behind the restriction imposed by the British Indian administration, the directors of the Cercle Littéraire, on the other hand, appeared confident about achieving their objective, which they believed was linked to the irreversible process of modernization that their country had embarked upon:

. . . The Cercle's Board of Directors has just sent a letter requesting His Excellency, the Viceroy . . . against the Commission's recommendation. You may note therein that the Board has provided unchallengeable arguments about how the French language has been useful everywhere and deserves a place as one of the best modern languages [...].

I am sure that His Excellency, the Viceroy, will not turn a deaf ear to our appeal and that he will not allow this language to be struck off the list of classical languages in the University.[16]

Arguments and Refutations

The Cercle Littéraire wrote to the Bombay University Senate requesting that French should remain accessible to all students following the University's syllabus. This letter did not fail to pinpoint the inherent contradictions in the Commission's decision: 'French has long been admitted among the optional subjects for the Indian and Ceylon as well as English Civil Service.'[17]

On the topic of the supposed easy-to-learn nature of French, which made the language suitable particularly—even exclusively—for women students, the Cercle Littéraire opposed this view in unequivocal terms:

The popular idea doubtless is that it is a language easy to master; but we would assert without fear of contradiction, that this is a popular fallacy and hallucination, based as most hallucinations are, on ignorance or an unverified data. The assumption, too, that the French language is easy enough to suit the intellectual calibre of girls and women, is as fallacious as it is gratuitously insulting to them.[18]

The commission's second argument was that students opted for French to the detriment of other 'classical languages of the Province'. First of all, the authors of the letter defending French argued against the significance attached to this statement and concluded that the languages being designated were Sanskrit, Arabic, and Persian. However, according to them, teaching French could in no way undermine Sanskrit or Arabic as for students learning those languages, they were indispensable for their future careers. Therefore, French would have entered into competition with the teaching of Persian, a language chosen by default by students who wished to avoid studying Sanskrit and Arabic. There followed a long brief comparing the two languages, and concluding finally with the many advantages that the learning of French offered:

It will suffice, if we place before them briefly the many advantages a study of the French language and literature offers to our students, to deprive them of which constitutes an argumentation without valid grounds, in our understanding, regarding a matter of serious importance to the educational and intellectual advancement of this country.[19]

In their letter, the authors also stressed the comparative status of French in other European countries and the prime position it held in England itself, where French language teaching enjoyed an important position and was recognized in the field of higher education. This claim was backed by a number of quotations taken from eminent British intellectuals referred to by the authors of the letter, hence arguing that the decision to prohibit access to the language for Indian students was made even more inexplicable:

It appears to us then incomprehensible that it should even be contemplated to bar the doors of such a temple of light to our Indian Undergraduates. . . . The advantages of learning French are so apparent and so manifold that we earnestly trust that those responsible for the spread of Education in this country will never be wanting in their endeavours to encourage and advance it.[20]

Moreover, the authors underlined in great detail the serious harm that the exclusion of French would cause to students of medicine, a large number of students in the Arts Faculty who planned to pursue their education in England with the aim of passing their Civil Services examinations, those wishing to enter the Bar or seeking to earn higher degrees from a British university, as well as those who wished to be a part of the liberal professions.[21]

The authors also supported their arguments by quoting other special cases. They emphasized, in particular, that French provided a passport to the commercial professions and to teaching, observing that the latter sectors 'offer nowadays many openings, with the general spread of education and the increasing intercourse with Europe'.[22]

Apart from the arguments related to socio-professional issues, the authors of the letter defending French teaching advanced moral and civic arguments too. According to them, French teaching provided a: 'means of moral and mental improvement and of social equipment and finish, such as few other studies could so completely bestow, and such as cannot but make him a good citizen and a useful member of society'.[23]

Finally, the letter of protest written by the members of the Cercle Littéraire to the university authorities stressed the usefulness of the French language for staying in touch with European thought and science, and concluded that it ought to be 'one of the functions of the university to place within the Indian student's reach, rather than to snatch it away from his grasp'.[24] French was then shown as a language that provided access to moral and social development, as well as to scientific and technical knowledge. At the beginning of the twentieth century, it was a vehicle of progress and modernity. The trade then being carried out between Bombay and France also played an important part in making it attractive.

On 24 January 1903, the committee constituted by the Bombay University's Senate to look into the letter of the Bombay government, arising out of the report of the Indian Universities Commission 1902, issued a report containing 16 articles.

In Article 12, the Senate stipulated that it found it: 'in the impossibility to approve (i) the exclusion of history and political economy from compulsory classes in Arts, (ii) the exclusion of French as an alternative to classical languages except for girls (...)'.[25]

The Cercle Littéraire's action, therefore, helped Bombay University to withdraw the discriminatory measures taken unilaterally by the Indian Universities Commission against the teaching of French. However, it was discontinued as an examination option for male students in Calcutta and Bombay universities.

In 1907, Elphinstone College appointed Louis Peltier, an Alliance Française delegate, to take French classes within the university curriculum, which indicated the importance attached to the teaching of this language in an institution held to be one of the most prestigious in the city. However, while the battle to save French from being discontinued in Bombay University's curriculum had been partly won, administrative conditions for its teaching remained precarious. More so as the British authorities had not given up and would soon find new allies in their campaign.

A New Threat: The German Jesuits' Campaign in 1911

Even as the Société des Amis de la France dans l'Inde britannique (Friends of France in British India), constituted by representatives of the British Raj, was being created, attacks against French education intensified, as indicated by the Consul:

> As the Department knows, the Governor of Bombay Presidency has recently exhibited a very determined opposition to French teaching in its university. But his action was limited to the administrative field.

Though the British established the Société des Amis de la France dans l'Inde britannique, this did not prevent the authorities from pursuing a discriminatory policy *vis-à-vis* French teaching in the course of the same year. Their hostile stand was declared publicly during a speech made by the Governor in 1911:

> Until now, the Governor had not made any public statements on this topic but, at the inauguration of new buildings of the 'Sirdar Dastur

Nosherwan Girls' High School' in Poona, he declared in the part of his speech pertaining to the fact that there were too many subjects in the curriculum, the text of which I have enclosed: 'I am bound to say that the study of French is of no use and could be harmful.'

The contradiction between the respect that the British had for French culture in private and the actions of the British authorities in India in public was, therefore, quite evident.

In reply to a letter to the Governor of Bombay on the stand he had taken on the teaching of the French language, Consul Barret, received the following justification: 'We cannot encourage the teaching of this subject, in consideration of the much more urgent obligations of Public Instruction, but we would not think of abolishing it if it could be taught without the government having to provide any financial support.'

Despite the attitude of the British authorities, a healthy sign of French language teaching in western India in the early twentieth century was the appointment of a second French teacher—Professor Charlier—at the Government High School in Ahmedabad and the Ahmedabad College, in 1910. Following the example of Louis Peltier, he stayed with his family in the city for several years, and taught French. The teaching of French in the Bombay Presidency and nearby areas once again sparked off attacks both by the British authorities and by German Jesuits.

In 1893, the Consul in Bombay had drawn attention to the hostility of the German Jesuits to French language teaching in the Bombay Presidency:

> The only establishment that has so far refused to accept the spread of our language is the one run by German Jesuits, where Latin is being taught, essentially. Consequently, many Hindu and Parsee students have forsaken it, preferring by far a living language over a dead one, as it would be much more useful and would help them obtain jobs that were more likely to be gainful.

The new campaign against the teaching of French was to once again take the form of curricular reforms. When it became a teaching institution in 1911, the University of Bombay undertook fresh curricular reforms in order to set the syllabus for the BA

(Honours) degree. The Parsees remained at the forefront in defending the teaching of French:

> I have the honour of informing the Department that during its discussion on teaching, the University of Bombay's Senate has decided to institute a degree that will be higher than the BA degree. It will be called a 'BA with Honours'.
>
> Professor Wadia, seconded by Mr. Mody, Secretary to Bombay's Parsee Panchayat, requested that French, Avesta and Pahlavi be introduced as subjects for this exam. The Director of Public Instruction opposed the proposal strongly, and it was finally rejected. It appears that Mr. Sharp who, as I pointed out in my preceding paper, had requested the Governor of Bombay to include French in the study programme, finally gave in to Sir George Clarke's wishes, who did not wish to encourage the study of French.[26]

When this reform was undertaken, the Jesuits of Saint Xavier's College, Bombay—whose influence predominated in the University's Boards—managed to convince the Governor, Lord Sydenham, to do away with French language teaching. They took up the arguments used in 1902, stressing the competition with Persian and Sanskrit. At the request of the Presidency's Director of Public Instruction, the Governor decided not to grant his approval to the secondary-level curriculum, established by Charlier and Peltier, which enabled students of French to qualify for the university entrance examination.

However, the German Jesuits did not stop there. They tried to get French language teaching eliminated from secondary schools falling under the government. However, in response to an enquiry instituted by the government, teachers and students of French managed to prove that the allegations concerning French language teaching remained unfounded. Nonetheless, the new campaign still had serious consequences. When examinations were instituted for BA Honours in English, Sanskrit, Latin, and Persian, the government representative demanded that no such examination be instituted for French. His request was supported by a large majority of the University's Senate. Thus, the development of French language teaching in university curricula in India ran into rough weather, preventing students of French from having access to the highest university degree. The request made by the Governor of Bombay *not to promote French* thus appeared to be a euphemism used to cloak the desire of the British authorities to dissuade the Indian élite from studying French, thereby putting an end to any changes or dialogue that French language could have led to. In addition, Lord Sydenham further aggravated the measure adopted by the University of Bombay's Senate by deciding to no longer recognize French language teaching in secondary schools after almost half a century during which the language had been taught officially.

Since they no longer enjoyed the official status of professors, the situation of French teachers became precarious. Further, the attacks by the German Jesuits seemed to have succeeded in convincing members of the Muslim community of the harmful consequences of French language teaching with regard to the teaching of Persian, as well as of the immoral nature of the French language.

However, on the whole, these discriminatory measures and the denigration campaign did not seem to have affected the interest of Indians in the French language. The Consul in Bombay noted: 'It must be pointed out that, despite all the opposition, there was no perceptible change in the study of French. Our language was frequently chosen in examinations, in which it could be selected as an optional subject.'

THE FRENCH LANGUAGE IN INDIA AFTER FIRST WORLD WAR

Between 1914 and 1940, French language teaching was gradually re-incorporated in different universities—such as Calcutta and Madras—from where it had practically disappeared following its partial exclusion. It also established itself in other universities, such as in Dacca and Allahabad. Its re-incorporation coincided with the gradual establishment of departments of Modern European Languages, in which French was taught along with German and, sometimes, Dutch. Henceforth, in the eyes of the Indians, German and French emerged as equally important languages, with the spread of German influence being acknowledged. This was supported by an active policy of university exchanges and, more generally, by effective cultural action. Nonetheless, it seemed that French still enjoyed the status of the 'first second European language' in India, thanks to its early establishment, its importance in Bombay, and its intellectual prestige in Bengal. On the eve of Second World War, it appeared to be part of the curriculum in India's main universities, although no French department or chair had yet been set up.

A second general observation concerns the committees of the Dacca, Calcutta, and Allahabad universities. There, French language classes were intended to provide access to specialized publications for research purposes. So the extent of the usefulness of the language seems to have been less than the Cercle Littéraire's members had attributed to it in response to the measures of exclusion instituted by the University of Bombay's Senate. For there was a self-evident linguistic reality that no one could ignore—the confirmation of the influence of English in India.

After the war, the situation of the French language remained paradoxical, to say the least. Following a decision of the former Governor of the Presidency, Lord Sydenham, although French was being taught extensively, it no longer enjoyed official recognition. For several consecutive years, the latter had refused to grant official recognition to the French curriculum in secondary schools, which was 'based on a more varied and extensive study of the language and literature', prepared by French teachers, at the request of the Director of Public Instruction: 'Officially, French was not recognized as being taught in secondary schools—but it was. It was a truly abnormal state of affairs, to say the least!'[27] remonstrated the manager of the Bombay Consulate.

The situation of French teachers was, therefore, highly precarious because of the attitude of the British authorities. Peltier describes the difficult conditions prevailing in his profession:

> In 1893, the University of Bombay included our language in its curriculum and placed it on the same footing as other second languages.

However, the study of French was just about tolerated by the government of Bombay. That is why there is no French chair in its colleges, and why Mr. Charlier in Ahmedabad since 1910, and myself, in Bombay since 1902, only occupy temporary posts and can be dismissed at any time. That is why we get a fixed salary, with no chance of a raise—three-tenths of what official teachers get, without any right to paid leave or retirement benefits, which are provided to everyone else.

Despite the hostile attitude of the British authorities and its punitive consequences for French language teaching, the latter continued to spread. It was reportedly being taught in 50 secondary schools out of the 200 recognized by the University of Bombay.[28] The French course in these schools lasted four years. French courses included grammar and translation into and from the language, and those who completed four years were considered to have a 'reasonable grasp of our language'.[29]

The Official Reintroduction of French into the Syllabus

In 1918, following the Franco–British alliance during the war, the British authorities agreed to introduce a course, in the form of a series of 24 public lectures, for the preparation of a MA degree.[30] The decision elicited the following comment from the director of the Consulate in Bombay: 'It is quite clear that before the war, the University would have rejected such a decision.'

In 1918, the University of Bombay entrusted one of its professors with teaching sixteenth-century French literature to its MA students. Peltier made the most of the change in the attitude of the university authorities by trying to consolidate the institutionalization of French in the university curriculum: 'I started an academic campaign to institute an honours degree in French, such as the one that exists for English, Sanskrit, Latin and Persian.'[31]

In 1919, Peltier noted a weakening of prejudices against French teaching, and hoped to see signs of an end to '. . . this evil and widespread slander concerning the so-called immorality of the French people'. A little over a year later, he witnessed the happy outcome of his campaign. The University of Bombay's

Senate declared the following with regard to the registration of French among the honours courses:

> We recommend [. . .] that French be added to the list of languages for which an honours degree is granted. The close relationship that is destined to continue between France and the British Empire seems sufficient reason to go back on the decision taken eight years ago.[32]

The link between the decision of the University of Bombay's Senate and political events was, therefore, clearly expressed. Peltier was pleased with the decision made and took an optimistic view of the future: 'This is a step forward, and we can hope to succeed.'

At the same time, after a study conducted between 1917 and 1919, the following was noted in the report of the University of Calcutta's Commission:

> We are glad to find that the university has arranged for classes in French, German, Dutch, Modern Tibetan, Chinese and Japanese for the benefit of advanced teachers and students, and the eagerness with which admission is sought into some of these classes by university teachers and research students is a hopeful sign of the success likely to be achieved under judicious management.[33]

Among the conclusions drawn by the University of Dacca with regard to the same commission's work, the following was stated: We agree fully with the suggestion of our predecessors that provision should be made for the teaching of French and German so as to enable the students to read in those languages relating to their studies.[34]

In April 1919, the University of Bombay introduced nine new courses. Among them, it proposed to have one for ancient French. Three months later, Peltier became the first professor in India to be officially entrusted with the teaching of a French course in an Indian university. The course was called '17th century French literature'.[35] In July 1919, French teaching appeared to be on the verge of regaining its position in the official curricula of Indian universities. However, it was still just a course in ancient French.[36] In 1920, five candidates presented themselves for the MA examinations with French. Ten students registered for the 1919–20 BA (Honours) courses. Two students passed the examination, and five new candidates registered for the examination the following year. Peltier clarified that the two other courses offered at the same time—economics and Persian—each had just two students.

The Significant Presence of the French Language in Bombay

In Bombay, in the 1920s, French teaching continued to draw enthusiasts. It had a special place among foreign languages, and in 1929, almost half a century after its introduction in the University of Bombay, the Consul was able to note the following: 'Of all European languages, apart from English, which is the official language, it is French that is the most known, most popular and the best studied in India and especially in the Presidency of Bombay.'

In the 1920s, in the Bombay Presidency, university curricula were broadened. French language teaching was no longer limited to women and the number of second languages went up—along with Sanskrit, Persian, Pali, Prakrit, Avesta, Pahlavi, Greek, Latin, and Hebrew. Languages such as Portuguese, German, Gujarati, Marathi, and Sindhi were also taught, among many others. The expansion of second language curricula did not harm the spread of French, which seemed to consolidate its position in the University of Bombay. Furthermore, French could now be taught as a second language from the age of twelve years. Thus, the French course could now last up to ten years—four additional years as compared to other regions, where, except for a few private secondary schools, it was generally only accessible at the level of higher studies, i.e. after Matriculation.

In 1929, in the Bombay Presidency, 12 per cent of secondary school students chose French as their second language. Out of a total of 25,000 students, 3,000 chose French classes that year. Of them, 800 opted for it as their second language for the Matriculation examination, as against about 3,000 for Sanskrit and 900–1,000 for Persian. In university colleges, the teaching of a second language was not compulsory for those who opted for the science, medicine, commerce, technology, and agriculture streams. The second language remained compulsory for students of the humanities in the second year, and then became optional. About 60 students opted for French for the BA degree, with English and one more subject; 12–15 students took it as the main subject for a BA (Honours) degree. Thus, there was a definite improvement over 1920, as the Consul also pointed out: 'French found a place in the official University of Bombay curricula, gaining in importance over the years.'

Those who passed the BA (Honours) examination generally continued for another two years for an MA degree. Thus, French became an integral part of higher studies. Each year, about 60 students chose it for a six-year course and about a dozen students opted for the eight-year cycle.

TABLE 3.6: INCREASE IN THE NUMBER OF STUDENTS OF FRENCH IN THE UNIVERSITY OF BOMBAY (1921–9)

Examination	*BA*	*BA (Honours)*
1920	40	10
1929	60	12–15
Increase	50%	20–50%

Moreover, the Consul in Bombay deemed that the level of education was the same as the level in universities in other Anglo-Saxon countries: 'The official University curricula in the city of Bombay are of the same level as those of British universities and higher than American ones.'

To the number of students in universities must be also added those in private establishments or European schools that did not fall under the University of Bombay, for instance, schools that prepared students who were 'children of Europeans *or* Parsees' for the examinations held on the completion of secondary school, for English universities.[37] In these schools, the medium of instruction was English, and French was reported to be the main second language: 'In the Bombay Presidency, students from these schools generally opted for French as the second language, preferring it over Latin or German.'

While competition with German increased, French still remained one of the primary choices of students in the Bombay Presidency at the end of the 1920s.

As far as Calcutta and its region were concerned, there are no reports specifically devoted to the issue of French teaching available in the diplomatic archives, which makes it impossible to carry out any quantitative assessment. Nonetheless, French was taught, more in association with the prestige of French culture.

Calcutta and Bengal: Erudition and the French Language

Despite recommendations by the universities of Calcutta and Dacca aimed at introducing Modern European Languages, essentially French and German, the conclusions of the Calcutta University Commission in 1919 proved to be cautious:

> We do not recommend the establishment in the first instance of a department of Modern European languages, but we think a competent teacher should be appointed to give instruction in French and German to those students who will require tuition in those languages in order to pursue their special studies, whether in science or in arts subjects. The teaching of modern European languages should be developed gradually.[38]

Despite its timorous acknowledgement, the poet, Rabindranath Tagore, introduced French teaching in Santiniketan in 1919 itself. The consequences of the lifting of restrictions imposed on French in Calcutta University are difficult to assess. While the archives failed to provide any specific answers to this question, several accounts have testified to the fact that French was in vogue in certain intellectual and literary circles. The widespread use of French among the élite in Bengal's capital was confirmed by Désirée Lévi, the wife of the great philologist who noted the existence of 'proper French literary circles'[39] in 1922. In 1928, Kalidas Nag, a historian, a professor at Calcutta University, and a former Sorbonne scholar, referred to the fact that many of his students could read French books.[40] The same year, he set-up an Indo–Latin Society centred on French. Indeed, the translation of certain French works became the subject of controversy among even the city's Francophile circles. The careers of personalities such as Ruby Palchoudhury confirm that certain religious congregations that were running schools frequented by European and Indian children from Calcutta's high society, such as Loretto College, offered French classes.[41] Furthermore, after the War, French soon found its place in the education offered by the university set-up by Rabindranath Tagore in Santiniketan. Professor Morris, of Parsee faith and a member of the Cercle Littéraire, was appointed as a French teacher in 1919.

When the Lévis reached Santiniketan in 1921, French language teaching in Visva Bharati still seemed to be in an embryonic stage. Their stay was to give some impetus to its growth. While no precise figures are available, several renowned personalities can be identified among the French students in Tagore's university. There were, for instance, Dinendranath Tagore, the poet's nephew, Prabodh Mukhopadhyaya, Seyad Mustapha Mujtoba Ali, who was to become a famous writer, Bidusekhar Bhattacharya Sastri, a Sanskrit scholar, and Kshitimohan Sen. In 1924, French was offered from the primary level up to the BA (Honours) level in Santiniketan. From 1935 to 1940, it was Professor Christine Bossennec from Sainte Marie de Neuilly, a former tutor of Alain Daniélou and Zaher Shah, who took over the French classes. Bossennec's subsequent appointment as a French teacher in New School, Darjeeling confirms the existence of French classes outside Calcutta.

As in Bombay, French was taught at Calcutta University up to the MA level.[42] Thus, French language teaching definitely existed in both schools and universities in Bengal. However, the number of students was probably lower than it was in Bombay. From 1940 onwards, the success of the classes held by the Alliance Française would confirm the existence of an enormous potential for French teaching in Bengal.

In Lahore's Punjab University, there are no records of French being taught in 1933.[43] However, when the Franco–Indian Centre was set-up in 1938, Lahore became a hub of French culture. In Ajmer (Rajasthan) and Mhow (M.P.), where a significant French missionary presence has been noted,[44] French was imparted at the primary level, up to Classes 8 and 9.

The case of Aligarh and André Weil is interesting. The future eminent mathematician, a co-founder of the Bourbaki group,[45] met Sylvain Lévi several times, which gave him a taste for Indian philosophy.[46] In 1929, the philologist introduced him to Syed Ross Masood, Vice-Chancellor of Aligarh Muslim University, in the United Provinces near Delhi. The latter offered to entrust the young mathematician with a chair of French civilization that he planned to institute, as he believed that the study of French culture should have a place in Indian universities along with the study of British culture. However, the project for introducing a French civilization chair failed. Instead, Weil was invited to occupy the mathematics chair left vacant in 1930. Thus began a stay lasting more than two years in India for this young enthusiast of Indian culture. Weil was officially incorporated as a member of the Indian university's faculty.[47] Along with the Jesuits, Caius and Racine, he contributed to cultural exchanges through the promising realm of the sciences. Indeed, this great intellectual's thinking was considerably influenced by his stay in India, as was the case with his sister, the philosopher, Simone Weil.

When he left Santiniketan in 1925, this French professor of Swiss origin apparently first settled in Benares, before moving to Allahabad, probably in 1930. His qualifications as a teacher of German and French made it possible for him to be selected when the university sent a call for nominations to the Quai d'Orsay that year.[48] Soon after India's Independence, he was found to have been living there for several years, having created a French cultural hub around him, which included leading professors and intellectuals. Indeed, his presence encouraged several of this university's graduates to complete their studies in France.

South India

The annual reports of the Saint Joseph College of Trichinopoly, Ignatius Loyola of Madras, and Saint Francis Xavier College of Palamcottah reveal new reforms in the BA examinations, instituting a 'BA new regulations' examination. This led to the reorganization of curricula and increased the number of second languages. The curriculum now offered a choice of languages from among three groups: the classical languages group (Sanskrit, Greek, Latin, Arab, Persian, and Hebrew), the Indian languages group (Tamil, Marathi, Telugu, Oriya, Malayalam, Burmese, Kannada, Sinhalese, Urdu, and Hindi), and the Modern European Languages group (French and German). English was the main language and was compulsory. The initial students of French were able to choose it as a second language for the BA examination at the end of 1931–2.

It is interesting to note that 687 reference works related to French culture could be found in the Madras Loyola College library catalogue in 1927. Of them, a little under a 100 were in English.[49] However, a comparison should be made between this figure, the 5,459 titles of works in English and the publications related to other second languages: 396 for Latin and Greek combined, 78 for Sanskrit, 362 for Tamil, 99 for Telugu, 75 for Malayalam, 8 for Russian, and one for each of the following languages: German, Italian, Malay, Malagasy, Provençal, Serbian, and Spanish. For Italian, Malay, Malagasy, Provençal, Serbian, and Spanish, the publications were, in fact, in French, along with three reference works concerning Russian. Thus, French unquestionably emerged as the second European language in this prestigious establishment, founded in 1925. For the year 1930–1, references can be found to a French department headed by Reverend Saulière, presented as an assistant teacher of French for diploma courses, not for French as a second language in the BA curriculum.[50] This confirms that French was certainly taught as an optional course before it was introduced as a second language following the reform of the BA degree curricula in 1931–2. This explains the presence of so many references to French literature in the Loyola College library in the 1920s.

A few remarks need to be made for a deeper understanding of the list of students. First and foremost, the success rate of students of French in examinations was often much higher than that of students of other languages. Further, among students

TABLE 3.7: BREAKDOWN OF STUDENTS WHO PASSED THE BA FINAL YEAR EXAMINATIONS (NEW VERSION) AT LOYOLA COLLEGE, MADRAS (1932–4; 1937–8)[51]

Year	*Second languages in the curriculum (BA final)*					*Percentage of students of French*
	French	*Tamil*	*Telugu*	*Malayalam*	*Sanskrit*	
1932	4	16	13	4	11 + 1 (Latin)	9%
1933	4/101	N.I.	N.I.	N.I.	N.I.	4%
1934	7	37	16	11	17	8.6%
1937	21	42	37	13	22	18.5%
1938	15	57	23	7	23 + 1 (Persian)	13.5%

Note: (N.I.: Figure not indicated).

of French at the Ignatius Loyola College in Madras, a significant proportion of candidates with names of British or even Portuguese origin can be noted. From 1930 onwards, in the Madras Presidency, French was elevated from non-compulsory classes to the BA study programme, as an optional second language, which enabled it to consolidate its position as the second European language in India. However, the study of French did not seem to reach the élite in the Madras Presidency and remained almost marginal.

French and the Evolution of Indian Society

Between the two World Wars, the public education system was Indianized in reaction to the domination of English. In 1922, Ashutosh Mukherjee abolished the use of English as a medium of instruction for higher education in Calcutta University. Other universities followed suit. In 1929, according to the principal of Saint Francis Xavier's College in Palamcottah, one Indian language also became compulsory in secondary schools. Relaying the news from the rector of Saint Xavier's College, the Consul General expressed his concerns with regard to French language teaching: 'The few students who gave preference to French, which was accepted as a second language so far, will now have to give up studying our language, which is already not very widely spoken in India.'[52] The principal clarified his concern by pointing out the practical consequences of the change in regime: 'So far, our students found opting for French advantageous, as they could dispense with the need to take up a local language. Now, this privilege has been taken away and we cannot hope to get any new candidates for French, at least for some time.'[53]

It was not long before the consequences of this measure surfaced. In a society where English was necessary for several jobs, French was relegated to the ranks of a possible third language in the educational curricula. Except for the Bombay region, French tended to disappear from the curricula of Indian public secondary schools, where the regional Indian language and English started being taught.

Yet the information available points to an overall increase in French language teaching in India between the two Wars. This was the result of the broadening of curricula, especially once the ban on French for male students was ended. In addition, from 1919 onwards in the Bombay and Calcutta universities, and from 1931 onwards in Madras University, French was accepted as a second language for the BA examinations. In Bombay and Calcutta, the teaching of French had been vouched for up to the MA level.

Molière's language came to be considered increasingly as an alternative language to English by the end of the nineteenth century. Mastering English, the Indian élite looked forward to mastering another modern European language in order to deal freely and, independently with the West. In that sense, the history of the Indian élite and the French language provides a measure of the process leading from cultural assimilation to cultural emancipation: 'The power to narrate, or to block other narratives from forming and emerging, is very important to culture and imperialism.'[54] The British attitude towards the spread of the French language among the Indian élite has to be seen through this relationship between imperialism and culture described by Edward Saïd. That French itself was the medium of another imperialistic culture did not really matter in so far as the Indian élite had given to it their own interpretation, selective and articulate. They were about to form from French culture a kind of autonomous cultural area and therefore a rival to the one under British control. This explains the virulence of the British propaganda against France and its language. By the second decade of the twentieth century, the French language remained fairly well spread in the high schools and colleges of the Bombay Presidency, but its position was rather precarious elsewhere. Official steps taken by the British administration and the lack of French support restricted the growth of the French language in India. Eventually, the teaching of French did not take the shape of a national reaction among the élite against the cultural control imposed by the Raj. From the 1920s onwards, if French prestige remained, it had, on the one hand, to face the increasing attraction of the cultures of other nations such as USSR, Japan, and Germany. On the other hand, Anglo–Saxon influence was reinforced by the growing political and economic power of the United States on the international scene.

NOTES

1. Archives of the Alliance Française in Paris, *Bulletin de l'Alliance française*, no. 38 (10.12.1991), pp. 132–3.
2. S.J.S. Noti, J.E. Davar, *A Letter From The Bombay Cercle Littéraire Français, Bibliothèque Dinhaw Petit. On the subject of the exclusion of the French language from the University course as recommended by the Indian Universities Commission*, p. 3, 20.10.1902, Bombay.
3. AMAE/P – Série C administrative, 1876–1907/C35/Alliance Française (G-M)/138 consul in Bombay to AE, 05.07.1893.
4. Archives of the Alliance Française in Paris, *Bulletin de l'Alliance française*, no. 38 (1991), pp. 132–3.
5. Série C administrative, 1876–1907/C35/Alliance Française (G-M)/ 138 – Consul in Calcutta to AE, 10.10.1893.
6. Ibid. See also H.J.S de Barthélémy, *l'Inde anglaise et son état actuel*, op. cit., p. 174.
7. MAE Archives in Paris, Série C administrative, 1876–1907/C35/ Alliance Française (G-M)/ 138 – CG to AE, Direction des Consulates et des affaires commerciales, sous-direction des affaires consulaires, 23.08.1893.

8. AMAE/P – Série C administrative, 1876–1907/C35/Alliance Française (C-M)/ 138, Consul in Bombay to AE, 05.07.1893.
9. Throughout this period, Ceyo was included in the region covered by the French Consulate General in Calcutta.
10. MAE Archives in Paris – Série C administrative, 1876–1907/C35/ CG de Calcutta to AE, 10.10.1893.
11. Evaluation from the figures given by the French consulate for the city of Bombay. Students of other schools should be added, included those studying in Pune, Ahmedabad, and Karachi.
12. This figure includes neither students from the Alexandra Native Girls Institution, where two teachers are appointed to teach French, nor those taking private tuitions.
13. Archives of the Alliance Française in Paris, *Bulletin de l'Alliance française*, no. 52 (10.12.1894), pp. 199–231.
14. Archives of the Indian Office/V/26/864/1 Indian University (Raleigh Commission), vol. I: *Report*, Simla, 1902, and V/26/864/2, vol. II: *Abstract* (divided into separate sections for each university, all sections with their own numerotation).
15. S. Sarkar, 'L'entrée dans the siècle, la première révolte', in J. Racine (dir.), *Calcutta 1905–1971*, op. cit., pp. 38–40.
16. The honorary secretary of the Cercle Littéraire to the French Consul in Bombay, Bombay, 28.10.1902.
17. S.J.S. Noti and J.E. Davar, *A Letter From The Bombay Cercle Littéraire Français, Bibliothèque Dinhaw Petit. On the subject of the exclusion of the French language from the University course as recommended by the Indian Universities Commission*, 20 October 1902, Bombay, p. 7.
18. Ibid., pp. 4–5.
19. Ibid., p. 6.
20. Ibid., p. 7.
21. Ibid., p. 8.
22. Ibid.
23. Ibid.
24. Ibid., p. 9.
25. *Report of the Committee appointed by the Senate to consider and report on the letters from the Government of Bombay communicating the observations of the Governor General in Council on certain points dealt with by the Report of the Indian Universities Commission.*
26. AMAE/P – Correspondence politique et commerciale no. 32 (ff. 174–5), Consul in Bombay to AE, Bombay, 21.10.1911.

27. Ibid.
28. The main colleges being the Elphinstone College, the Wilson College, and the Saint Xavier College in Bombay, the Gujarat College in Ahmedabad, the Baroda College, the Sindh College, and, in Junagadh, the Bahudin College.
29. AMAE/P – AO 1918–1940, PB no. 23, Consul in Bombay to AE, 24.09.1918.
30. Ibid.
31. AMAE/P – AO 1918–1940, PB no. 23, Peltier to AE, 07.12.1918.
32. Ibid., 18.04.1919.
33. Archives of the Indian Office, V/26/864/6, *Calcutta University Commission, 1917–1919*, vol. II, part I, chaps. XIV –XX, Calcutta: Superintendent Government Printing India, 1919, p. 108.
34. Archives of the Indian Office V/26/864/7, *Calcutta University Commission, 1917-1919*, vol. IV, part II, chap. XXXIII, Dacca University, p. 168.
35. AMAE/P – AO 1918-1940, PB no. 23, Peltier to AE, 10.07.1919 (Cours de littérature française institué par l'Université de Bombay).
36. Almost in the meantime, French classes were started in Santiniketan. But in its initial stage, Visva Bharati was not granted official recognition by the British authorities.
37. *Oxford ou Cambridge Junior et Senior Local Examinations.*
38. Archives of the Indian Office V/26/864/7, *Calcutta University Commission, 1917–1919*, vol. IV, part II, chap. XXXIII, Calcutta University, p. 175.
39. D. Lévi, *Dans l'Inde*, op. cit., pp. 53–4.
40. K. Nag and R. Rolland, *Correspondence, The Tower and the Sea*, C. Guha (trad. presentation and notes), Calcutta: Papyrus, 1996, p. 245.
41. Private Archives – Henry Bourgeot.
42. Archives of the Indian Office/ V/11/799: *Calcutta Gazette*, 3.10.1940, part 1 B, Educational notice.
43. Archives of the Indian Office/V/26/864/4: *Punjab University Enquiry Committee, 1932–1933*, report, Lahore Superintendent Printing, 1933.
44. J. Despont, *Nouvel atlas des missions*, op. cit., p. 16.
45. Groupe créé en 1933 par des mathématiciens de l'Ecole Normale Supérieure dans the but d'unifier les différentes branche de cette science. On doit notamment à ce groupe la publication du gigantesque ouvrage de référence, *Éléments de mathématiques*, paru en 1939.

46. V.S. Varadajan, 'The Apprenticeship of a Mathematician – Autobiography of André Weil', in *Notices of the AMS*, vol. 46, no. 4, pp. 448–56. www.ams.org/notices
47. AMAE/N – SOFE no. 219, Indes anglaises, MIP to AE, 04.01.1930.
48. Ibid., ENLOV, Paris, 12.05.1930.
49. Archives ofs jésuites à Paris - *Catalogue of the College Library*, Madras: The Hogart Press, 1927.
50. Centre des Archives des jésuites à Paris, *Annual Report*, Madras: Loyola College, February 1931.
51. Centre des Archives des jésuites à Paris. From data collected from the *Annual Report*, Loyola College.
52. AMAE/N – SOFE no. 219, CG to AE, 11.02.1930.
53. Ibid., the Sg. A. Gnanapragasam à CG, 05.02.1930.
54. Edward Said, *Culture and Imperialism*, op. cit., p. xiii.

CHAPTER 4

The French Community in India

From 1870 onwards, cultural initiatives became an issue of major importance in the rivalry between European states throughout the world. Indeed, cultural activities were increasingly incorporated into their expansionist strategies.[1] Thus, India's representation on the world stage and the perception of the stakes involved in establishing the presence—or at least the influence—of France in the subcontinent played a decisive role. In the early twentieth century, this rivalry assumed an increasingly global dimension, with the growing involvement of the United States, Japan, and the USSR, in particular.

REPRESENTATIVES AND AGENTS OF THE FRENCH CULTURAL PRESENCE IN INDIA

France's cultural initiatives in various countries of the world between 1870 and 1914 were essentially led by the Alliance Française and missionaries. French nationals in general and French teachers, engineers, scientists, and artists residing abroad in particular also played their part. Indeed, throughout the world, they played a significant role in representing French culture, in the wider sense of the term. As groups or individuals, these representatives have been categorized as private players, as distinct from the officials who implemented direct state action.[2]

General Description of the French Population in India – Regionwise

The French community of metropolitan origin in India in the nineteenth century was noted for its modest size, referred to several times in diplomatic correspondence. In 1912, a census carried out by the British administration in its Indian empire, including Burma, described a French population of metropolitan origin of 1,478 persons. If we exclude the French community in Burma, the French population of metropolitan origin in British India stood at 1,267 nationals. The majority lived in the Madras Presidency, with 504 French nationals (40 per cent), followed by Bengal with 175 (14 per cent), and Bombay with 164 (13 per cent). The French nationals listed as living in the 'Central Provinces and Berar', estimated at 101 persons, must also be noted, along with around 90 persons living in the princely state of Mysore. These five regions together harboured 1,034 French nationals out of the total of 1,267, i.e. about 82 per cent.

Thus, south-eastern India, particularly the Madras Presidency, was the primary region where the French community had settled down in British India. It was also the place where French missionaries first settled in India. The archdiocese of Pondicherry included several suffragans working outside the geographical limits of the French colony, in Coimbatore and Mysore, followed by Kumbakonam and Salem, which fell under the Madras Presidency in administrative terms.[3] The distribution of the French community, therefore, largely corresponded to the settlement of French missionaries in India. They had a limited presence in south-western India, except for the state of Mysore, entrusted to the Société des Missions Etrangères (Society of Foreign Missions). The difference between the south-western and the south-eastern regions of the Indian subcontinent should certainly be related to the fact that the south-west had generally escaped the influence of Roman clergy, due to the schismatic tendencies of the Goa clergy and the size of the Syrian–Malabar cult.

Consequently, outside the cities of Bombay and Calcutta, the French community in the British Indian empire consisted almost exclusively of missionaries. Furthermore, as Table 4.1 shows, an over-representation of women in the Central Provinces and Berar, Bihar and Orissa, the Bombay Presidency, and even the Madras Presidency may be noted. The predominant presence

TABLE 4.1: FRENCH NATIONALS RESIDING IN BRITISH INDIA (1912)[4]

Province, State or Agency	*Born in France*			*French Establishments in India*		
	Total	*Men*	*Women*	*Total*	*Men*	*Women*
Ajmer–Mewar	29	24	5	3	3	0
Andaman and Nicobar Islands	0	0	0	1	1	0
Assam	0	0	0	17	14	3
Baluchistan	6	3	3	0	0	0
Bengal	175	104	71	1,606	714	892
Bihar and Orissa	26	10	16	80	37	43
Bombay	164	68	96	60	36	24
Burma	211	113	98	224	170	54
Central Provinces and Berar	101	29	72	88	39	49
Coorg	6	1	5	5	4	1
Madras	504	240	264	21,206	9,173	12,033
North-West Frontier Province	10	7	3	0	0	0
Punjab	51	28	23	7	5	2
United Provinces of Agra and Oudh	36	26	10	25	24	1
Baroda	6	3	3	0	0	0
Central India Agency	24	20	4	15	12	3
Hyderabad	12	6	6	71	32	39
Kashmir	3	3	0	4	0	4
Mysore	90	52	38	360	186	174
Cochin	2	2	0	11	7	4
Travancore	2	1	1	85	49	36
Rajputana	20	17	3	2	1	1
Sikkim	0	0	0	0	0	0
Overall Total	1,478	757	721	23,870	10,507	13,363
Total (without Burma)	1,267	643	619	23,646	10,330	13,309

of women can be explained by the fact that several congregations of women had settled here. This was also true for Burma. France had a consulate and a consular agency there for a while—two consular agencies for most of the time. It is well known that in Burma too, the French community was not very large and essentially consisted of missionaries.

A Very Limited Presence in Urban Centres

Only two censuses of the French community in Calcutta have been recorded in consular and commercial correspondence registers in the archives of the Ministry of Foreign Affairs. The first, in early 1891, referred to the presence of six people: the acting director of the Comptoir National d'Escompte, an officer and a clerk of the Compagnie des Messageries Maritime, a trader, an employee of George Lockhart & Cie, and a cobbler. In the following year's census, there were seven individuals; a trader who was passing through was added to the list of six persons mentioned above. Information gleaned from French travellers to Bombay also provides a picture of a patchy, almost invisible, community:

> It must be noted that in Bombay, French-speaking Europeans are almost all Swiss or Belgian. 'In establishments bearing French names in the city, there are people from all over, as the British tell us, perhaps even your compatriots.' The consul confirmed that he knew, at the very most, seven French residents in Bombay. There was a Parsee who used to say, 'We are Bombay's French people'.[5]

At the same time, the emergence and spread of the influence of other countries such as Russia, Japan, the United States, and Germany was noted. The presence of representatives of German trading concerns as also that of technicians and teachers was behind the increasing German influence, often pointed out by consuls, as for instance in the extract below from 1898:

> It is a German, Dr. Hoernle, who heads Calcutta's college of Asian dialects; and again, it is a German, Dr. Führer, who manages the archaeological survey department in India.
>
> In this context, I admired the liberal approach of the British, who opened the doors of their private domain wide to people from a competing nation.
>
> 'Don't you believe it', I was told 'it is not because of their liberalism that the British welcome the influx of foreigners. Jobs in purely scientific departments are very badly paid in India; no Britishers wanted them. They don't pay. That's the reason behind the arrival and settlement of Germans, who were only accepted because of the lack of British candidates.

This explanation of the tolerant attitude of the British authorities with regard to filling administrative posts with other European nationals can be related to their liberal attitude towards missionaries from other European countries, especially France. Indeed in the absence of British candidates, these other European nationals, who were trained and closely supervised, played a role in the administration of the British Raj.

TRAVELLERS, TOURISTS, AND ORIENTALISTS

Working Missions or Leisure Missions?

At the end of the nineteenth century, the number of French travellers on exploratory study trips to India rose. According to the Consul General, however, as it turned out, tourists took advantage of such trips to a much greater extent then the other visitors, treating them more like pleasure trips that were rarely justified by their professed scientific objectives. Further, travelling facilities to and within India did not necessarily mean an increase in social contact with Indians, especially since a strict segregation between Europeans and Indians had been a distinct feature of British Indian society, in particular since the 1860s. In addition, India had become a sort of preserve of the British in the scientific field.

Artistic Missions

The archives do not reveal any travels related to the arts in India that were subsidized by the French government and that were of any major importance in furthering cultural relations between the two countries. In 1910, a visit by the painter, Albert Besnard, as well as one by Marie Bermond, also a painter, were scheduled, but there are no details available about them. The most interesting cultural mission about which information is available in the Foreign Ministry's archives took place in 1895. This was a visit by the painter, Druet. This 'archaeological painting' mission, entrusted by the Ministry of Public Instruction and Fine Arts, brought the painter from Ceylon to Calcutta. It led to an interesting event, as he exhibited works he had brought from France to the Indian public and he also did some graphic studies. His paintings were exhibited in the Fine Arts School's museum in Calcutta, between December 1895 and January 1896, and led to the publication of a catalogue and several articles. Therein it was stated that Druet was 'The first French painter who had brought his country's art to Calcutta.' Druet was to become familiar with the region, as he also took part in the Prince of Orleans's expedition from Tongking Bay to Calcutta, in 1896.[6]

India Investigated from the Outside

In 1896, after a long journey, an expedition led by Prince Henri of Orleans reached Calcutta. The prince ended his expedition with a stay in India. This was his second visit to India, the one being in 1888. The expedition, organized in collaboration with Paris's Société de géographie (Geographical Society), left Tongking Bay in Hanoi in January 1895, travelling up the Songkoi and the Mekong along an unexplored 1,700-km. long route for four months. The expedition then visited Tsei-Kou, Tibet, and Assam. It then went up the Irrawaddy, where it surveyed the sources of the river, before reaching Bengal's capital. From Calcutta, the prince continued his journey to Bombay, after passing through Chandernagore, Benares, Gwalior, Agra, Delhi, and Jaipur. While travelling across the subcontinent, Druet planned works in Benares, in particular, for his next exhibition in Paris. However, the journey across India was just a tourist epilogue of the exploratory expedition from the Songkoi to the Mekong.

Again, in 1896, Dutreuil de Rhins undertook a topographical and geographical survey of Tibet. The same year, Alfred Foucher a young professor of the École des Hautes Études (Institute of Higher Studies) and a former student of Sylvain Lévi, was entrusted with an archaeological research mission to India by the French government. He stayed in Kashmir from 1895 to 1897. He brought several objects for Sénart and Chavannes, the latter being a teacher of Chinese at the Collège de France: casts of Sanskrit seals, impressions and scumbles of stone sculptures in the Calcutta, Bodh-Gaya, and Benares museums, books and catalogues, as well as negatives and photographic prints of engraved stones and Hindu antiques. Among the documents he brought back was a particularly interesting collection of texts on the *Siva-Arsana*, a philosophico-religious system popular among Kashmiri pandits. Foucher's report for the Académie des Inscriptions et Belles-Lettres (Academy of Inscriptions and Fine Arts) mentioned several prospects for research on contemporary Hinduism in Kashmir and in India's holy cities. His studies took him to the north-west of the subcontinent. He distinguished himself by his work in Swat and Chitral, laying the groundwork for research on Gandhara art, which he contributed to the Louvres Museum. He was later appointed head of the Ecole Française d'Extreme Orient (EFEO).[7]

Sylvain Lévi and Nepal: The Beginning of a Friendship

The desire of the Nepalese government to establish relations with other European countries, especially France, surfaced in 1875. That year, Sir Jung Bahadur, prime minister of Nepal, planned to visit Europe with his brother, Nepal's commander-in-chief, six of his sons, five nephews, ten senior officers, and 'perhaps also a few ladies from his family'. However, a fall while riding in Bombay forced Sir Jung Bahadur to cancel his trip. In 1897, Sylvain Lévi's visit to Nepal—he was then a teacher at the Collège de France—laid the foundations for Franco–Nepalese friendship.[8] The Consul General recalled the exceptional nature of the authorization granted to Lévi for his visit to the Himalayan kingdom. According to him, it was an 'uncommon favour (that he was granted) to travel and stay for the necessary duration for the completion of his mission'.[9] A short extract from a letter that Lévi sent to the Consul General gives an idea of the links he established during his first visit itself, which also marked the beginning of friendship between Nepal and France:

> I am not just *persona grata* but even *gratissima*. I am overwhelmed with kindness and considerations [. . .]; the troop commander—the acting Maharaja—sent Pundits on an official visit to monastery libraries in search of works that I was looking for, of his own volition,

and offered to take impressions and inscriptions for me from places to which I would have no access. It was not friendship—it was affection.[10]

The Nepalese authorities did not take long to once again demonstrate their friendship. Consequently, Deh Shamsha, Nepal's acting maharaja, presented a collection of manuscripts to the French government. This first visit highlighted the desire of the Nepalese government to increase collaboration with partners other than the United Kingdom, which was trying to incorporate the Himalayan kingdom into the Raj, on the same footing as other princely states. Hence, the British authorities had no intention of allowing contacts between Nepal and other foreign representatives to increase. That is what the Consul General emphasized with regard to permits granted for visiting the Himalayan kingdom:

> In such matters, we normally take the opinion of the Indian government beforehand. . . . Sir Edward Grey added that, generally speaking, the Durbar of Nepal in no way encouraged visits by European travellers.[11]

The sponsorship of archaeological expeditious and the study of civilizations was a crucial factor in rivalries between European nations. At the end of the nineteenth century, when there was talk of setting up a counter-institution on the lines of the Asiatic Society of Calcutta, the EFEO and French Indianists put together a project to set it up a few kilometres away from it, in Chandernagore.[12] Nonetheless, setting up a centre such as the EFEO in the former trading post with its sandy banks—an investment, a reaffirmation of France's presence, and, possibly, a certain authority—seemed essential unavoidable. It was, therefore, in Hanoi that France established its great academic centre in Asia in 1898, although India remained at the forefront in its thinking: 'The old dream of EFEO's founders to study India on its own soil and among its people'.[13]

Although it was located outside the subcontinent, the study of Indian culture remained the Institute's main purpose.[14] According to Sénart, one of its founders, the institute had to establish a vast network of correspondents working in the neighbouring countries of Indochina. Consequently, the EFEO was set-up to provide France with a tool that would enable it to compete with the British effectively in the scientific field.

When he devoted himself to research on Nepal, Sylvain Lévi too had India within his sights. This was the view he expressed in the introduction to his book, published in 1905, *Le Népal, étude historique d'un royaume hindou* (Nepal, a historic study of a Hindu kingdom):

> I believed that it was opportune to draw a composite picture of the extraordinary destinies of this corner of the earth, where a miniature version of India's larger destinies seemed to be playing itself out. For me, Nepal's history thus conceived seemed less like a local monograph than a prelude to a general history of India.

Therefore, French scientists decided to approach India from its peripheries, where the field was free of any British presence. This is also seen in Alfred Foucher's archaeological investigations in Afghanistan[15] and, before him, those of Darmesteter. It was also the case, much later, with a woman traveller, Alexandra David-Néel, who was initially quite enamoured of India but who later devoted her energies to Tibet. Although these projects conducted on the peripheries of the Indian subcontinent had the study of India's culture as their main objective, they distanced French Indology from its source, its raw material. Besides, the British authorities did everything possible to thwart and discourage contacts or studies by scientists of other nations within their empire.

India, a Private Hunting Ground of the British Crown

When, in 1898, the Consul General passed on a gift from the Assistant Resident of Kashmir to the Institut de France (a bundle of manuscripts,[16] a few copper coins, and some fragments of pottery from towns buried in the sands of the Takla Makan desert), he stressed the generous character of the gesture, specifying that the British Residents could have easily kept the documents in their possession, as they were obtained as a result of research studies carried out on Indian soil, for the exclusive use of British Indian societies.[17] The activities of the British Indian authorities with regard to the Burma expedition organized by General de Beylié,[18] planned for 1906 under the supervision of Gérard,[19] says a lot about their attitude *vis-à-vis* conducting research within their empire. The purpose of the expedition was to study the history of the expansion of Hindu civilization to Indochina, on the site of the ancient towns of Prone and Moulmein—unexplored sites from where the organizers intended to '. . . bring back hitherto unknown documents on the civilization, religion, art and literature of the population'.[20]

Only General de Beylié finally decided to go on this expedition. He asked to be assigned the services of Duroisel, a member of EFEO and a professor of Pali in Rangoon.[21] The question of authorizations then came up.[22] The conditions laid down by India's central government for authorizing excavations 'were not really very encouraging', noted the general. Indeed, the British Indian authorities stipulated that the permission granted was:

> . . . revocable at any time. All objects discovered would remain the property of the Indian government. It was obligatory to send a report every month to the Lieutenant Governor, who would have the right to publish it in the Special Reviews on India, along with any photographs taken.[23]

This led the Consul to conclude the following: 'That was as good as saying that official Indian archaeologists cared little about seeing their French colleagues compete with them in their own territory.'

Drawing conclusions from the requirements laid down by the British authorities concerning his archaeological expedition, General de Beylié that the '. . . only intended to spend a month at the excavation site, just enough time to "save face"'.

The mission finally took place without General de Beylié being able to conduct the excavations he had planned. The modest investigations carried out were done under the supervision of British authorities, especially the Director of the Archaeological Department of India, who had rushed to the site. The Consul reported that General de Beylié

> found the authorities there quite pleasant and the supervisors anxious. He was even the cause of a secret visit by the Archaeological Department in the person of the Director General[24] who rushed there sensing danger, but remaining in the shadows—invisible, yet present.

Unable to pursue his excavations, this was how de Beylié concluded his letter to the Consul concerning his mission: 'In short, it was all over in nine days.' Finally, the initial investigations were for the most part put aside so as not to have to hand over their findings to the Archaeological Department of India. This was what Beylié wrote about the Director of the ASI: 'He planned to pull some dirty work on me and painlessly crown himself with laurels. He was to return empty handed.'

The Consul had the final word on this affair: 'It was clear from this exposé that the valiant General took his Burma adventure in good spirits—the way it should have been taken.' Thus, in the face of British prerogatives in the Indian Empire, a preserve of its scientists, France decided to remain in the background.

In 1908, a scientific mission was entrusted to Lunet de Lajonquière in the Malayan peninsula, Ceylon and southern India. The purpose was to conduct research on the origins of Cambodian art. The missions to the southern part of the Maydan peninsula between 1906 and 1908, led by Gabriel Jouveau Dubreuil and Jules Bloch, the latter a student of Meillet and Lévi, must also be mentioned. Jules Bloch's announcement of the purpose of the mission provoked sarcastic reactions among French scientific circles. These reactions reflected the lack of understanding of many scientists in the early twentieth century concerning the usefulness of Indianists conducting field research, as Sanskrit was considered a dead language, and hence any contact with Indians was considered pointless.[25] However, this did not stop Bloch from conducting research studies, which became milestones in the study of the Marathi language. Another pioneering aspect of his work concerned south Indian languages. He conducted a part of his work from Pune, at the Deccan College Research Institute. One of his students continued his work later, under the aegis of the same institute.[26] Thus, Bloch may be considered as the initiator of Franco–Indian collaboration in Indology, in Pune. But, despite the fascinating nature of his work, it must be emphasized that Bloch, like any orientalist, was bound by the rules of exclusivity concerning the dissemination of his works, as it was only the institution to which he was attached, i.e. the EFEO, that had any rights in this regard. Obviously, this made the development of a Franco–Indian partnership more difficult. The division of geographical areas by major European schools of Indology, supported by their respective governments, draw scientific investigation further into the colonial fold.[27]

In 1909, ashes that were believed to be those of the Buddha were discovered in Shahji-ki-Dheri, near Peshawar, based on indications furnished by Foucher.[28] The same year, the Consul reported the visit of one of the first group tourist excursions, organized by the agency Voyages d'études, which proposed an itinerary through Russia and Russian and Chinese Turkistan, up to India.

In 1911, after a first trip in 1891, and making the most of recommendations from the highest authorities in the French government, Alexandra David-Néel once again set-off for India. She was entrusted with an assignment by the Ministry of Public Instruction. This trip, which was to become one of the most amazing journeys through the Indian subcontinent—more especially the edges of the Himalayas—only took place after several approaches were made to the British authorities in London. This gave the Ambassador of France to London the opportunity of explaining the reasons behind the reluctance of the British authorities to issue authorizations for travel in these regions, as well as their request for additional information on the achievements and works of David-Néel:

I believe that it is my duty to draw the Department's attention to this issue because of the situation that currently exists in India, where political unrest has many points in common with religious movements by individuals [. . .].

In fact, we must be very prudent in the missions we send to India in these times, as the sensitivities of the British authorities are a bit ticklish with regard to any expression of interest from abroad concerning ideological movements there.

In 1914, the request by David-Néel to return to Nepal from Tibet was rejected by London:

Sir Edward Grey has just informed me, that after having consulted the competent authorities, His Majesty's government regretted that, in the present circumstances, it would not be in a position to grant any facilities to European travellers to enter Tibet and, consequently, it was not possible for it to grant Mrs. David-Néel the permission she was seeking.

In 1921, Sylvain Lévi's long stay in the Indian subcontinent led to the strengthening and deepening of the friendship and recognition that Indian and Nepalese scholars had extended to him.

Despite the outcome of the visits of Lévi, Foucher, and Bloch, French works on Indian civilization at the end of the nineteenth century focused on the Indian subcontinent peripheral areas rather than its centre. While the British Indian authorities were careful to allow only the least possible amount of scientific investigation to be conducted within its borders, it was much more liberal regarding the activities of missionaries. Indeed, this liberal spirit was frequently praised by French missionaries.

NOTES

1. B. Piniau, F. Roche, *Histoires de diplomatie culturelle des origines à 1995*, Paris: La Documentation Française, 1995, p. 14.
2. A. Salon, *L'action culturelle de la France dans the monde Analyse critique,* Université Paris I, 1981, pp. 103-26. Il n'est ici fait mention que de l'action des acteurs privés et on de celle de l'Etat also analysée dans Berthet S., La culture française en Inde, op. cit.
3. J. Despont, *Nouvel atlas des missions*, Paris et Lyon: Bureaux de l'œuvre de la propagation de la foi, 1951, p. 16, 19 cartes.
4. Compiled from the data of the Census of India given to the Consulate of France - AMAE/P – Correspondence politique et commerciale-Nouvelle série: Inde no. 33 (ff. 20–1).
5. A. Metin, *l'Inde aujourd'hui*, op. cit., pp. 22–3.
6. AMAE/P CCC – Cal no. 15 – 1896.
7. AMAE/P – Correspondence politique et commerciale-Nouvelle série, Inde no. 48 (f. 247), Bruxelles, 15.03.1912.
8. C. Caillat, *L'hindouisme étudié dans les textes et sur the terrain*, op. cit.
9. Ibid.
10. AMAE/P – CCC – Cal no. 17 (ff. 219–20), 12.02.1898.
11. AMAE/P – Correspondence politique et commerciale-Nouvelle série, Inde no. 48 (ff. 145–51) ambassadeur de France en Angleterre, 26.07.1898.

12. See P. Singaravélou, *L'Ecole française d'Extrême-Orient ou l'Institution des marges (1898–1956), essai d'histoire sociale et politique de la science coloniale*, Paris: l'Harmattan, 1999.
13. Jean Filliozat quoted in Fussman, 'La route de l'Inde', in Ambassade De France En Inde *50 ans de coopérations scientifique et technologique entre la France et l'Inde*, Delhi, 1998, p. 146.
14. Ibid.
15. J.-M. Laffond, '1930 André Malraux en Gandhara', in Ambassade De France En Inde, *Malraux et l'Inde, itinéraire d'un émerveillement*, Delhi, 1996, pp. 35–7.
16. Introduced then by Sylvain Lévi as the oldest manuscripts in the world.
17. AMAE/P – Correspondence consulaire et commerciale-C17/205-206/15.01.1898.
18. Member of the technical council of the colonial troops.
19. Architect, Secretary of the Society of Fine Arts.
20. AMAE/P – Correspondence politique et commerciale – Nouvelle série no. 48, fouilles de Birmanie (ff. 84–91).
21. Ibid. (f. 96).
22. Ibid. (ff. 99–101), Darjeeling, 04.01.1907.
23. Ibid. (ff. 102–5), Darjeeling, 13.01.1907.
24. M. Marshall, Director of the ASI.
25. P. Singaravélou, 'Les Indianistes français et the *Greater India*', op. cit.
26. C. Caillat, *L'hindouisme étudié dans les textes et sur the terrain*, op. cit.
27. Pierre Singaravélou, in his study of the EFEO, mentions a 'nationalist *science and an international division of the orientalist work*', underlining that, as early as 1898, the division into various zones of research in South Asia and South-East Asia is achieved: India being the territory of British orientalists, with the creation of the Royal Asiatic Society of Bengal in 1784, Indonesia of the Dutch orientalists, through the Bataviaasch Genootschap van Kunssten en Wetenschappen created in 1778, and Indochina the domain of the French orientalists with the creation of EFEO.

    P. Singaravélou, *L'Ecole française d'Extrême-Orient...*, pp. 86–7.
28. AMAE/P – Correspondence politique et commerciale – Nouvelle série no. 48 (ff. 175–7), 13.09.1909 (Pièces-jointes: coupures de presse). This discovery will open a debate regarding the authenticity of the ashes.

CHAPTER 5

Élite Mobility: The Indian Diaspora and France

During the nineteenth and twentieth centuries, several members of the Indian élite visited the French capital, sometimes only as a stop over on a trip to the United States or Germany, or while travelling to England. These visitors added to the few rich Indian residents in France, staying for varying lengths of time.

Increasing exchanges with other countries presented a major aspect of British control for the modernization of India and the emancipation of the Indian élite. In these exchanges, the issue of the education and training of the élite occupied a central place. The tide that carried Indian students abroad first took them to England, soon followed by the USA, Japan, and Europe. A small Indian student community also established itself in France.

THE FIRST INDIAN STUDENTS ABROAD: ORGANIZATION AND MOTIVES

The speech given by Pankristo Chaudhuri on 24 August 1884 illustrates the challenges before the children of the Indian élite pursuing higher education abroad:

> The Universities of Calcutta, Bombay and Madras train a very large number of graduates every year. The time is not far when many of them would have to start to look for a livelihood outside India. We see the number of young people leaving for England increase every year, although the results they obtain are unfortunately out of proportion with the bother and expenses they incur. It is true that a young Indian can earn a lot in England by preparing for the bar, public office, medical services, civil engineering services, etc. However, life is

expensive in England, in all respects, and the examination programmes are so strict that few have the means to spend so much money and time and, often, many are obliged to return disappointed and discouraged. Moreover, India cannot benefit much from candidates who succeed, because they all enter the services. What would truly benefit the country would be if a large number of the youth went to Europe to study arts, trades and practical sciences. Since that is the case, our youth should direct its attention towards the Continent.[1]

Chaudhuri's wishes soon came true. An increasing number of Indian students started choosing destinations other than Great Britain. In Bengal, an association was formed to help candidates to study abroad. In 1907, the Consul General, who witnessed the emergence and growth of this movement, took note of its scope and quality. He recognized in it a facet of the swadeshi movement:

In Bengal, an 'Association for the promotion of scientific and industrial education of Indians' has been formed, which intends to facilitate and help young people—students of secondary or higher education—to go and study abroad in different branches of industry. It is basically putting into practice the advice given by Gulkovar of Baroda at the last industrial conference. It is also a striking proof of the gravity and future of the swadeshi movement, from an economic perspective.[2]

THE FIRST INDIAN STUDENTS IN FRANCE

The sole assessment concerning Indian students in France came from the British secret services, at a time when they were taking a close look at the Indian community for reasons of security. It refers to about 250 people—a community that was described as essentially consisting of brokers and students.[3] However, Indian students arrived in France before the Indian nationalist movement started to expand to Europe. From the 1870s onwards, the new route linking India to Europe facilitated the establishment of an Indian community in France. Thus, in the early 1870s, the future author, Toru Dutt, did her secondary school studies at a boarding school in Nice.[4] In September 1890, Mihirbai Ardeshir, who was keen to enter a medical college in Paris, sent a request to the consulate in Bombay asking for the admission conditions for courses in French faculties for foreign students.[5] The Ministry of Public Instruction and Fine Arts, vide its decision on 13 November of the same year, gave a favourable response.[6] That is how the faculty of medicine in Paris had an Indian woman among the ranks of its students.

Again, in 1890, the University of Paris launched French courses for foreigners. In the early twentieth century, a growing number of universities had begun to offer such classes. Indian students could be easily found in the French language courses of the Alliance Française de Paris, for instance, Bajorji Sorabji in 1899.[7] The case of the young prince of Kapurthala can also be mentioned. These are but a few examples that the archives have allowed us to find, but we can affirm that these examples marked the beginning of a trend at the end of the nineteenth century that took the first Indian students to France to complete their studies. Paul Coèdes's account of the open houses held at Sylvain Lévi's home, at rue Guy de la Brosse, at the beginning of the century, which brought together personalities from the world of intellectuals and Asian students, has confirmed the presence of Indian students:

> Surrounded by his family, he used to invite his students. Louis Finot, Alfred Foucher, Antoine Meillet, Marcel Mauss, Henri Huber, François Macher and Isidore Lévy were always there, along with Indian, Chinese and Japanese students.[8]

This account was confirmed by another guest at the home of the great philologist—the sociologist and ethnologist, Marcel Mauss:

> During the fifteen or twenty years that preceded the war, Monday evenings at (Sylvain Lévi's) modest house on the rue Guy-de-la-Brosse, where he lived, acquired universal fame. You could meet the viceroys of India, Maharajas, poor students, Antoine Meillet, Marguerite Moreno and Marcel Swob, Vandervelde, Yvonne Serruys and Pierre Meille, Rabindranath Tagore, Jean Perrin, Langevin, Pelliot, Paul Boyer, Philippe Berthelot, Foucher, Finot, explorers, Buddhist priests, various Mission priests, scholars from all the continents and young people crowding around. The buffet hardly ever offered more than

blue cigarettes and cold beer. Gaiety, wit, culture, information, youth and genius transformed these evenings into unique interludes in the life of Paris and the world.[9]

Consequently, at the turn of the nineteenth century, an important Indian community in the political, social, and intellectual arena saw the light of day in France.[10] The Tata family, Krishnavarma, S.R. Rana, the Maharaja of Kapurthala, and the philosopher Vivekananda, who stayed with the writer Jules Blois at the end of 1900 are some of those who stopped by or were more or less permanently established in the country and were members of this 'Indian France'.[11]

Soon after First World War, several Indian students, artists, and researchers visited France again. Paris and the Sorbonne were a centre of attraction for students of the humanities and the arts. Other universities, such as those of Strasbourg, Montpellier, and Grenoble, for instance, and other specialized schools also attracted Indian students. The names of the universities of Belgium and Switzerland could also be added to the list. Louis Vallée de la Poussin of the university of Gand was a well-known authority in the field of Indology, which drew some Indian students towards it. Several theses were also defended by Indian students at the University of Lausanne, in scientific fields—essentially in medicine.[12]

In Paris, Lévi's scientific activities and authority continued to encourage Indian students to come and complete their studies. He sometimes worked through the Association française des Amis de l'Orient to request scholarships from the Service des Œuvres françaises à l'Étranger (Overseas French Works Department).[13] That was the case, for instance, with the extension of Sivasunder Deb's stay; he was a student of applied geology in France, in 1933.[14] In the 1920s, several doctorates were defended by Indians—for instance, the theses in the humanities by Professors Nag and Parashuram Vaidya of Bombay in 1923.[15] Theses were also published by Ishwari Prasad entitled *India from the 7th to the 16th centuries*, Gopal Advani on the geography of Sindh, and Hem Chandra Joshi on political and economic concepts in ancient India,[16] among others. To mark the more than one century of exchanges between Zoroastrian culture and France, the University of Paris created a chair of Parsee history and religion in 1924, which was held by a person called Katrak.[17] At the École des Langues orientales (School of Oriental Languages), two Indian teachers came to study Indian art and archaeology under the guidance of Alfred Foucher, most notably B.C. Sen. A student at the Faculty of Arts in Paris, as well as the École pratique des Hautes Études (Institute of Higher Practical Studies), he took charge of the Bengali language classes as a temporary teacher in 1930.[18] For the Hindustani classes, the presence of Jamil was noted as a temporary teacher in 1924–5, followed by Ali Rahmat, a student in Paris since 1927, and a doctoral candidate in 1933. The latter then occupied the post of assistant professor, from 1934 to 1940.[19]

Among student associations in Paris, the existence of an Association for the development of Indo-French friendship must be noted, along with that of the Tagore Society.[20] There was also a Krishnavarma Foundation, named after the Indian nationalist and intellectual, which provided assistance to Indian students to come to France, and a Sylvain Lévi grant was also created after the philologist's demise.[21]

The regular presence of Indian students—one to four of them—at each session of classes at the Alliance Française in Paris has also been recorded.[22] Between the winter of 1928–9 and the spring of 1934, there were 36 'Hindu' students participating in different sessions of French classes at the Alliance Française de Paris.[23] Indian students in France did not just stay in the capital. In Montpellier, for instance, Patrick Geddes developed a building within the university's residential campus, the 'Cité universitaire', which included a hall of residence and offered French language classes in English for foreign students. Later, in 1927, he set-up an Indian college. This university college took in Indian doctoral students, in particular those from the Bombay region.[24] Gopal Advani was its secretary for a while.[25] Raja Rao, a native of Mysore and later a student in Hyderabad, stayed there at the end of the 1920s, before moving on to pursue his research in Paris.[26]

When the college was set-up, the Bengali Nobel laureate became its honorary president. In 1931, Patrick Geddes wrote these words to Tagore:

> I have great hopes that our Indian College here—which you have honoured by becoming its president and which I hope you will one day visit and inspire anew—will convey your educational message and give impetus to future sister-colleges of our university campuses.[27]

Having grown up on Avenue de l'Opéra, J.R.D. Tata joined the Lycée Janson-de-Sailly (higher secondary school) and later did his military service in Lyon. He went to England in the 1920s, and joined the family business, becoming its chairman in the 1940s.[28] In Ahmedabad and Bombay, the University of Grenoble acquired quite a reputation among Indian professors who had studied in France, which seems to imply that several of them had been there.

SCIENTIFIC RELATIONS

Developing its relations with the West in the spheres of training and research, India put itself in touch with Western modern science at the end of the nineteenth century:

> The remarkable advances in science from the last quarter of the 18th century and the progress made in the 19th century in Europe provided echoes for interest in modern science in India. These date from the last quarter of the 19th century in Europe. The establishment of college education and institutes for training of engineers in Roorkee, Poona, Calcutta produced new aspirations. The Indian Association for the Cultivation of Science at Calcutta created entirely new opportunities for scientific research. The advances in France made by Becquerel, Marie Curie, and later by Irène and Joliot-Curie made strong impact in India.[29]

India followed closely the scientific progress achieved in France, which changed the face of research, from Marcelin Berthelot to Irène Joliot-Curie.[30] At the same time, the Indian élite set-up specialized institutes. The Indian Association for the Cultivation of Science, established in January 1876 by the physician, Mahendralal Sarkar, was the first modern scientific research centre in India. It was founded entirely by Indians. The chemist, P.C. Ray, was one of the young students who benefited from the courses offered by this establishment. In 1907, it was the turn of the future Nobel laureate for physics, C.V. Raman, a native of Madras, to take advantage of this institution for his research.[31] Sir J.C. Bose set-up the Bose Institute in 1901 in Calcutta. Again, at the beginning of the century, Calcutta University became the first premier institution to offer post-graduate scientific education. The Indian Institute of Science was established in 1909 in Bangalore by J.N. Tata, in collaboration with the Maharaja of Mysore, while an organization called the great Indian Science Congress began to hold annual meetings from 1913 onwards.

The history of scientific collaboration between the two countries began with the great chemist, P.C. Ray, and Berthelot, also a great French chemist and politician.[32] Berthelot's work on chemistry in ancient Greece encouraged his Indian counterpart to take a keen interest in the history of ancient India's knowledge of this field. P.C. Ray wrote an article on a famous Sanskrit treatise—the *Rasendrasara Sangraha*—and sent it to Berthelot. The latter published it with an introduction, which he penned himself, in which he stressed how deeply the text had interested him. He requested P.C. Ray to pursue his study of ancient texts and include his findings in a book on Indian chemistry. After several years of research, P.C. Ray published *The History of Hindu Chemistry*, which found favour with the scientific community. This collaboration was later sealed by a meeting between the two men in 1904, during a trip to Europe by the Indian chemist. The role played by Father Lafont, of Saint Xavier's College in Calcutta, must be noted. The activities of the latter—who died in 1908, while demonstrating the function of the gramophone to his students—certainly played a role in building bridges between several young scientists in Calcutta and France. It was under Father Lafont that a young student from Faridpur, J.C. Bose, started his higher studies. In 1896, an article he had written on electro-magnetic waves earned him international recognition. In 1900, during the International Conference of Physicists in Paris, the presentation of J.C. Bose's work on radio waves caused a sensation. The two greatest

Indian scientists of these times, P.C. Ray and Sir J.C. Bose, maintained contacts with France, which the following generation developed further, in particular Satyendranath Bose, Meghnad Saha, and the Nobel laureate, C.V. Raman.

In 1921 the Sarkar and Basch project stressed the need to institute a framework for such intellectual exchanges, so that they could lead to cooperation on the ground:

> 2. Sciences: Certain facilities would be offered in laboratories, hospitals, factories and the *Écoles des Arts et Métiers* (engineering schools) in Paris, Lyon, Strasbourg, Bordeaux, etc., to Indian students and scholars coming to France to do research under the guidance of French experts, on subjects that are of particular interest to India.[33]

In the 1920s, Sir J.C. Bose's works on plants were translated into French. At least five such works were published in France between 1926 and 1934.[34] Bose visited Europe quite frequently, especially France, and met Rolland on several occasions in Switzerland. In 1924, Satyendranath Bose, the author of a statistical description of radiation, which he depicted as a gas of identical and imperceptible particles, which Einstein reiterated, received a scholarship from the University of Dacca to do research at the Marie Curie Research Laboratory and the Institute of Radium for one year. The following year, he joined Einstein in Berlin. His contacts with France did not stop there. He maintained correspondence with several French scientists and, in 1926, he was back with Marie Curie for some new work. This exceptional scholar was also a polyglot. He had mastered French and used it in his conversations with Marie Curie. He also translated French short stories. Indeed, the reason why the Swedish Academy overlooked this scientist, who had paved the way for some of the most advanced developments in modern physics, remains a mystery.

On the other hand, it did not overlook the physicist, Chandrasekhara Venkata Raman, born in Tiruchirapalli, on the banks of the river Cauvery. Consequently, India was honoured by a second Nobel Prize in 1930. In 1929, C.V. Raman became an associate foreign member of the Académie française des sciences (French Academy of Sciences), and a doctor *honoris causa* of the Paris University.[35] Taking advantage of his trips to the United States and Germany, he visited France several times.[36] Other notable Indian scientists also had more or less sustained contacts with France. M.N. Saha visited his friends among the Indian community settled in France, while S. Ramanujam was in regular correspondence with his French counterparts.[37] Sisir Kumar Mitra and Nikhil Ranjan Sen pursued research at the Sorbonne University and at the Collège de France from 1920 onwards, before obtaining their senior doctorate (doctorat d'état) in 1925.[38]

Finally, in what may be seen as a sign of the Indianization of the administrative machinery of British India, an increase in requests for information regarding and missions to France by members of Indian institutes especially from 1930 onwards, was noted in the archives. These queries came from the most varied of sources: sylviculture—mostly from the Forest Institute of Dehra Dun, viticulture, agriculture—through the Poona Agricultural College, the Zoological Department of India, the United Provinces' Legislative Council, Punjab's Department of Public Works for the study of road networks, a study of night shelters by the Bombay Municipality, and many others.[39]

A trail-blazing example of cooperation in the technical field was initiated by J.R.D. Tata, a French national at the time, along with the famous aviator, Louis Blériot.[40] Blériot gave the young Frenchman of the Zoroastrian faith his first flying lessons. In 1929, J.R.D. Tata became the first Indian to get a private aviator's licence. In 1930, he flew solo from Bombay to London.[41] He then set-up India's first commercial airline company, Tata Airlines. In October 1932, connecting Bombay and Karachi, he himself inaugurated the first Karachi–Bombay–Madras flight, at the controls of a Puss Moth.[42]

Hence, links between Indian and French scientists were relatively numerous. However, they essentially developed through private initiatives.

THE TECHNICAL COOPERATION

In 1912, a technical cooperation mission in the agricultural field—specifically sericulture—was sent at the request of Bengal's silk producers. A scientific sericulture establishment in

Berhampore wrote to the sericulture station of Montpellier's National Agricultural Institute, with the Bengal Silk Committee—a body falling under Bengal's Chamber of Agriculture—acting as the intermediary. The Berhampore establishment, which was 'keen to give an impetus to Bengal's silk industry', offered Lafont—the head of practical works at the Montpellier sericulture station—a three-year contract. In Secunderabad, a Frenchman called Vinay attached to the Deccan Railway Company seemed to have pointed to France's involvement in the biggest railway developments of India's princely states.[43] The main scientific and technical cooperation project between France and India was based on work done at the Institut Pasteur. The desire of the Indian élite to develop national-level modern scientific structures was clearly in evidence. At the end of the nineteenth century, Indians attempted to take charge of the field of medical research, as investments in it by the British administration had proved inadequate. Epidemiological research was a case in point.[44]

In particular, this approach took the form of the organization of an annual national congress—the Indian Medical Congress. It took place in Calcutta on 24–29 December 1894. It brought together more than 500 doctors, half of whom were of Indian origin. Dr Gallay, the Chief Medical Officer of the Colonies, also participated, and his presence was deemed to have left the best of impressions on the Indian medical corps.[45]

At the end of the century, British military officers and officials in India who had fallen prey to rabies were sent to the Institut Pasteur in Paris for treatment.[46] The research conducted by Louis Pasteur and his institute aroused a keen interest among Indians, particularly his work on rabies, cholera as well as water treatment. In 1895, the Russian doctor, Valdmar Haffkine, a scientist affiliated with the Institute, began to work on a cholera vaccination in India.[47] The same year, a Central Committee of the Institut Pasteur was set-up.[48] In December, the Consul General underlined the deep-felt feelings that Louis Pasteur's death had aroused.[49] In 1896, Indians started planning to set-up an Institut Pasteur.[50] The same year, collaboration in the fight against epidemics was envisaged between the Director of the Institut Pasteur, Dr Calmette, and Calcutta. Finally, in

1897, it was in Bombay—thanks to Dr Haffkine and with the participation of the University of Paris—that collaboration in the field of epidemiological research was started.[51]

Again in 1897, the Darjeeling Municipality inaugurated the Pasteur system for the city's water filtration.[52] As for the Institut Pasteur, there was a delay in its establishment in India. British authorities, which were not ready to allocate the necessary budget, delayed the procedures required for it to be set-up.[53] Consequently, in 1898, it was the Nizam of Hyderabad's government that took up the project. The Consul took a favourable view of this initiative, while condemning the British attitude:

> It would be better to have an Institut Pasteur in Hyderabad than wait for such projects to come up on British territory. It was a point in the Nizam's favour, at a time when a marked indifference was observed on this issue on the part of the Indian Government and the Committee that had been entrusted with the establishment of an Institute in India for the last seven years.[54]

At the end of 1898, the Anglo-Indian press launched a campaign against Pasteur's anti-rabies treatment.[55] In 1899, the British government still did not seem to have decided on significant financial measures in order to deal with the serious health problems that were rampant in India at the time. Indeed, in order to set-up an Institut Pasteur in India, the Viceroy decided to grant really modest sums. These resources consisted of an allowance, which was the equivalent of the average funds spent annually to send soldiers and officials suffering from rabies to Paris.[56] The Institut Pasteur was finally set-up in Conoor, thereby enabling India to become a large-scale producer of vaccines. As for Dr Haffkine, he continued his work in India. In 1907, he settled down in Calcutta to produce vaccines. In 1911, The Governor of Bombay invited him to settle in the Presidency's capital to pursue research work.[57]

THE FRENCH HEART BEATING TO THE RHYTHM OF INDIAN ARTS

The translation of a part of Tagore's works and the publication of books devoted to India's architecture and sculpture contributed to the recognition of its art and civilization. This recognition took the form of visits by artists. In 1914, concluding the initial period of cultural exchanges between France and India, an exhibition of Bengali painters brought together by Abanindranath Tagore was held in Paris with the help of Suzanne and Andrée Karpelès, marking the beginning of the rich history of artistic exchanges in the French capital.[58] Translations of works by Ananda Coomaraswamy also helped disseminate knowledge about Indian art in the early 1920s. The first of these works to be translated into French was published in 1921. It was a book entitled *Scupltures çivaïstes de l'Inde* (Sculptures of India), written in collaboration with E.B. Havell, the art collector, Victor Goloubew,[59] a member of EFEO, and the sculptor, Auguste Rodin. The following year saw the publication of an anthology of essays, *La danse de Çiva* (The Dance of Shiva), in collaboration with Romain Rolland, in particular. This was followed by *Les arts et métiers de l'Inde et Ceylon* (1924) (Arts and Crafts of India and Ceylon), *Pour comprendre l'art hindou* (1926) (Understanding Hindu Art), and *Les miniatures de la collection Goboulew au Museum of Fine Arts de Boston* (1929) (Miniatures in the Goboulew Collection at the Boston Museum of Fine Arts).[60] Progress in the knowledge and understanding of India's art history and civilization in France led to the issue of a remarkable joint publication under the guidance of Paul Masson Oursel.[61] The translation into French of works by Abanindranath Tagore was part of the same trend of dissemination of knowledge about Indian art and culture: *L'Alpona ou les décorations rituelles du Bengale* (Alpana or the Ritual Decorations of Bengal) and *Arts et Anatomie hindous* (Hindu Arts and Anatomy) were published twice, in 1921 and 1935, and *Sadanga ou les six canons de la peinture hindoue* (Sadanga or the Six Canons of Hindu Painting), was published in 1935. These works were translated by Andrée Karpelès, while Victor Goloubew wrote a preface for the latter. To these publications may be added the university work carried out in France by Subodh Chandra Mukherjee for a thesis published in 1926 called *Rasa, essai sur l'esthétique indienne* (Rasa: An Essay on Indian Aesthetics).[62]

In the 1920s, a young Indian student is mentioned as being present in France, whose experience with the stage was soon to change his own destiny as well as that of his younger brother. Uday Shankar first studied at the J.J. School of Arts in Bombay, followed by the Royal College of Art in London, from 1920 to 1924. In 1923–4, he joined the troupe of the great dancer and choreographer, Anna Pavlova, for a show on an Oriental theme.[63] This marked the beginning of the career of one of the most famous contemporary dancers of India. His career as a choreographer proper began in Paris, in 1924. Here, the performance of Indian dance occupied pride of place—from Théophile Gautier's *Bayadere* to Mata Hari shows before President Clémenceau, to displays and exhibitions at the Guimet Museum. Between the two wars, several French artists enjoyed presenting themselves as Indian dancers.[64] Uday Shankar associated himself with one of them, Simkie, whose real name was Simone Barbier. They stormed the Parisian stage with their dance until 1929, with shows based on themes inspired by Indian mythology.

Uday Shankar's meeting in 1929 with Alice Boner, an artist from Zurich and a rich heiress settled in Paris, marked the second phase of his career.[65] They returned to India together in January 1930 to study Indian classical dance. They formed a troupe with musicians and dancers, hired on the spot,[66] then returned to Paris in the autumn of the same year.[67] They formed the Compagnie des Danseurs et Musiciens Hindous d'Uday Shankar (Uday Shankar's Company of Indian Dancers and Musicians). Among the members of the troupe, which consisted of the dancer's friends and family, was Ravi Shankar, one of his younger brothers. Daniélou, himself a young dancer at the time, began to follow the career of the two brothers, first in Paris and later in India.[68] The troupe took up residence in a house in Boulogne-sur-Seine. After five months of rehearsals, it gave its first show on 3 March 1931 at the Champs Elysées Theatre. It captured the hearts of Parisians, succeeding far beyond their wildest imagination. It marked the beginning of a long tour of Europe and the United States, from 1931 to 1938. Indeed, an entire episode in the history of contemporary dance was written between France and India.

The Indian artistic scene in France was not limited just to Bengali artists, although they did occupy a prominent place. When an artist from north-west India came to Paris, her stay was also noteworthy. She was the first painter from India to earn recognition internationally—Amrita Sher-Gil, born in 1913 in Budapest, to a Sikh father and a Hungarian mother. In the 1920s, she followed her family to Florence and later to Paris.[69] In Paris, between 1930 and 1934, she studied painting at the Grandes Chaumières and later at the Beaux-Arts.[70] Lucien Simon and Pierre Vaillant were her professors. In 1934, she was the first Asian and the youngest artist to be distinguished by the Grand Salon's international prize for her painting, *Conversation*.[71] She returned to India that year. Despite her death at an early age, Sher-Gil's works made a long-lasting impression.[72]

Indian and French art also met in the field of jewellery. Between 1910 and 1920, many contacts developed between jewellers in Place Vendôme and Indian princes. In the mid-1920s, the latter no longer hesitated to send their jewels to the House of Cartier or to the Parisian jeweller, Boucheron, for having their jewellery designed in the Art déco style, while respecting traditional Indian shapes.[73] That is how Indian Art déco emerged. The high point of this encounter took place in 1928, when, during an exhibition on the rue de la Paix, the Maharaja of Patiala's Indo-Art déco jewels were showcased. The exhibition was a great success, with well-off Europeans and Americans making it a point to visit. The press also covered the event extensively, their coverage being later published in the form of a 36-page photo album.[74]

In the inter-War period there was a work from India whose light spread widely in France and in many other countries. It was, of course, a work by Tagore. It may be recalled that in 1914, the day War was declared, Clémenceau sent the *Offrande Lyrique* (Lyrical Offering) to the Countess of Noailles,[75] and when the Germans entered Paris, French radio broadcast *Amal* or *Lettre au Roi* (Letter to the King), a piece that was also penned by the Bengali poet.

AN INDIAN VOICE IN FRANCE: TAGORE

The incomparable poetic purity of this little book shone so brightly in my eyes that I consider it an honour to offer France a tiny echo. Throughout the war and beyond our political and inter-denominational dissensions, this stationary star continued to glow and radiate a peaceful light of love, trust and peace to the world. I am happy to be able to add my contribution to this homage and express my gratitude to this great personality. . . .[76]

At least thirty-three works of Tagore were translated into French before 1940.[77] In 1930, the Librairie Française, in its catalogue of publications on sale, noted more than sixteen titles, including seven literary works published by the N.R.F., as well as four essays: *A quatre voix*, with a preface by Romain Rolland, *La Religion du Poète*, *La Maison et le Monde* and *Nationalismes*.

There were also at least six studies in French devoted to Tagore during this period. While this was not much, given the entirety of his corpus, it represented a large part of Indian literature translated into French between the two Wars.[78] In fact, it was extraordinary for a non-Western contemporary author.[79] Outside Santiniketan, another page in the history of his work was written in France—the dissemination of his pictorial work. Tagore's popularity after 1913 is difficult to figure out nowadays. No wonder his name was associated with those of personalities such as Perse, Bergson, Gide, Clémenceau, Yourcenar, Cocteau, the Countess of Noailles, and Rolland, among many others.[80] The study of the authors of letters that Tagore received from France is revealing in this context.[81] Along with letters from well-known personalities, there were also letters from country schoolteachers, soldiers, activists for peace, etc. They reveal how deeply the poet had touched the French emotionally. Tagore was on the list of must-reads for the entire French readership, across all classes. In a France traumatized by the horrors of war, these letters also underscore the hope aroused by the vitality that emanated from his writings. These seem to echo with a heart-rending lyricism and harmony from a lost world.[82] Indeed, Saint John Perse wrote,

'His ageless, rootless poetry, in love with the eternal, seeks familiar roots in the gait of man and the clay bank where man's night shuffles off its mortal coil.'[83]

Tagore made only short trips to France, but each of them turned into major events that not only recalled the enthusiasm aroused by his persona, but also the stakes involved in the dialogue between France and India. During his many travels throughout the world, which took him to thirty countries, Tagore visited France three times—in 1920, 1921, and 1930. He also made a stop over in 1924, before continuing his journey to South America, and again in 1926, while engaged in a major conference tour in Europe. His several more or less brief trips corresponded to various stages in the itinerary of his international activities. In 1920, he proposed the idea of Santiniketan University; in 1921, he prepared for its inauguration; and finally, in 1930, the first major exhibition of his paintings took place.

Tagore's first visit was in the summer of 1920, after a trip to England, for the purpose of establishing his university.[84] He stayed six weeks in Boulogne-sur-Seine, with Albert Kahn, the Director of Cercle Autour du Monde (Around the World). Tagore's reputation was already well established. After a trip to England that had left him somewhat bitter, his visit to France aroused his enthusiasm. Apart from Lévi, Tagore met Henri Bergson, Anna de Noailles (who was to prove a loyal friend), Georges Clémenceau, and several other personalities.[85] He visited the Guimet Museum. He also visited the frontline during First World War. The Association française des Amis de l'Orient made the arrangements for his stay during this trip.

In 1920, Sylvain Lévi informed Tagore about the formation of the Association française des Amis de l'Orient and, in 1921, the association invited him to present a lecture.[86]

Suzanne Karpelès, the association's secretary, recalls an incident that indicates that Tagore's arrival was considered a major event:

> To avoid any difficulty with the British government, the Ministry of Foreign Affairs entrusted our association with the organisation of receptions worthy of this Nobel laureate (. . .). I will never forget the crowds that pestered us for an invitation to one of these receptions—

> to the extent that we were even offered money in exchange for invitations to see Tagore.[87]

This confirms the semi-institutional role of the Association française des Amis de l'Orient as well as the extreme discretion demonstrated by the French government in its relations with the British authorities. Indeed, official cautiousness was driven to an astonishing extent, especially since we know that Tagore was received officially and invited by all the heads of government of the countries he visited in Europe, America, and Asia.

Tagore's visit to France in April 1921 took place when preparations for launching Visva Bharati were in their last stages, before the inauguration of the university at the end of the same year. Once again, Tagore stayed at Albert Kahn's house. In Paris, he met Romain Rolland. Then he went on to Strasbourg on 27 April, where he met Sylvain Lévi.[88] Under Lévi's guidance, Strasbourg University sponsored Visva Bharati University, which was described as a 'sister university' in the course of a tribute paid to the poet.[89] The friendship between the two universities was sealed by the formation of a Tagore Committee.[90] The purpose behind the Tagore Committee was to collect the necessary funds to offer a collection of classic works of French literature to Visva Bharati University. In June 1921, the Students' Circle even celebrated a 'Hindu festival' in honour of the 'unforgettable memory' Tagore left in his wake,[91] where Indian and Orientalist personalities gathered together. Sylvain Lévi gave a lecture on Tagore and the Hindu tradition. Among the Indian personalities present were Francisco de Bragança da Cunha,[92] Kalidas Nag, V.G. Paranjpe, B. Mukherjee, and J. Gauba. They recited texts along with a poem 'from their glorious country'. The example of Strasbourg illustrates how much the poet's prestige reflected on his country. Indeed, through his persona, a dialogue between the two countries that went beyond the East–West divide seemed possible.

In addition, during the 1920s, Tagore's work paved the way for several publications: plays, poetry, and essays, among others. While Pierre Jean Jouve co-translated *La Machine* (The Machine) and helped stage many plays from Tagore's repertoire, André Gide translated another of his plays, *La Lettre du*

Roi (The King's Letter). Also in Paris, a Tagore Society was presented as one of the capital's most dynamic student associations. In 1931, it presented a drama by Tagore, *Le Sacrifice* (The Sacrifice).[93] Finally, a series of glossy art publications, *Les Feuilles de l'Inde* (Leaves of India), was issued by Dal Högman, Andrée Karpelès's husband. These publications devoted a large section to the poet's works and to Santiniketan.

In 1926, the Guimet Museum once again played host to Tagore for a lecture in front of a packed hall. When Tagore visited France in 1930, it was not on a stop over on his way to Europe and America, as in the past. This time, it was for his first exhibition of paintings. It was held in the avant-garde artists' gallery, the Pigalle Galerie, from 2 to 10 May. The catalogue was written by the Countess of Noailles, who used all her poetic eloquence to evoke the dreams—both conscious and hallucinatory—rendered by the painter on canvas. The exhibition was a success, and brought the poet worldwide recognition as a painter. Tagore gave this account to Daniélou on the genesis of and proceedings at the historic exhibition of his works in Paris:

> Kahn, the banker, with whom I stayed, told me: 'Don't show your paintings in Paris—people are too critical, you have a good reputation, don't ruin it.'
>
> An Argentinian friend[94] took such a keen interest in my paintings that she gathered together an élite group of writers and artists. Paul Valéry, André Gide, etc. They were in the hall, I was feeling too nervous and was waiting in the other room. When I returned, a critic—Rivière,[95] I think—told me: 'I knew that you were a great man, but I would never have imagined that you were so great.'
>
> The reviews were very good, but I could not sell because the Franc was too low. Berlin too was a great success. The National Gallery wanted to buy five of my paintings, but I offered them as a gift.[96]

Victoria Ocampo compared the event to an exhibition of drawings by Victor Hugo or Jean Cocteau.[97] The Paris smart set made this exhibition a 'huge success'.[98] The warm reception in Paris gave Tagore, then sixty-nine years old, the necessary confidence to pursue his work as a painter.

From the painting exhibition of Bengali artists in 1914, to Amrita Sher-Gil's recognition at the Grand Salon in 1934, including the exhibition at the Galerie Pigalle in 1930, performances by Uday Shankar's troupe, and Rabindranath Tagore's plays—Indian contemporary arts all contributed to France's artistic ferment between the two Wars. Many other pilgrims followed in their wake to what long remained the Mecca for contemporary art in the eyes of Indians.

A WELL-STRUCTURED COMMUNITY

On the eve of First World War, an initiative christened the Franco-Indian Committee saw the light of day. Its aim was to establish a framework for the exchanges between France and India, both in the cultural as well as in the scientific and technical fields:

> A Franco-Indian Committee, which drew inspiration from the affinities that brought the two countries close, will be formed in Paris in order to work towards an increasingly close understanding between India and France.
>
> On my recent trip to India, I got the impression that France could play a significant role in this vast country, both because of its intellectual and moral prestige and its commercial activities.[99]

The originator of this first attempt at organizing exchanges with India was an Indian, Dr Krishna. That year, a proposal for the establishment of a committee was submitted to the French authorities by Krishna, supported by several French personalities. The reason put forward was as follows: France must take part in the competition that the world's biggest nations were engaged in India, in order to further their influence.

An article in the newspaper, *Le Temps*, of 5 June 1914, reported on the formation of the committee as follows:

> Under the inspiration of Dr. Krishna, a Franco–Indian Committee has just been formed in Paris. Its aim is to develop intellectual, scientific, artistic and economic relations between France and India, promote the sending of Hindu students to France, popularise the use of the French language in India, etc.[100]

Important French personalities involved in French activities in Asia were the main stakeholders in the project. They included

Philippe Berthelot, Director for Asia in the Ministry of Foreign Affairs, Paul Doumer, the former Governor of Indochina, Lebon, the former Minister for the Colonies and Director of the Maritime Express Company, and Morel, the former Minister for the Colonies. Luminaries of the Franco–Indian Committee who were representatives of French India were also mentioned as members: Etienne Flandin, the Senator of French India and several representatives of France's commercial interests, such as Henry Gabelle, a member of the Council of State, the Director at the Ministry of Trade and Industry, and the Chairmen of the Chambers of Commerce of Lyon, Le Havre, and Paris. Finally, representatives of the state such as Deschanel, the Speaker of the Chamber of Deputies, and Albin Bozet, a deputy and President of the Foreign Affairs Commission. Thus, the initiative received the support of representatives of France's foreign policy establishment.[101] The association's honorary chairman was a fervent defender of the Oriental cause in France, and a writer and member of the Académie Française: Pierre Loti. At his side was the explorer, Gervais de Courtemont.

The project thus called for mobilization in the face of the expanding influence of competing nations, by evoking the glorious past of India and thereby trying to convince France that it still had a role to play in India:

> These forward-looking men were rightly concerned to see a large number of Indian students proliferate in all other countries, except France; they knew that these young people would return from Japan, America or Germany with a destructive impression of the genius of their own race and that they would later become bad leaders for the Indian multitude, no longer able to understand their aspirations.
>
> Logically, the initiating role should have gone to France alone. Pierre Loti said it in so many words: 'The genius of France is such that it alone can be associated with that of India.' France has left quite glorious memories in India, it is still admired and loved enough for it to be able to draw Indian youth keen to study modern culture, which France would be able to impart without destroying the genius of their own race.

The project also attracted attention towards nationalism in Asia. According to Gervais-Courtemont, who wrote the introduction to the project programme, these movements found a reference and hope in France and its culture:

> . . . Indians are turning their eyes towards France, which they consider, among all Europe's major nations, as the land that chose Liberty. Our Revolution seems to fascinate them, just as it has won over the Japanese, the Turks, and the Chinese.[102]

This was how the first Franco–Indian association was born in France, with the declared aim of forging a link between the two countries. Much more than being merely a national reaction as such, this initiative highlighted the dynamism of the Indian community in France, which sought to encourage exchanges between the two countries. Unfortunately, the tragic events that were soon to dominate all international relations put a premature end to the Franco–Indian Committee. In the context of First World War and the presence of a large number of Indian troops on French territory, Great Britain's demands with regard to the surveillance and extradition of members of the Indian community increased in terms of both intensity and intransigence. The Franco–Indian Committee could hardly expand in these conditions.

What is interesting to note was the aspiration of the Indian élite to foster and strengthen cooperation with France and, in particular, to provide a framework for university student exchanges. The Indian community in France exhibited the same aspiration and dynamism in the period between the two wars. Through its diaspora in France, India projected an image of a modern nation in the process of building itself. The Indian presence in France was the result of the initiatives of Indians themselves, and not the result of a policy of the French government, unlike the case with the Chinese student community, for instance.

From 1914 to 1940, the Indian community played an important role in the scientific and artistic ferment in France, particularly in the period between the two wars. Its social composition was similar to that of the preceding period, i.e. businessmen, students, and aristocrats. However, the number of businessmen seemed to have risen. In addition, Paris remained a centre of attraction for Indian artists, scientists, and writers. Those who were settled in other European countries, particularly Great Britain and Germany, never missed an opportunity to visit France. Admittedly, Paris was the main centre of attraction, but it was not the only one. In the early 1920s, Nag wrote:

(Back to Paris: 23 September 1921–31 October 1921) From Ceylon reached Paris via Marseille, exactly a year ago in September 1920, when Tagore was there to cheer me. Now I re-enter Paris to take up my thesis work on Kautilya. Three of my friends from the Calcutta University will be with me. Dr S.K. Chatterji, Dr S.K. Mitra and Dr P.N. Ghosh and other friends from London, Oxford, Cambridge, Birmingham, etc., used to visit me on holiday terms. So my Paris 'dig' was humming with life and we managed to develop an 'Indian centre' as it were, whence responsible French professors, publicists, authors and artists could be given reliable information about developments in India in those critical years (1920–1) (. . .). Mon. and Madame Rana kept me in touch with the leading Indian businessmen of Paris like Mehta, Banker, Shah, etc., and Miss Khurshed-behn Naoroji (granddaughter of the great Dadabhai) used to visit her Indian brethren frequently and entertain them with music. She had then with her Miss Indira Bhagwat, a girl of the Royal house of Indore, who fled the ease and comfort of the palace to get herself trained for national work (. . .). So a new generation of Indian women also appeared on the horizon (. . .). Mrs Cole, Miss Bloch, Miss Karpelès and other European ladies also began to get deeply interested in India and help us in every possible manner, developing a rare tradition of cooperation and camaraderie possible only in the cultural milieu of Paris. Professor Lévi was living in his son Abel's country house at Andilly where I took Suniti and we returned to the dig of Amitava Ghosh (Lévi's adopted son and partner of Abel) who gave us *kichuri* cooked on his stove ! (. . .) M.N. Saha and K.P. Chattopadhyay often came to me and Suniti to discuss their recent studies on Physics and Anthropology. I began collecting information on the facilities for Indian students at Lyon, Nancy, Bordeaux and other provincial universities of France.[103]

In 1930, the Indian community in Paris gathered together whenever major events took place in India. According to a note compiled by the Ministry of the Interior:

The Hindu colony in Paris organised a meeting yesterday in a small room of the 'Petit Journal', attended by eighty people, mostly residing in the locality and dealing with diamond-merchants. The room had been hired by a man called Dalal, to enable a lawyer from the Bombay bar, Mr. Mazumdar, to give a lecture on the events currently taking place in India to his compatriots (. . .).

Based on the information gathered, it seemed that Mr. Mazumdar came to France on business and also to launch an appeal for the 'Gandhian' party. Besides, most of his compatriots residing in Paris were supporters of their country's independence.[104]

It is difficult to provide a precise estimate of the size of the Indian community in France. The above document—the only one in the archives of the Foreign Affairs Department to provide a numerical estimate—speaks of a community of at least eighty individuals in Paris. Of course, their family members have to be added to their ranks, along with those who did not attend the meeting and other Indians living far away from Paris.

The community's dynamism was manifested in particular in its desire to construct a framework for the development of relations between the two countries. The Association Sociale et Commerciale Hindoue (Hindu Social and Commercial Association), formed in Paris on 2 March 1921, was an example of this dynamism. The formation of the association should be seen in relationship to that of the French Chamber of Commerce for Western India and the Persian Gulf, which was set-up in Bombay on 21 June of the same year. The Consul in Bombay spoke of the structure aimed at 'offering the services of a consular organisation on a small scale', describing it as having 'significant clout and means' at its disposal.

The Association des Hindous de Paris (Association of Hindus in Paris), formed in December 1920, may be added to the list. Its office was at 17, rue de la Sommerard. The police chief sent the Quai d'Orsay a report on the group as well as on the Association Sociale et Commerciale Hindous, which had similar objectives and common members at its head.[105] The report, like the one sent by the Consul in Bombay, mentioned members who often enjoyed a very high social status. When it was set-up, the President of the Association des Hindous de Paris was Raghumath Karve Dhondo, a teacher from Bombay who had come to France in October 1919 in order to improve his

French.[106] The two vice-presidents, Ambalal Bahabal Mehta and Sobharam Hariram Khanna, were both dealers in oriental pearls. The Prefect's report informs us that Mehta had been residing at 26, rue Lamartine since 1909, and noted that 'seems to be comfortably off'. As for Khanna, he worked for Bombay's Khanna House, lived in Garches, in Seine-et-Oise, and his offices were in Paris at 15, rue Bleue. The association had its head office at the house of the treasurer, Rama Edakrow, at 17, rue de Sommerard. The latter, the son of a rich planter, was pursuing medical studies in Paris. He had also come to Europe to learn French and seemed to be doing business as well.

The police chief described the association's goals. They seemed to be essentially directed at providing services for Indians in France. Of these, the publication of a magazine in French is to be noted in particular, since it was certainly the first Indian magazine in France, written in French:

> Its objective is to encourage and take far-sighted measures for social relations and mutual assistance to Indians coming to France for business and studies. The association is an information bureau from the literary, scientific and industrial perspective, initiating Hindus who come to Paris in the material and social life of our country. It holds meetings and conferences and even has a publication, printed from time to time—the *Bulletin d'information indienne* (Indian Newsletter). Refraining from being in touch with nationalist organisations in India, it limits itself—in the magazine—to recounting current issues of public interest in India, without making any comments of its own.[107]

One of the association's secretaries was Amitabha Ghose, recruited as a volunteer in Pondicherry in 1916 for the duration of the War; he had fought in Argonne and Verdun.[108] He lived at 19, rue Saint-Vincent de Paul, in an apartment from where he set-up a company called Comptoir d'Extrême-Orient in partnership with a Frenchman named Lévi.[109] It is noteworthy that Amitabha Ghose was also the founder of an organization called Association des Étudiants Hindous (Association of Hindu Students) in Paris.[110] Thus, in the 1920s, different initiatives emerged seeking to organize the Indian community and to help Indians settle down in France. These organizations also attempted to strengthen Franco–Indian exchanges over time.

With regard to the Association des Hindous de Paris and the Association Sociale et Commerciale Hindoue, the police chief observed, 'These groups are headed by perfectly honourable persons, but imbued with Anglophobic sentiments (. . .).'[111] The dynamism of the Indian community manifested itself once again in Paris in 1934:

> A Hindu delegation, led by a person called Kabil from Calcutta, along with a deputy and interpreter called Marry, arrived in Paris three weeks ago.
>
> All the delegation's members are staying at the Ambassador Hotel on Boulevard Haussmann.
>
> Mr. Kabil, who is financially supported by several Chambers of Commerce of his country, represented moderate national trends.
>
> The mission's objectives are to:
>
> 1. Gather all the documents that could serve as the basis for intellectual and economic exchanges between India and Europe.
>
> 2. Examine all possible means that could help in bringing about a rapprochement and collaboration between India and Europe (correspondence, research, travel).
>
> The delegation is currently searching for premises to set-up offices. Discussions will shortly be started with the 'Maison France' (France House) on Avenue des Champs-Élysées in this regard. Mr. Kabil envisages publishing a newspaper in several languages, along with propaganda brochures. Further, he is preparing for a trip to Europe next August, with representatives of the Chamber of Commerce of Hindustan.[112]

The history of the Indian diaspora in France remains by and large unknown. These episodes form an important stage in both the history of Indians abroad and of the Indian nationalist movement. The Indian cultural contribution to the history of French thought, arts and sciences has similarly been underestimated, if not ignored, by historians. This Indian presence took part in the vibrant cosmopolitan and intellectual life of France during the 1920s and the 1930s. The history of the Indian diaspora in France displays its capacity in setting up a well-structured community and the opportunities that it offered to France to establish real cooperation even before India's independence. But France was by that time too focused on safeguarding her own colonial empire and on strengthening its relations with Great Britain to really seize them. Nevertheless, these episodes show how the broad chronological framework of Indo-French relations has to be analysed in the context not only of major currents and a long-term perspective, but also through personal links, achievements, and failures.

NOTES

1. Archives of the Alliance française in Paris, *Bulletin de l'Alliance française*, nos. 3-4, January-March 1885, pp. 20–4.
2. AMAE/P – Correspondence consulaire et commerciale, Calcutta no. 12 (ff. 2-5), 06.03.1907, *Les boursiers de voyages indiens.*
3. R.J. Popplewell, *Intelligence and Imperial Defence*, London: Frank Cass & Co., 1995, p. 126.
4. M. Renouard, *La littérature indienne de langue anglaise*, Paris: PUF, 1997, p. 46.
5. AMAE/P - CCC-B, no. 5 (f. 275), 27.09.1890.
6. AMAE/P - Correspondence consulaire et commerciale, Bombay no. 5 (f. 280), 20.11.1890.
7. Archives of the Alliance française in Paris, *Bulletin de l'Alliance française*, no. 76 (15.10.1899), p. 193.
8. P. Singaravélou, *L'Ecole française d'Extrême-Orient,* Paris: l'Harmattan, 1999.
9. *Archives privés* – VERMEIL. Letter of Marcel Mauss, dated 19.11.1935.
10. Samuel Berthet, 'Indian Diaspora in France', in S.D. Singh and M. Singh (eds.), *Indians Abroad*, Gurgaon: Hope India Publications, 2003.
11. Some handwritten letters in French of the philosopher have been found.
12. For instance, the PhD dissertation in medical sciences of Ambaj Nath Bose in 1928, or the one of Taha Taha in 1929, both in the University of Lausanne.
13. AMAE/N – Service des Œuvres françaises à l'étranger, no. 298, Sylvain Lévi to AE, 31.03.1933.
14. Former student at the Ecole des Mines, who graduated from Calcutta University, he became an active pioneer in the movement of Indo-French cooperation.
15. K. Nag, *Les Théories diplomatique de l'Inde ancienne et l'Arthaçâstra*, Paris: Maisonneuve, 1923.

V.L. Vaidya, *Etudes sur Ayurdeva et son Catuhsataka* (chaps. VII- XVI), Paris: Paul Geuthner, 1923.

16. H.C. Joshi, 'Recherches sur les conceptions économiques et politiques aux Indes anciennes d'après les Rig-Veda', PhD dissertation for the Faculté des Lettres de Paris, Paris: Jouve, 1928.
17. AMAE/P – AO 1918–1940, PB no. 36, Bombay, 04.05.1926: 'Lecture at the Sorbonne on history of Parsis'.
18. P. Labrousse, *Langues'O 1795–1995, Deux Siècles d'Histoire de l'École des Langues Orientales*, p. 222, Paris: INALCO-Hervas, 1995.
19. Ibid., p. 215.
20. Ibid., p. 222.
21. Created by Indians living in Paris, it is aimed at sending French students to India.
22. Archives of the Alliance française in Paris - *Revue de l'Alliance française.*
23. Ibid.
24. The PhD dissertations at the University of Montpellier by Gopal Advani on the rural areas of Sind in 1926, and by Arthur Geddes on rural Bengal in 1927.

    G. Advani, *Etude sur la vie rurale dans the Sind*, Impr. De la Manufacture de la Charité, Montpellier, 1926, A. Geddes, *La çivilisation rurale du Bengale Occidentale et ses facteurs géographiques*, A. Demangeon (préf.), Université de Montpellier 1927, Paris: Armand Colin, 1928.
25. P. Boardman, *The Worlds of Patrick Geddes Biologist, Town planner, Re-educator, Peace-Warrior,* Henley-on-Thames: Routledge & Kegan Paul.
26. M. Renouard, *La littérature anglaise de langue indienne*, op. cit., p. 58.

    Raja Rao served as interpreter for a meeting between Nehru and Malraux in Paris in 1936, organized by Jean Guéhenno.

    R. Rao, 'Quand Malraux rencontre Jawaharlal Nehru', op. cit., pp. 44–6.
27. P. Geddes in K. Nag (ed.), *The Golden Book of Tagore*, Calcutta, 1931, pp. 83–7.
28. http://www.indiancultureonline.com/indian_hero/JRD_Tata; K. Mahindra, 'The Visionary', in *India Today, 100 People Who Shaped India in the 20th Century*, Delhi, 2000, pp. 94–5.
29. S. Varadarajan, 'the point de rencontre', in Ambassade De France

En Inde (ed.), *50 ans de coopération scientifique et technologique entre la France et l'Inde*, Delhi: Service Culturel, 1998, p. 4.

30. During the nineteenth and the early twentieth century, the Indian seeds and information on Indian cultivation are sent to France and French colonies.
31. He quit Calcutta to join the Indian Institute of Science in Bangalore in 1939.
32. Marcelin Berthelot Paris 1827; Id. 1907. Chemist and politician. Made major discoveries in the field of chemistry. Ministry of Public Education (1886–7), and of External Affairs (1895–6).
33. AMAE/P – AO 1918–1940, PB no. 24, *La France et l'Inde*, Par M. Benoy Kumar Sarkar, 26.01.1921.
34. *Réactions de la Matière Vivante et Non Vivante*, 1926, *Physiologie de l'ascension de la Sève* (Préface de M. Mangin de l'Institut) and *La Physiologie de la photosynthèse*, 1927, *Electrophysiologie comparée par Sir Jagadis Chandra Bose*, 1931, *Les Autographes des Plantes et leurs révélations*, 1934. See les catalogues de la Librairie française.

    K. Nag, R. Rolland: *Correspondence, The Tower and the Sea*, C. Guha (trad., intr. and notes), op. cit.

    The physiologist J.C. Bose (1859–1937) is also mentioned many times in the correspondence between Romain Rolland and Tagore, as well as in the account of Désirée Lévi, *Dans l'Inde*.
35. Varadarajan, 'Le Point de Rencontre', in Ambassade De France En Inde (ed.), *50 ans de coopération scientifique et technologique entre la France et l'Inde*, Delhi, 1998.
36. S. Varadarajan, ibid.
37. Ibid., p. 4.
38. Ibid.
39. AMAE/P – AO 1918–1940, PB no. 73.
40. http://www.indiancultureonline.com/indian_hero/JRD_Tata
41. K. Mahindra, 'The Visionary', pp. 94–5, *India Today*, op. cit.
42. AMAE/P – AO 1918–1940, PB no. 73, consul in Bombay to AE, 18.10.1932.
43. Archives in the Alliance française in Paris - Bulletin de l'Alliance française no. 83, 15.04.1901, p. 150.
44. From 1890 onwards, the epidemiological issue gained momentum in the French diplomatic mail. Various epidemics broke out that consuls reported to the French authorities, since maritime relations between Indian and French ports, particularly Marseille were intensive.
45. AMAE/P CCC – Cal no. 13 (ff. 394–406), Calcutta 24–29.12.1894.

46. Ibid., Cal no. 18 (ff. 476–8), 18.04.1899.
47. Ibid., Cal no. 14 (ff. 126–8), 30.08.1895.
48. Ibid., Cal no. 18 (ff. 397–8), 17.11.1898.
49. Ibid., Cal no. 14 (ff. 187–8), 16.12.1895.
50. Ibid., Cal no. 16 (ff. 2–3), 07.09.1896.
51. Ibid. (ff. 416–7), 28.02.1897.
52. Ibid., Cal no. 17 (f. 138), 18.10.1897.
53. The consul in 1897, though an Anglophile, describes the total lack of concern on the part of the British authorities compared to Dutch officials in Indonesia investigating the spread of plague in Bengal and concludes: 'I can certify the authenticity of this account which testifies to the deep indifference of the administration in India for every matter that do not affect directly its interests.' AMAE/P CCC, Cal no. 16 (ff. 438–9), 20.03.1897.
54. AMAE/P CCC, Cal no. 18 (ff. 397–8), 17.11.1898.
55. Ibid. (ff. 402–3).
56. Ibid. (ff. 476–8), 18.04.1899.
57. 'The residence was used later for research on immunology and cancer, the making of diagnoses and vaccines. To pay homage to Haffkine and his mentor, Louis Pasteur, the place was named, in 1933, the Institute Haffkine.' Ibid.
58. 'M.E.B. Havell had encouraged a core of artists who were in the circle of Abanindranath Tagore, and tried to free themselves from the imitation of the Occident and find their national tradition. He came to organize in Paris, in 1914, in the Salon de la Nationale, an exhibition of contemporary Bengali artists which was successful' AMAE/N – Service des Œuvres françaises à l'étranger no. 256 – 15e Assemblée générale de l'Association des Amis de l'orient, 29.06.1935 – Compte rendu pour l'exercice moral 1934–1935.
59. Regarding Goloubew, see: P. Singaravélou, *L'École française d'Extrême-Orient* . . ., op. cit., pp. 325–6.
60. See the various *Catalogues de la Librairie française* for all the references.
61. P. Masson Oursel, H. Stern and Willman-Grabowska, *L'Inde et la civilisation indienne*, Paris: Bibliothèque, 1933.
62. S.C. Mukherjee, *Rasa, essai sur l'esthétique indienne*, Alcan, 1926, Paris.
63. R. Shankar, 'Amar Dada', pp. 47–8, in *Desh*, 10 June 2000, Calcutta (Bengali).

    A. Danielou, *Les Chemins du Labyrinthe, Souvenirs d'Orient et d'Occident*, Paris: Rocher, 1993, pp. 101–2.
64. J.L. Erdman, 'Who Remembers Uday Shankar?', Annual Conference

of the Society of Dance History Scholars, Barnard College, New York, 21.06.1997, in *Interchange*, 1998 (www.danceadvance.org - 03archives/shankar).

65. She was instrumental in the renaissance of Indian classical dance and then devoted herself to the study of Hindu architecture.
66. A. Boner, *Alice Boner Diaries: India 1934–1967*, L. Soni, G. Boner (co-ed.), Delhi: Motilal Banarsidass, 1993.
67. Ibid.
68. Alain Daniélou did some of the first recordings of Ravi Shankar.
69. Amrita Sher-Gil (1913–41).
70. A.E. Menon, 'Passion Flower', in *India Today, 100 People Who Shaped India in the 20th Century*, op. cit., pp. 168–9.
71. Ibid.
72. Ibid.
73. A. Garde, S. Rault, *Salon indien, L'influence de l'Europe sur l'architecture, les arts décoratifs et l'art de vivre en Inde*, op. cit., pp. 29–31.
74. Ibid.
75. K. Dutta, A. Robinson, *Rabindranath Tagore: The Myriad Minded Man*, Delhi: Rupa, 2000, p. 228.
76. A. Gide, in R. Chaterjee (ed.), *The Golden Book of Tagore*, quoted in K. Kripalani, *Rabindranath Tagore: A Biography*, Calcutta: Visva Bharati, 1980, p. 380.
77. Chartier, 'Bibliographie' dans *Santiniketan: legs de Tagore – Rencontre avec l'Inde* Conseil Indien pour les Relations culturelles, vol. 30, no. 2, Delhi, 2001, pp. 299–306. See also the Catalogue de la Librairie française.
78. See the entry 'Littérature indienne' dans *Catalogue de la Librairie française*.
79. One should note the fact that almost all his works were translated from the English.
80. S. Liné, *Tagore: Pèlerin de Lumière*, Paris: Le Rocher, 1987.
    F. Chartier, *Rabindranath Tagore, l'Unité dans la Diversité*, op. cit.
81. Archives of Rabindra Bhavan in Santiniketan, correspondence Tagore–France.
    F. Chartier, 'Rapports épistolaires entre Tagore et la France', in *Rencontre avec l'Inde*, vol. 30, no. 2, *Santiniketan: legs de Tagore*, Delhi: ICCR, 2001, pp. 270–92.
82. S. Berthet, 'Santiniketan, ou les avatars du rêve d'un poète moderne', in *Rencontre avec l'Inde*, vol. 30, no. 2, op. cit., pp. 101–18.
83. Quoted in F. Chartier, *Rabindranath Tagore, l'Unité dans la Diversité*, op. cit., p. 106.

84. K. Dutta, A. Robinson, *Rabindranath Tagore: The Myriad Minded Man*, op. cit., pp. 227–8.
85. Ibid.
86. Ibid.
87. S. Liné, *Tagore: Pèlerin de Lumière*, op. cit., p. 181.
88. N. Dé, *Madame Lévir Diary*, op. cit., p. 18.
89. Ibid.
90. Ibid., p. 18.
91. Archives Rabindra Bhavan in Santiniketan.
92. Braganca Da Cunha Francisco (11.01.1887, Chandor/Goa, 25.09.1954, Paris). Student in the EPHE (Sorbonne). Stay in France from 1908 to 1912, 1918 to 1921, and then 1950 onwards. Close to Léon Blum and Nehru. Brother of the nationalist Tristan Braganca Da Cunha, who wrote *L'Inde et l'avenir de l'Europe* (Paris: Maison Deuvel), and *La Danse de l'Inde* (Paris: Maison Deuvel), and philosophical works in the magazine, *Les Quatre vents*. See AMAE/N – Consulate Bombay, no. 8.
93. Ibid.
94. Victoria Ocampo, intellectual, translator, publisher of the international review, *Sur*, which published, among others, the first works of Jorgé Luis Borges.
95. Georges Henri Rivière from the Musée de l'Homme.
96. Private Archives – Jacques Cloarec.
97. K. Kripalani, *Rabindranath Tagore: A Biography*, op. cit., p. 365.
98. K. Dutta and A. Robinson, *Rabindranath Tagore: The Myriad Minded Man*, op. cit., p. 289.
99. AMAE/P – Correspondence politique et commerciale, Nouvelles série, no. 33 (ff. 49–52).
The signature is unclear, but it seems to be most probably that of the explorer Gervais-Courtemont.
100. Archives of the Alliance française in Paris, *Bulletin de l'Alliance française*, p. 316, no. 137 (15.07.1914).
101. AMAE/P – Correspondence politique et commerciale, Nouvelle série, no. 33 (ff. 49-52): Krishna (Dr), *Projet du Comité franco-indien*.
102. Ibid., G. Courtemont, *Présentation du Projet du Comité franco-indien*.
103. K. Nag, *Memoirs*, Calcutta: Writers Workshop, pp. 9–11.
104. AMAE/P – AO 1918–1940, PB no. 73, Ministère de l'Intérieur à Ministère à Affaires de l'étrngère, 19.08.1930.

105. AMAE/P – AO 1918–1940, PB no. 24 (émigration hindoue), the Préfet de Police à Ministère AE, 19.01.1922.
106. Probably a relative of the reformist, Dhondo Keshava Karve (1858–1962).
107. Ibid.
108. Ibid. The other secretary, Vasudev Gopal Paranjpe, 'is a teacher in India. He came to Paris in September 1920. Some months later he went to Strasbourg, then came back to Paris to go to Berlin, 29 October 1921, holding a six month passport (return) to Germany'. Ibid.
109. Most probably Abel Lévi.
110. AMAE/P – AO 1918–1940, PB no. 24, The Préfet de Police to MEA, 19.01.1922. Amitabha Ghose is described as one of the most active members of the *Association des Hindous de Paris*. He also organized the *Société des Amis de la Liberté des Indes*, branch of the Friends of Freedom for India in New York.
111. Ibid.
112. AMAE/P – AO 1918–1940, PB no. 24, the Préfet de Police to MEA, 05.1934.

CHAPTER 6

France and the Indian Nationalist Movement: From Sovereignty to Solidarity

One unexpected event in the year 1907 was the appearance of Indian revolutionary parties in London, Paris and Vancouver.[1]

When the Indian nationalist movement spread to Europe and the USA, the British authorities suspected Paris and New York of having been turned into bases for anti-British activities. Indeed, some of the main activists found refuge in the cosmopolitan capital of France, with activists such as Mme Cama, 'Generals' Bapat and Hemachandra Das, the editor of the *Indian Sociologist*, Shyamji Krishnavarma, Sardar Singh Rana, and even Vinayak Savarkar. This community met with other revolutionaries in Paris and received the support of a rich and well-organized Indian community. In 1907, Mme Cama and a group of Indian revolutionaries exhibited the second version of the Indian national flag in Paris, after the flag had been raised in Calcutta on 7 August 1906. The British authorities reacted quickly through political pressure and by settling for some time their intelligence service headquarters in Paris in order to handle the matter. The case of Savarkar shows the efficiency of their action. Gradually, Indian nationalists found better conditions for conducting their activities in Europe in Switzerland and Germany. First World War marked the peak in the collaboration of the French and the British authorities in dealing with the Indian community.

The Indian nationalist movement was political, material, and cultural all at once. The increasing speed in the transmission and the exchange of both ideas and men, within India, on the one hand, and between India and the rest of the world, on the other, were determining elements in its development. Students being instrumental in the radicalization of the nationalist movement, it was carried along with its leaders within the Indian community, first in England itself, and very soon, in France.

In 1907, the intensity of violence had reached its climax in India. It was then that the British secret services realized the existence of intermediaries, if not strongholds, that participated in the organization of violent activities outside the Empire. One of the reasons for the development of these organizations outside the empire was the immunity granted to their leaders, including, in the first place, in England, where the police and the London secret services were anything but willing to spy on the Indian community. And when this same police did cooperate with the secret services of the British empire in India, France appeared a natural haven.

One of the forerunners and main leaders of the Indian nationalist movement in England, and later in France, was Shyamji Krishnavarma, a rich merchant of western India, described by the secret services as one of Tilak's disciples. In 1897, after the imprisonment of the latter, Krishnavarma left for England. In 1905, he started the publication of the magazine, *Indian Sociologist*. In the same year, he created the association, 'Indian Home Rule Society', as well as the India House, which the secret services considered to be a hotel for nationalist students.[2] In September 1907, as British officials began to investigate the Indian community, Krishnavarma embarked for France, where he settled.[3] The Indian community in France was then an estimated 250, comprising mainly rich brokers and students.

The Director of Criminal Intelligence (CDI)[4] evinced an interest in the Indian community in France. In 1907, the revolutionaries tried to derail the train of the Lieutenant-General, Sir Andrew Fraser, on French territory. French officials then issued a notice revealing that a Russian anarchist called Nicholas Stranski was teaching some Bengali students bomb manufacturing techniques.[5] It was actually an entire terrorist network that had developed between India and France, via Chandernagore. However, this incident did not lead to any cooperation between the French and the British authorities.

From as early as 1908, the embassy of England in Paris interceded directly with the French government regarding the surveillance of the Indian community in France, following a scandal involving a Parisian house that had provided explosives to a Chandernagore-based house.[6] British officials suspected 'a few Hindus living in Paris and who were classified as militant revolutionaries'. These suspicions proved to be groundless. Nevertheless, the Indians residing in France came under increasing surveillance. A second police report thus remarked on certain meetings held on rue Richer, 'which sometimes as many as 15 to 18 Hindus attended', and where 'discussions are reported to be rather spirited'.[7] This was followed by a report on Hindus in France, which stated that:

> the residence of John Varma (Indian) was a true den of Hindus, where he himself had offered shelter to ten of them in 1906 and 1907, (...) all individuals who appeared to be in a somewhat precarious situation, and the landlady Levallard believes that they used to receive help from various fellow countrymen, particularly Krishnavarma, Tata and Rana.

From then on, the embassy of England in France informed the Ministry of Home Affairs about the 'the visit of a probable Hindu anarchist',[8] requested the surveillance of a 'Hindu anarchist' spotted in Tangiers, and suspected to be on his way to Paris,[9] asked for reports on the activities of other Indian residents,[10] demanded special protection for the Viceroy then returning from India to England via France,[11] and finally referred to French officials the case of suspected 'anarchist' networks thought to be supplying weapons to the nationalists in India,[12] an affair much discussed in several inquiry reports.[13]

The year 1909 was marked by the assassination of Sir William Curzon Wyllie, aide de camp of the Secretary of State for Indian Affairs, the first act of this kind on British soil since the 1880s. The claim that the main centre of terrorist activities by Indian nationalists was located in Paris then appeared in the British press, in England proper, in the first few days of 1909: '*The Indian Agitation. Headquarters in Paris. A dangerous conspiracy*.'[14]

The Ambassador of France in London addressed a note to the French Ministry of Foreign Affairs in this regard:

> The *Morning Post* has published in its 22nd December issue a news item from its Paris correspondent according to which the anarchist unrest in India which, as H.E. is aware, is of grave concern to the British government, would have its general quarters in Paris.[15]

A reader of the newspaper accused by name Shyamji Krishnavarma,[16] who responded in the same *Morning Post* as follows:

> He defended himself in a letter addressed to the *Morning Post*. He denies the existence of the said plot but expresses at the same time, in rather brisk terms, the anti-British feelings of the Hindu nationalists. Do note that Mr Krishnavarma, in spite of his hostility against British domination, declares that it would be pure madness for his fellow countrymen to attempt an assassination in Paris, violent means being in his view only a last resort, even in India.[17]

The Ambassador of France in London then concluded: 'These rumours may be completely unfounded.'[18] However, from then on, the British embassy in Paris regularly sought the cooperation of the French government for the surveillance, and even the arrest, of Indians settled in France. The British authorities increased their investigative machinery in Great Britain, but in France they stumbled over the issue of the right of asylum, one of the foundations of the concept of state sovereignty in Europe. Lord Morley[19] himself mentioned this fact when the British authorities asked for Krishnavarma's extradition.

The French government then did not seem ready to face the storm provoked by a breach in the right to asylum, and the French authorities responded to their British counterparts by instructing them to follow more official channels.

The Savarkar affair, which took place in 1909–10, marked a turning point in Franco–British relations. In June 1909, Vinayak Savarkar, one of the most dreaded Indians according to the British authorities, had Sir William Curzon Wyllie assassinated because he had refused a court appeal against his brother, Ganesh, who had been sentenced to deportation for his terrorist activities. By June, Savarkar's extradition had became an issue for the British authorities. In November 1909, Savarkar launched the Free India Society and called for an immediate uprising in India.[20] On 21 December 1909, in Bombay, Judge Jackson, who had sentenced Ganesh, was also killed.[21] In January 1910, while proof of his implication in the murder was being collected, Savarkar took refuge in France. Shortly after, he foolishly returned to England where he was arrested.[22] While being deported from London to Bombay in a ship of the Peninsular Company, he managed to escape the British authorities at the port of Marseilles. The French maritime police had him apprehended.[23] The English press protested strongly against the detention in France of a prisoner belonging to the British and denounced it as an obstruction of British justice. However, according to French law, a judicial trial was necessary for deciding the fate of each prisoner. This presupposed a certain delay before the eventual release of the prisoner to the British authorities. The English press decided to protest vehemently against France for what they called a diplomatic incident and threatened to take it to the Houses of Parliament. The French Ambassador in London[24] noted that the episode of the escape of the young Indian nationalist had become, in effect, in England the 'Savarkar Affair'.

British pressure eventually overcame the principle of the right of asylum in France. As indicated by the *Madras Time* of 20 September, the French government 'did not seek to put to the test the question of his rights' and praised this conciliatory attitude.[25] In this article, entitled 'France and the anti-English movement', the Indian newspaper published in English described the French attitude of the last few months as follows:

> France has always, whether voluntarily or involuntarily, given asylum to conspirators against the English Government (. . .). In the last few years, the Indian anarchist party, at the head of which is the infamous Shyamji Krishnavarma, has found refuge in Paris (. . .).
>
> The cordial relations were a true 'Entente Cordiale' and the French government, supported by the majority of its subjects, did not want to tolerate in its territory an anti-English crusade.

> The first act of friendship of the French government towards Great Britain was the tacit agreement of the former on the arrest of Vinayak Savarkar on French territory (. . .) On this issue, the French government in order not to delay British action 'did not seek to put to the test the question of his rights'. (. . .)
>
> The second example of the desire of the French government not to block the United Kingdom in the difficult task of crushing anarchy in its territories, is the recent prohibition of the meeting of the Egyptian National Congress in Paris (. . .). Many times in these columns, we have called attention to the close parallel between Indian and Egyptian nationalist movements, and the similar nature of the dangers they present. While the nationalists approved the assassination of Boutros Pasha, one proclaimed the assassin Dhingra a hero in the streets of Cairo.
>
> A long time before the discovery of the revolutionary clubs in Calcutta, the Indian political chiefs cited the Egyptian chief Mustapha Pasha as an example the Indian patriots should follow. By prohibiting the Egyptian Nationalist Congress in Paris, it was hoped that they would profit from the lesson and would go to other shores where they would encounter less freedom in the impious alliance between pan-Islamism and the Hindu religious awakening.
>
> Now that France has made it known that they disapprove of anti-English crusades in their own country, they can adopt measures that, even while tolerating the presence of refugees on French territory, will not permit them to pursue their 'scélérat' occupations.[26]

The obvious objective of this article was to discourage Indian nationalists from going to France to find asylum there, to continue their activities against the English government. It also informs us about the attitude of France, in particular the shift in policy during the year 1910. The change in the attitude of France since 1910 corresponded to the beginnings of French cooperation with the British secret service, namely the CDI. In 1909, this organization was in-charge of monitoring the Indian community in England, which improved the effectiveness of its functioning. In January 1910, the Superintendent of the Police force of Bombay, John Arnold Wallinger, was named 'itinerant officer' of the secret service network in-charge of surveying the activities of Indian nationalists in Europe. He began his mission in France. The results came quickly. By the end of the year, he had succeeded in setting up a network of informers. Wallinger succeeded through his personal and direct interaction with the authorities in overcoming the problems posed by the official procedures concerning extradition. The French police force was described in February as being of only 'very little assistance in the monitoring of Indian suspects in Paris'. Two months later, they were described as being of 'valuable assistance'.[27] The explanation given by Wallinger for this success is as follows: 'The continental police dare not correspond officially on matters political, except through the recognized channels, which would really mean a waste of everyone's time.'[28]

From 1910, therefore, Indian nationalists no longer had a French platform for the organization of revolutionary activities against the British authorities. Following the 'Savarkar Affair', one no longer finds any traces in the diplomatic dispatches concerning the political activities of Indian nationalists in the French cities.

Henceforth, the British authorities in France intervened directly in the surveillance of its citizens of Indian origin. In a 'non-official' two-page document of 3 September 1913, the British embassy in Paris questioned the French authorities about the activities of Mrs Cama, a Parsee lady from Bombay residing in Paris. The letter stated:

> It is well known that she is at the centre of the Indian revolutionary movement. She is a founder of the newspaper *Vandé Mataram*, a newspaper violently anti-English, provoking assassinations, and prohibited in India.[29]

The letter referred to her presence at the International Women's Congress held at the Sorbonne in June. 'It is known that she has been seen at a reception given by the President of the Republic at the Élysée, and at another given by the MAE. She has been photographed with others on the steps of the MAE'. . . .

The French Home Minister confirmed the participation of Mrs Cama along with participants from other countries at this Congress. He also confirmed that Mrs Cama was the editor of the newspaper, *Vandé Mataram*, specifying that this newspaper was published from Geneva. Finally, it seems that Mrs Cama was an intellectual Indian, certainly committed to the nationalist cause, like practically all her Indian compatriots, above reproach, however, of taking part in the organization of acts against the Indian government.

From 1910, the Indian community under surveillance in France was thus no longer a base, for Indian revolutionaries. These centres moved to Swiss Europe, through which Germany operated actively and where many Egyptian nationalists resided.[30] In 1914, the principal centre of Indian revolutionary movement was, according to the CDI, in North America. Nevertheless, First World War brought India to the centre of British–French relations. The August 1914, Indian troops embarked for France, and disembarked in Marseilles seven weeks later. In all, there were approximately 138,000 Indian soldiers who fought at Flanders.

By the end of 1915, the Indian troops, after more than fourteen months of combat in Flanders were sent to fight in Turkey.[31] Wallinger was put in-charge of combating the nationalist anti-British propaganda among the Indian troops in Germany. By 1915, Wallinger had established his headquarters in Paris. On the European continent, it was through Switzerland that Germany carried out its propaganda targeting Indian nationalists and troops. There was complete collaboration between the French police force and the British authorities. The French agreed to extradite, or to expel, the suspects identified by the British authorities. Thus, the veteran leader S.R. Rana was expelled along with his German wife and his son to Martinique. The British even went so far as to prevent his return for medical reasons, although the French authorities were willing to allow his return for cancer treatment.[32]

After the departure of the Indian troops, the British–French collaboration continued. Thus, the French War Minister in a letter of 3 January 1916 gave his consent for the arrest and the handing over to the British authorities for purposes of deportation 'undesirable British subjects without these individuals being the object of an expulsion warrant or the regular procedure of extradition'.[33] This is confirmed by Popplewell, who writes:

In January 1916, they [the British] put forward far-reaching measures, which the French Ministry of the Interior and the Sûreté (Sécurity) approved. These gave Indian agitators who had penetrated into the camps, but also any British subjects whose presence the military authorities considered a danger to the army.[34]

We thus see that the Indian issue was an international problem even before the War, and in a way became more serious during the War. Within the framework of control of the Indian nationalist movement and the repression of terrorist activities, the Franco–British alliance was concretized, primarily from the year 1910 onwards, by a collaboration on the surveillance and extradition of members of the Indian community suspected of nationalist activities. This accord prevented any possible independent positioning of France with respect to the Indian issue, which came to the forefront of the international scene from the very beginning of the twentieth century. In the second half of 1910, France thus chose an attitude of solidarity with the English government. The fear that the nationalist movements of India and Egypt were heading towards an alliance of the colonized countries to counter the colonial powers, to which the English press drew the attention of France, certainly contributed to this shift in policy. India and Egypt were then at the forefront of the anti-colonial movement. The colonial issue sealed the Franco–British alliance. Moreover, Germany during First World War made use instrumentalized the nationalist movements, particularly the Indian, as in their European rivalries. Indeed, Germany actively encouraged Indian nationalism, in particular via Switzerland, by propagating among the Indian troops fighting in France.

NOTES

1. Richard J. Popplewell, *Intelligence and Imperial Defence: British Intelligence and The Defence of the Indian Empire 1904–1924*, London: Frank Cass & Co. 1995.
2. Ibid., p. 125.
3. Ibid., p. 126.
4. The Director of Criminal Intelligence is in-charge, since the reform brought about by Lord Curzon in 1903, of the Central Agency

of the Secret Services of the Raj, as much for internal affairs as for external. It is complemented by the Criminal Investigation Department (CID), appointed for undertaking intelligence missions in the Indian provinces. Ibid., pp. 42–3.

5. Ibid., p. 135.
6. Ibid., pp. 69–73 / The President of the Senate, Minister of Home Affairs, to the Minister of Foreign Affairs / 8 February 2005.
7. Ibid. Then follows this description of three people considered to be the main supporters of the visiting Indians along with John Varma: 'Krishnavarma Shyamji, founder of the *Indian Sociologist*, writes for various newspapers against British influence in India. A big private fortune. Tata, residing rue Halevy, director of the house called "Tata Son & Cie", a broker in pearls and Indian silks. Great fortune. Rama Sardarsinhji, 46 rue Blanche, lapidary for the Tata house.'
8. Ibid., pp. 78–80.
9. Ibid., pp. 104–10.
10. Pages 111–12 / Minister of Home Affairs to Minister of Foreign Affairs. The AAP asks for a report on someone named Acharya Tirumal, student, 22 years old, born in Madras. The report states: 'As a student, he probably stayed during three years rue Lafayette, then, from November 1909 onwards, as he was a pearl broker, rue du Faubourg du Temple. No apparent political activities.'
11. Ibid., pp. 148–52: When Lord Minto came to France and travelled from Marseille to Calais, between 11 and 12 December on his way back to Great Britain, special protection was requested to prevent assassination attempts by Indian nationalists. The issue was taken very seriously by both sides: 'Protection from any attempt or annoyance or molestation by any Hindus, now sojourning in your country, who may feel dissatisfied with his rule in British India.'
12. Ibid., pp. 113–16: Minister of Foreign Affairs, Paris, 12 January 1910. The weapons used in the assassination of Mr Jackson in Nasik will also be identified as coming from France.
13. Ibid., pp. 117–20: Minister of Home Affairs to Minister of Foreign Affairs. Mr Rana has apparently been identified by the British services as 'being an intermediary for two Indian fellow countrymen at the time of the purchase of the weapons. Mr Rana is known to be in contact with the Hindu anarchists visiting Paris. His name is linked to the various inquiries motivated by the actions of Hindu revolutionaries.'

14. A Minister of Foreign Affairs, P / Correspondence Politique et Commerciale Relations avec la France / 45, 16.08.1910.
15. Ibid., London, 14.1.1909, pp. 43–4.
16. Ibid., pp. 43–4.
17. Ibid.
18. Ibid.
19. Secretary of State for Indian Affairs from 1900 to 1910.
20. Popplewell, pp. 133–4.
21. Ibid.
22. Ibid., pp. 138–9 fn. 75, 175.
23. A Minister of Foreign Affairs, P / Correspondance Politique et Commerciale Relations avec la France / 45, 16.8.1910.
24. Ibid., 6 October 1910.
25. Popplewell, pp. 137–40.
26. A-MAE-P – CPC.
    But, according to Wallinger, Mme Cama, though listed by the CDI from 1907, would not represent a serious threat, the intelligence agent looking at her as 'brainless'. Popplewell, op. cit., p. 221.
27. Popplewell, op. cit., p. 141.
28. In that instance, Mme Cama who went to Marseille with the aim of discouraging Indian troops from taking part in the War, was ordered to quit the city on 27 October.
29. One should add to those numbers the Indian soldiers recruited by the French army about whom little is known. Mention is made in the archives of the campaign to recruit Indian soldiers by the French from their Indian settlements.
30. Popplewell, op. cit., p. 221.
31. Ibid., p. 221.
32. A Minister of Foreign Affairs / Politique Correspondance et Commerciale Relations avec la France / 45, f. 221.
33. Ibid., f. 121.
34. Popplewell, op. cit., p. 221.

CHAPTER 7

Foreign Influence and French Culture in India

The power struggles that were already shaping up before 1914 erupted during First World War. New propaganda methods were developed, and their use continued even after the conflict. The emergence of Asian powers was confirmed, while the advent of the USSR was to further harden the East–West divide. In these circumstances, how could France—which was in the victors' camp, though weakened and bruised—manage to hold on to its cultural prestige, to which part of the Indian élite had demonstrated its attachment? Would it be able to withstand the changes and upheaval taking place? The response depended greatly on the prospects of dialogue and cultural exchanges that France was capable of offering India.

During the conflict, European countries made the most of the Indian nationalist movement. In Europe, the movement's centre moved from Paris to Switzerland, a country where a number of Egyptian nationalists lived, and which Germany was using for its own propaganda.[1] Germany was very actively spreading anti-British propaganda among the Indian troops stationed at the frontlines in France. Thus, the term 'Germano-Hindu' was being used for the propaganda.[2] At the same time, First World War marked a period of intensified collaboration between Great Britain and France. Immediately after the War, this momentarily gave rise to a conciliatory attitude on the part of the British authorities. However, the change in attitude did not last long and the English-language press generally remained Gallophobic or anti-French—at times even extremely vituperative.

Concerning the period between the two wars, there are no reports in the records of a mission to India. Yet, one such mission did take place, entrusted to Maurice Pernot by the Ministry of Public Instruction, according to an account he wrote in 1927: *Sur la Route de l'Inde: Inquiétude de l'Orient* (On the Route to India: Concerns about the Orient). Not only were missions few in number, but so were French publications related to India, as noted in the *Catalogue de la Librairie française* (Catalogue of French Publications). However, this should not lead to the conclusion that India was absent from the intellectual and artistic scene. Tagore, Gandhi, and some Indian artists and princes established India's presence in France to some extent. References to India can be found in the works of several intellectuals: Daumal, Weil, Guénon, not to forget Lévi and Rolland, of course, who always gave the country pride of place. However, in general, images inherited from British literature and propaganda dominated.

Orient–Occident, an Overplayed Antagonism and its Cultural Implications

At the turn of the century, the recurring theme of the irremediable cultural antagonism between the Eastern and the Western civilizations had a specific political objective: supporting the colonial cause. Great Britain's efforts in trying to gain the support of its neighbour from across the Channel with regard to the danger faced by the empire in the aftermath of the 1904–5 revolt contributed a great deal to it. Great Britain was, in fact, trying to link the unrest it was facing in its colony to the situation prevailing in the French colonies, by presenting the Indian nationalist movement as the expression of a general revolt against all colonial powers—an anti-European revolt, a revolt by the East against the West. Thus, the East—hitherto a realm of fantasy, emerging from romantic imagination—assumed a clearly political character in the colonial context at the end of the nineteenth century and the early twentieth century.

Besides, the Asian political context in France had become

increasingly worrying, as noted by Ernest Pirion in his book on India in 1905:

The movement is so powerful and so contagious that it may cross all borders. A student in Lahore told me: 'It is horrifying for the government to send Sikh regiments to fight against the Chinese. For the Chinese are our brothers!' It was a rather curious term to use. What a prospect if Japan or China were to one day form an alliance of the whole of Asia against Europe![3]

Following Japan's victory over Russia in 1905, England and France began to fear a general movement of Asian emancipation in the form of a general and violent uprising of Asia, or even the whole of the 'East', against European domination. Indeed, the contents of political correspondence from French diplomatic posts in India that developed in the early twentieth century were very instructive.[4] Henceforth, France's interests in India would be limited essentially to the repercussions that the events unfolding there could have on its own empire. There was no definite political strategy apart from this, and its relations with India were subjected to the imperative of not undertaking anything that could jeopardize the interests of the British authorities. Since the nationalist movement in India had begun to be perceived as part of a global Asian threat against Europe, the Raj emerged as the first line of defence against the revolt. In the face of the threat posed the Indian nationalist movement, the British authorities tried to seek France's support. Consequently, the British authorities sent the following despatch to the French authorities in 1907:

According to our intelligence, they have received pamphlets from Paris and New York. The objective of all these documents is the overthrow of the British government, but I believe that you will readily agree with me when I say that those who are organising this campaign will not be satisfied until they have destroyed all signs of European domination in India.[5]

Besides, Martineau, the Governor of Pondicherry, seemed to support the British:

As my own government was no less shocked by a similar assassination [to that of Tinnivelly] in Karikal, I am quite obliged to agree with you hat there is truly quite a strong solidarity between the European nations present in this country and that, to use your own expression, there are advantages in cooperating with each other to crush dangerous organisations. . . .[6]

At the same time as this political development was taking place, a cultural event marked the perception of India in France at the turn of the century—the recognition given to Rudyard Kipling, who was henceforth established as an unequalled and incomparable reference point concerning India. The Anglo-Indian writer's popularity is difficult to measure today.[7] In 1899, *Jungle Book*, *Naulakha,* and the second *Jungle Book* were published one after another, followed by *La Lumière qui s'éteint*, and *La Plus Belle Histoire du Monde* in 1900. The latter received an award from the Académie Française the same year.[8] The East–West divide depicted in this Anglo-Indian vision triumphed. Between 1900 and 1905, nine new novels by Kipling were published, along with a new edition of *Captain Courageus*. Prints and reprints then appeared endlessly.[9] The University of Paris added to Kipling's popularity and fame by awarding him the degree of Doctor *honoris causa*. France recognized him as the 'spokesman and bard of imperialism',[10] well before he gained international recognition with the Nobel Prize for literature in 1907. Kipling's work established this antagonistic relationship in people's minds—a relationship that was to influence both cultural and political ideas in France.

The success of Kipling's work was symptomatic of France's support of the concept of an East–West clash. In 1924, in one of his books condemning the values of the modern Western world, even the traditionalist philosopher, René Guénon, began his foreword by commenting on the famous works of the English author on the gap between East and West:

Rudyard Kipling once wrote: *East is East and West is West, and never the twain shall meet*. . . . We are used to quoting just the first verse in isolation, as if all that has remained in readers' minds is the idea of an insurmountable difference expressed in this verse; there is no doubt that this idea does represent the opinion of most Europeans, and in it we can feel all the conqueror's bitter disappointment when obliged to admit that those he believed to have vanquished and subdued, possessed something over which he would never have any control.[11]

Between 1914 and 1940, whenever anything concerning India came up in France, outside Indianist circles, Kipling was quoted as the indisputable reference—unique and absolute. From 1919 to 1921, there were more than eighteen editions of his works in France, over sixteen from 1922 to 1925, and over thirty-six from 1934 to 1939.[12] Claude Farrère, a member of the Académie Française, a former naval officer and a student of Pierre Loti, referred to the author of *Kim* for any representation of India: 'What is India, exactly? Excuse me for quoting Kipling twice in this book, from its second page itself. However, the truth must prevail over all lies. And, we are only talking about the truth here.[13]

Maurice Pernot also increased the number of references to Kipling in the book he wrote at the end of the mission entrusted to him by the Ministry of Public Instruction. These references evidently served to support descriptions that portrayed irreconcilable differences between the two worlds—the East and the West. Indeed, the last but one article devoted to India in the *Illustration* in June 1938 bore no less than the title 'Aux Indes de Kipling' (In Kipling's India)![14]

Indian nationalism: A Danger for the Colonial Order

Perceived as a key element in an 'oriental tragedy' in the making, India saw itself attributed the epithet of a 'land of dangers'.

Uprising in Asia and the Spread of Communism

Of the nationalist movements in Asia, Dr Legendre—one of the main players in French cultural activities in this continent—wrote in 1936:[15] 'Never has our civilisation and even our country's economy been more under threat.'[16] As it happened, the Indian nationalist movement was the main nationalist movement in colonized Asia. The idea of an India threatened by communist expansion then became recurrent. Therefore, the communist ideology served as a framework for demands by 'return students', as they were called at the time. Graduates from colonized countries who had gone to the West for higher studies, they were direct witnesses of the contradictions between the Western egalitarian ideology, which they learnt about while pursuing their studies, and the social segregation they found on returning to their countries.[17] The USSR was quick to seize the opportunity of using these antagonisms for its own ends by proposing the thesis of rivalry between an oppressed East—while presenting itself as its leader and liberator—and a colonial, capitalist, and oppressive West.[18] Some members of the Indian nationalist movement, with Nehru as their leader, were not impervious to this rhetoric. Furthermore, Dr Legendre recalled the words uttered by Nehru at the Lahore Congress. Describing his speech as 'Bolshevik',[19] he concluded with the following words: 'Moscow's action has truly established itself among India's educated classes.'[20] The collusion between the Soviet movement and Asian nationalists became a major concern for political analysts in France. French supporters of the colonial order, of whom Dr Legendre was an eminent representative, did not hesitate to take the plunge and lump together the Indian anti-colonial movement, the broad rebellion by Asian peoples, and the opposition between communism and democracy.

Another fear was added to that of communist expansion. India had the largest Muslim population in the world, which further raised the risks of the spread of the nationalist movement into its own empire, in the eyes of France.

At the Heart of the Oriental Drama: The 'Muslim World'

In the context of the awakening of various nationalisms, there was a fear of repercussions and reactions on the part of Muslim communities in different parts of the world, particularly as the diversity of these regions could disappear behind the monolithic concept of a 'Muslim world'. Consequently, in December 1924, the Ministry of Public Instruction entrusted Maurice Pernot with a mission to '... study the feelings of the Muslim populations of Egypt, Ceylon, India, Afghanistan and Persia *vis-à-vis* the Europeans.'[21] In the foreword to the book Pernot published upon his return from the mission, he began his account with the following lines, which truly summarize the general feeling in France *vis-à-vis* India in particular and the East in general:

> The unease reigning in the East has led to greater disquiet and trepidation in the European world, which is itself in disarray (. . .). Disruptive forces and creative forces that had lain dormant for so long that we had forgotten their existence, suddenly awakened.[22]

Although he intended to get a clearer view of the situation through a study based on investigations and interviews, Pernot still described the events as an 'Oriental tragedy' at the end of his foreword. The entire drama had been played out largely to serve political views established before his departure and defined by the title of his mission itself. The East–West antagonism found an additional avatar here—this time, a politico-religious avatar, which was echoed in the titles of press reviews by French consular posts in India.[23] The British authorities favoured greatly the antagonistic relationship in their press campaigns, aimed at arousing anti-colonial reactions among Muslims, contrary to what France believed.

Therefore, several factors came together in India, all likely to arouse fear in a France that was attempting to convince itself that it was witnessing a colonial 'golden age'. More than ever before, the interests of its neighbour across the Channel seemed similar to its own. An illustration of this idea among French intellectuals is given by Dr Legendre, who wrote: 'Great Britain is undoubtedly the keystone of any colonial edifice.'[24] In the increasing sentiment of solidarity toward the British colonial interests lies France's prudence with regard to any actions *vis-à-vis* the Indian nationalist élite. In 1930, *Illustration* expressed the same opinion in an article entitled 'Les Indes anglaises menacées: la clé de voûte des empires coloniaux'[25] (British India under Threat: The keystone of colonial empires). These overlapping common interests with Great Britain at a global level are to be considered in the Occident *versus* Orient context. The fact that this may have been against French interests in India appeared to matter only to a very small number of French personalities committed to fostering cultural exchanges with India such as André Weil and Sylvain Lévi, for instance. Thus, while the notion of Indian civilization developed, in particular through the works of French Indianists, political issues increased in importance over scientific and cultural considerations.

NOTES

1. R.J. Popplewell, *Intelligence and Imperial Defence . . .*, London: Frank Cass & Co., 1995, p. 141.
2. The French Ambassador in the United States used the expression in 1916. AMAE/P – Correspondace politique et commerciale, Nouvelle série, no. 33, Relations avec la France (f. 160), Washington, 12.07.1916.
3. E. Pirion, *L'Inde contemporaine et the mouvement national.*
4. AMAE/P – Correspondance politique et commerciale, Nouvelle série, Inde (1896–1918).
5. AMAE/P – Correspondence politique et commerciale, Nouvelle série, no. 33, Relations avec la France (ff. 167–9).
6. Ibid.
7. M. Renouard, 'L'odeur de l'Inde dans Kim', in *Arts, Littérature et Civilisation du Monde Anglophone* no. 4, Pau: PUP, October 1994, pp. 197–201.
8. *Livre de la Jungle* and *Second Livre de la Jungle*, *La Plus Belle Histoire du Monde* au Mercure de France, *Naulahka*, et *La Lumière qui s'éteint* chez Ollendorff.
9. See *Catalogue de La Librairie Française.*
10. M. Renouard, *La Littérature indienne de la langue anglaise*, p. 36.
11. R. Guenon, *Orient et Occident*, Paris: Les éditions Vega, 1983, p. 7.
12. See *Catalogues de la Librairie française.*
13. Claude Farrère in *L'Inde perdue* (Lost India) makes Kipling the reference point for all knowledge on India. C. Farrere, *L'Inde perdue*, 1933, Paris, pp. 3-5.
14. A. Okada, *L'Inde, les dossiers de l'Illustration*, Bagnear, Le Livre le Paris, pp. 183–90. Literature and literature are so intertwined that we can see a photo of an Indian introduced as Kim.
15. As the former Director of the Imperial Medical School of Tcheng

Tou in China, and chargé de mission, the opinion of Dr Legendre is revealing.

16. A.F. Legendre, *La crise mondiale, l'Asie contre l'Europe*, Paris: Plon, 1932, p. 253.
17. Ibid., and C. Farrere, *L'Europe en Asie*, Paris: Flammarion, 1939.
18. In the meantime Japan introduced itself as the 'champion of the yellow race'.
19. Legendre, *La crise mondiale, l'Asie contre l'Europe*, op. cit., pp. 251–3.
20. Ibid.
21. AMAE/P – AO 1918–1940, Affaires communes no. 832 (Recommandations de Français), Londres, 02.12.1924. It is from this fieldwork that Maurice Pernot, professor of the university, former correspondent in Rome for the *Journal des Débats* wrote in 1927 for Hachette: *Sur la Route de l'Inde, Inquiétude de l'Orient*. Among the various areas covered, India, Egypt, Ceylon, Afghanistan, and Persia, the Indian subcontinent is the main focus.
22. M. Pernot, *Sur la Route de l'Inde, Inquiétude de l'Orient*, Paris: Hachette, 1927, p. v.
23. Ibid., p. 144.
24. Ibid., p. 253.
25. Okada, *L'Inde, les dossiers de l'Illustration. . .*, op. cit., pp. 152–

CHAPTER 8

French Indologists and the Debate about Indian Civilization

'Always the old hope of seeing scholars from both the two worlds united in the same great task of erudition.'[1]

From the end of the eighteenth century in France, with a renewed questioning of the Biblical historical saga, India, its history and sacred texts were drawn upon to rewrite the history of humanity. This idea was closely associated with the scientific trends of the nineteenth century. In the inter-war period, this erudite vision was dealt a serious blow by a plurality of opinions. In the early 1920s, the ambitions of the leading scholar of French Indology Sylvain Lévi, and a leading Indian cultural figure, Rabindranath Tagore, seemed to find common ground. However, as the changing political situation caught up with them, differences soon appeared between the two men.

Indian and French Visions of the Concept of Civilization and the Political Stakes Involved in the Debate

Much more than the term 'culture', it was the term 'civilization' that was of more recent vintage and that came to be linked to the notion of the development of Western civilization in the eighteenth century. 'Civilization' and 'culture'—the two terms started competing with each other towards the end of the eighteenth century. The claims of a foundational civilization played a key role in nationalist thinking. While it could serve as a cultural excuse for colonial ideology through the idea of the progress and hierarchy of societies, the notion of civilization could also serve as a tool for the nationalist ideology of colonized peoples. Indeed, the recognition of a state of civilization considered to be advanced made it possible to support demands for independence. While it may essentially be based on scientific and cultural considerations, the notion then covered several other issues of a political nature. However, in the period between the two wars, Indian civilization gained scientific recognition in French works, which made it possible to support and legitimize the nationalist demands of the Indian political élite. Ashutosh Mukherjee, the Director of the University of Calcutta, and Tagore did not take long to understand this. Sylvain Lévi's award of the degree of Doctor *honoris causa* and his invitation in 1921 should be placed in this context. The influence of the French philologist and, more generally, of the EFEO on Indian historians through the works of Georges Cœdès, Henri Parmentier, or even Jean Przyluski has already been discussed.

In 1913, Tagore was undoubtedly *the* living figure who dominated the dialogue between India and other countries. On the French side, it was Lévi who was considered an authority, concurrently holding posts at the Collège de France, the Sorbonne, and the École pratique des Hautes Etudes. In 1920, he co-founded the Association française des Amis de l'Orient, along with other great figures of French Orientalism—Pelliot,[2] Sénart, and Hackin. The association was established as an intermediary between various French institutions and Asia, whether it was the École des Langues orientales (School of Oriental Languages) or the Quai d'Orsay (Ministry of Foreign Affairs). It was located in the Guimet Museum and worked closely with it. According to the first article of its constitution, 'The purpose of the association called the "Association française des Amis de l'Orient" or AFAO, founded in 1920, is to develop intellectual and artistic relations between France and Eastern and Far Eastern Nations.'[3] According to the third article, 'It enables its members to participate in the life and spread of oriental art museums, in particular the 'Guimet Museum'.[4]

Andrée Karpelès and her sister, Suzanne, were also part of the original group that gave birth to the association, the latter as its secretary.[5]

Thus, the Association française des Amis de l'Orient was founded as the official institution for dealing with issues concerning the East, whether it was the organization of Tagore's conferences, for instance, or extending help to students from 'Eastern' countries. The activities of the Association française des Amis de l'Orient and the Guimet Museum were, however, directed largely at the Far East, Indochina, and Buddhism, rather than India and Hinduism. The Institut de civilisation indienne (Institute of Indian Civilization), set-up in 1927, provided an institutional tool for Lévi's scientific conceptions concerning India.[6] Of course, Lévi was not the only French Indianist of the period. The role and works of Alfred Foucher, Jules Bloch, Coèdes, Pelliot, and Hackin de Przyluski have been cited. The works of Demiéville, Grousset, Mauss, Masson Oursel,[7] Olivier Lacombe,[8] and the role of Pierre Meile must be also mentioned. French Indology continued to contribute enormously to the exploration of Indian culture. But France was not the only country to position itself in the field of study of Indian civilization. Indology was also a propaganda instrumental in the expression of rivalries between these powers. The direction taken by French Indology reveals the power struggle between competing nations during this period. Curiously, it was not England that prevented or restricted the expansion of France's presence in the Indian subcontinent, but Germany. Indeed, European rivalries seemed to have prevailed over any 'overseas' perspective. While Great Britain's domination took the form of both a moral and pragmatic imperialism, France and Germany competed in the context of an ideological imperialism, presented as universalistic idealism, bearing the stamp of romanticism. Based on the dynamics of the colonial context and rivalry with Germany on the French side, and on the building of a national identity aimed at gaining freedom from colonial domination on the Indian side, the perspectives of French Indianists and Indian intellectuals did not uphold the same interests, although they may have concurred over the *Greater India* concept.

The fear of seeing Germany take on the role of Asia's preferred interlocutor became a significant central theme in France's relations with India. In its propaganda in India, Germany tried to arouse sympathy by presenting itself as a victim of French colonialism. At the same time, it spread propaganda about the idea of the 'joint origin' of Indian and German civilizations, based on common Aryan roots. Gradually, under the influence of Sylvain Lévi, French Indology adopted a different stance from the German perspective, bringing together Sanskrit, Vedism, and Aryanism, and by offering its own 'republican' interpretation of India's culture and history.[9] Of course, the French perspective is riddled with ambiguities.

Thus, France pitted Dravidian studies against Sanskrit studies. Against the hierarchized model of Vedic society, promoted and reinterpreted by German Indology, French Indology offered a democratic model that was presented as an outcome of Buddhist philosophy. The model proposed by French Indology combined the fruit of its research in the peripheries of the Indian subcontinent with meritocratic and republican ideas, personified by Lévy in some way.[10] In this regard, he wrote:

> French Indology is essentially drawn to Buddhism, the only product of Indian genius that is universal in nature, both by its aspirations and by its history. Within Buddhism itself, it has a predilection for the so-called 'northern' Buddhism, which covered by far the widest area.[11]

In contrast to the notion of a conquering genius of an Aryan people idealized by Germany, France offered the idea of an Indian genius operating on the basis of a peaceful influence. Moreover, it was a genius that would only reveal itself through association with other cultures, capable of showing it to advantage:

> India only produced its classical masterpieces through foreign action or on foreign land (. . .). In India itself, the Taj Mahal in Agra—which a competent judge (Fergusson) placed on the same level as the Parthenon—was the work of a Great Moghul.[12]

In this conception of Indian culture, which took a stand differing from the German model of Indology, Indian 'genius' was presented as the product of a necessary association with a guardian culture. Lévi clearly expounded his conception of Indian culture, civilization, and history in a series of lectures published in 1926 under the title of *L'Inde et le Monde* (India and the World). They reiterate the importance that he gave to Buddhism and to the role of other civilizations in the development of Indian culture, presenting these civilizations as being the only ones capable of revealing to India its own genius.[13] It is difficult not to see a reflection of the French colonial ideal of an *association* in Lévi's view, as distinct from the *indirect rule* of the British. Thus, despite the anti-colonial stands taken by several French Indianists, including Sylvain Lévi, the positions adopted by French Indology coincided with French colonial thinking, both in the concept of an *association* as well as in its areas of research, for the latter were located in regions that France had colonized, in particular south India and Indochina, to which Hindu culture had spread. Franco–German rivalry over India was publicly revealed during Tagore's travels in Europe.

The propaganda term, 'Germano-Hindu', emerged during First World War. India's importance in the great East–West debate and the rivalry over the country between France and Germany seemed to reach its zenith during Tagore's travels in Europe. While the poet's prestige reflected on his country, the political and other important issues of his times played a role in the assessment of his artistic and intellectual work. In the spring and summer of 1921, the two countries tried to present themselves as India's preferred interlocutors, through Tagore. At a literary event organized in his honour in France in April that year, French writers rejected any 'ceremonies referring to works by Germans'. Hence, Conrad Hausmman, the writer and politician, was refused an invitation.[14] In retaliation, German authors protested against 'the exclusiveness of France's literary circles', and when Tagore went to German-speaking Switzerland, they presented him with over 400 works signed by their authors at a ceremony in Lucerne. At the same time, they set-up a German literature fund in his honour. In his letter of thanks, Tagore described the special links between Germany and India in particularly reverential terms:

> More than any other country, it is Germany that played a role in opening and expanding the channel linking Western forces of reason and intelligence with India, and the tribute of love Germany has spontaneously offered to a poet from the East will undoubtedly further strengthen these relations, making them more intimate and personal.

The French Consul General in Stuttgart further added:

It has been announced that Tagore will visit a number of German towns, where a very warm welcome awaits him. His visit will certainly be celebrated there, many Germans doing so with the thought, at the back of their minds, of favourably influencing the Hindu soul through its most modern representative, all of them wishing to show a Germany that is welcoming even in the face of defeat by the noblest forces of humanity, asking for their utmost understanding and offering them their own—in a word, playing the role of the misunderstood and persecuted genius of Europe before the Asian genius.

France's concerns were soon confirmed. In end May, Tagore visited Sweden for a lecture series on Buddhism and the need to seek an East–West rapprochement. On 1 June, reports of the poet's interviews with German journalists were received, '. . . in which he apparently praised German culture to the skies and, generally speaking, the character of the German people'.[15]

The affair was reported widely in France. The Quai d'Orsay informed the Ministry of Public Instruction and Fine Arts, and Lévi narrated the unfolding of events:

On 22 May, the *Roter Dag* published an article by Count Kyerserling on Tagore. Tagore had been his guest in Darmstadt on his arrival in Switzerland; before setting off on his visit to the Scandinavian countries, Kyerserling wrote in this article: 'Tagore, who has never visited Germany, believes that the future of Europe lies in this country. According to Tagore, it is Germany that will trigger Europe's intellectual and moral renaissance. America is more materialistic than ever. The victorious nations are struck with blindness. It is in Germany that the new human order can and will be reborn.' I'll keep the rest for later.[16]

Lévi explained how German newspapers reported the words attributed to the poet, one after the other, while he was in Scandinavia, 'officially welcomed and feted in Copenhagen and Stockholm'.[17]

On his return to Germany, to Darmstadt, where Kyerserling had gathered 'all of Germany's intelligentsia',[18] for a 'Tagore Week', the poet came to know about the publication of these articles. On 11 June itself, he wrote to Lévi:

I have been given to understand that certain statements, which have been attributed to me, were published in a German newspaper, and took my friends in France by surprise (. . .). I urgently request you to help me inform my friends that it was a false statement that was quoted, and one that surprised me more than anyone else. . . . The article came out while I was in Sweden, and it is only by chance that I came to know about it, long after it had been published. Marburg University's Dr. Otto has promised me that a corrigendum will be published. . . .[19]

The same day, Lévi wrote to Tagore to inform him about a donation of books for his institution, Santiniketan, on behalf of the Strasbourg Tagore Committee. Franco–German rivalry and the active propaganda revolving around the poet help us to better understand the implications of the following statement by this committee: 'It is very important for French thought and culture to have a significant presence in this university, which has a large role to play in East–West relations in the future.'[20]

On 14 June, while acknowledging receipt of Lévi's letter, Tagore reiterated the difficult situation in which he had been placed by the publication of the aforementioned articles in Germany:

You would have certainly received my last letter just as you had sent your own. The false statements that were published in the newspapers during my absence have caused a lot of problems for me and I have taken measures to ensure that similar offences against my person are not repeated in the future. That is why, I will make use of the last day I spend in Germany to tell people how much the distortion of facts has hurt me.[21]

We can gauge how burdened Tagore felt during his travels in Europe. Through him, it was India—'the Hindu soul', to cite the term used by the Consul General of France in Stuttgart—that was caught in the trap of European rivalry, especially the rivalry between France and Germany. It was a rivalry that weighed considerably on Franco–Indian relations. The Quai d'Orsay's refusal to support the project presented by Professors Sarkar and Bash in 1921 was another case in point.

The weight of the issues at stake and all the political rivalry also affected the supporters of a Franco–Indian dialogue. Thus, during Tagore's trips to France in 1920 and 1921, Lévi avoided introducing the Indian writer to Rolland in spite of the desire evinced by both men to meet each other. Rolland's global pacifism and idealized approach to India made the professor ill at ease, as he was a patriot and a fervent believer in republican values, both in his scientific and political outlook. Nevertheless, Rolland and Tagore did manage to meet. The poet visited the writer in Switzerland in 1921, and once again in 1926. They started collaborating on the issue of the condemnation of Western nationalism, which Tagore attempted to compare with an Eastern conception of the world and Rolland with his global pacifism. Very soon, differences emerged between the philologist, the poet, and the pacifist. In 1922, during a lecture delivered by Tagore on nationalism, Mrs Lévi emphasized the differences between her husband's views and those of the poet. The controversy was further exacerbated in 1923. During a visit to Japan, Lévi read an article in a newspaper that highlighted Tagore's enthusiasm for the German philosophical movement, *Zeitgeist*.[22] This led the Collège de France professor to write the following to Tagore: 'Ah Gurudev! Whatever you are born, you are not a prophet! You believe that West is waiting for a message of peace from the East. The East is lacking peace even more than the West.'[23]

Lévi referred to the unrest in India, 'the Chinese hell', 'the terrible crisis' that Japan was undergoing, where students were 'poisoned with Bolshevism', to conclude that the great Indian artist was incapable of understanding the political realities of his time:

> Yes, you are a dreamer, and the most delightful dreamer. But look down to ordinary men, and then you will not sneer any more at our passion for liberty, you will have to recognize that, for an ordinary man at least, dignity of life cannot exist without liberty.[24]

Lévi then painted a picture of an aristocratic, Brahmanical India—implicitly presenting Tagore as its representative—as opposed to a democratic, Buddhist India, which was very dear to him. He compared this Buddhist India, crushed by the Brahmanical India, with a West that was becoming 'more and more democratic' and that 'believed in Human Rights'.

Lévi's charges against Tagore were serious, more so as the poet belonged to a family of social reformers. Besides, Tagore took an active and personal interest in the revival of interest in Buddhism, both through his teachings and the research being done in Santiniketan, in which Lévi himself had been invited to participate. Lastly, Tagore's devotion to education in India—which lasted until his death—made him one of the rare examples in the history of contemporary artists and intellectuals in the world. At the end of his letter, Lévi tried to soften his criticism by declaring that he did not know who was wrong—whether it was he or Tagore, or even both. However, the relationship between the two men was considerably damaged.[25] Indeed, it began to deteriorate from that moment on.

In 1925, Tagore's anti-colonial statements, along with those of Rolland, once again provoked Lévi to launch an attack in *Les Appels de l'Orient*:

> Romain Rolland, who depicts Gandhi's India in the same vein as Philostratus depicted the Greece of Gymnosophists, does a great disservice to India whose glory he claims to portray. Tagore, who denounces the faults and crimes of the West to his compatriots, to China and to Japan, and who, in contrast, talks about a fantasy Orient, does a disservice to Asia, to Europe and his own ideals.[26]

In 1923, the origin of the controversy between the two men could be traced to Tagore's kind words with regard to Germany. It was in reaction to these statements that Lévi once again referred to an East brimming with revolutions and threatened by Bolshevism versus a democratic West, upholding the principles of individual liberty and human rights. The appreciation of an intellectual living in a society scarred by the racial discrimination imposed by a colonial power, of Western origin, would obviously be very different. For Tagore, a resurgent Asia held out the hope of establishing a more balanced power equation in the world. Which of these two great men was more idealistic? Pursuing similar goals, representing countries placed in different situations, it is logical that their positions, which once converged, now began to diverge. Politics finally gained the upper hand in the friendship nurtured in the field of culture.

Another divisive and discordant factor was the varied perspectives of India amongst French intellectuals. These perspectives covered approaches that stemmed from different concerns that were not simply scientific or cultural in nature.

THE DIVERSE APPROACHES OF THE PARTICIPANTS IN THE INDO-FRENCH DIALOGUE

India was not a subject of study reserved for Indianists alone. Since the eighteenth century at least, India was seen as a subject ripe for intellectual and romantic speculation, filled with its share of fantasy, even phantasmagoria.[27] At the end of the nineteenth century, alongside the academic Indianists emerged an increasing number of supporters of the idea of initiating a dialogue with India. The philosopher, René Guénon, was one of them. He was opposed to modern Western philosophy, adopting a perspective that was closer to Nietzsche and the German school of thought. He recommended a return to a society based on traditional concepts, whose real foundations he wished to reclaim. It was in this spirit that he took an interest in 'Oriental' cultures. India occupied an important place in his earlier works. He allied a certain erudition with dry reasoning. These works made him very influential amongst France's intellectual and artistic élite, especially in regard to his contribution to the 'great East–West debate', which he tried to place in an intellectual framework.[28] Topping the list of personalities who were influenced by him were leaders of the surrealist movement, especially Breton and Artaud, as well as fascist thinkers or 'nationalist revolutionaries'.[29] André Gide, Drieu La Rochelle, Raymond Queneau, and Jean Paulhan, who founded the *Traditions* series at Gallimard, also owed much to his work.[30] Although he attended Paulhan's lectures regularly, Lévi refused to guide his research work, thus demonstrating his differences with his philosophy. Later, Guénon drew closer to Sufism.

Neo-Hindu movements were also at odds with modern Western civilization, and proposed a reformative philosophy of syncretism as an alternative. The primary movement amongst them was the Theosophical movement. It struck a chord with the Westernized Indian élite and certain nationalist leaders especially Gandhi and Annie Besant. It enjoyed considerable and influential support in Western nations, particularly in France. At the end of the nineteenth century, many theosophical works were published in French. Another neo-Hindu movement was founded by the Bengali nationalist, Aurobindo Ghose, in Pondicherry, together with Mira Richard, the wife of France's Consul in Japan. The writer, Jean Herbert, helped to widen the reach of Aurobindo's works by translating them into French. More and more people in France were attracted to these works, among them certain Indologists such as Suzanne Karpelès. The ashram was to gradually become a focal point and an important partner in the Franco–Indian dialogue.

Although it no longer occupied the central position that it once enjoyed in the intellectual dynamics of the mid-nineteenth century, India was always present in the French cultural landscape and imagination. It still constituted an areaof interest for many intellectuals and artists, an interest that went well beyond the circle of Indologists. It would be impossible to list all the authors, musicians, dancers, painters, etc., whose works contained references to India. Daumal was one of the most well known amongst them. The young Malraux travelled across India in 1931 on his maiden initiation to a passion that would remain a topical thread throughout his life and in his works. Michaux devoted a major part to India in his *Barbare en Asie*. As for Paul Morand, he called one of his works that contained not even a single reference to India *La route des Indes*![31] India remained a presence in the French cultural landscape, but rather indistinctly, sometimes troubling, but rarely familiar, contrary to certain narratives of the eighteenth century.

Just after the First World War, Romain Rolland asserted his presence as an unavoidable interlocutor in France in the dialogue between the East and the West. Rolland, who was awarded the Nobel Prize in 1916 after his book *Au-dessus de la mêlée*, would soon distinguish himself with biographies of Indian personalities such as Gandhi and Ramakrishna. His journey from European pacifist thought to international pacifist thought brought him closer to Indian intellectuals.[32] It is in this context that he bonded with Tagore, with whom he collaborated from 1917,[33] and with Nag from 1922. He was also close to Tagore's friends, the Britons, Andrews and Pearson. Following the latter, he abandoned Tagore gradually and drew closer to Gandhi. The latter's rejection of violence would rapidly convert Rolland into one of his most steadfast supporters. Never having set foot in India, speaking neither English nor any other Indian language, Rolland was first and foremost a committed writer who put India at the service of his own ideals, which would earn him strong condemnation among Indian academic circles. They rejected a vision of India that they deemed as having nothing to do with any scientific reality. Moreover, the relations between Tagore, Nag, and Gandhi were not devoid of complexities either. Driven into a corner by Lévi on the question of the opposing values of an aristocratic East and a democratic West, it was natural for Tagore to strengthen his ties with Rolland. The latter differed from Lévi in his eagerness to highlight the weaknesses of West in the stranglehold of nationalist passions, confronted with the values of humanism and universalism of the East, whose incarnation he found in some of the legendary figures that strode the Indian stage.

However, relations with Tagore too gradually began to decline. First of all, there was the famous episode of Tagore's trip to Italy in 1926. During his sojourn, the poet was granted the status of a state guest, which did not prevent him from having clandestine meetings with intellectuals opposed to the fascist regime.[34] On his return from Italy, Rolland attempted to extract a public condemnation of Mussolini's fascist regime from him. The poet complied. However, the pacifist intellectual increasingly came to consider Tagore as an artist whose ideas were far removed from the reality of contemporary political issues.[35] He believed that the proof of this lay in Tagore's new passion for painting, considered a futile social nicety. Rolland stated this clearly in his diary, when the two men met for the last time on 28 August 1930 in Geneva. Moreover, Tagore was soon eclipsed by a rising figure in Indian politics—Gandhi. In the context of the rebirth of political passions, Gandhi found an audience that continued to grow and he slowly eclipsed Tagore. In 1925, Rolland wrote the following about the two Indians:

> At heart, one can feel the insurmountable antipathy between the free spirit enamoured by all forms of life (and possibly dilettante) and the puritan who imposes his regimen of mortification and asceticism on his disciples, to create a militia ready for any sacrifice. Tagore. Gandhi. Two worlds, between which the schism continues to widen.[36]

Initially, Rolland sided with the scepticism of some Indian opponents of Gandhi. Tagore was one of them, accusing the new political leader of obscurantism, mainly due to his avowed ability for manipulating crowds and for his opposition in allowing access to women in certain fields of education.[37]

It is interesting to note that in the French press, Gandhi was first portrayed as an agitator, as was the case in *Illustration*, in March 1922.[38] Then, in July 1924, he was depicted as a prophet.[39] His aura continued to grow thenceforth. He became a charismatic figure, recognized across the world. He soon found a number of supporters for his actions in the Anglophone world. Rolland's expansive essay on the 'Mahatma' owed much to the testimony of Andrews.[40] This hagiographic essay was issued in the magazine, *Europe*, towards the end of 1923 and published in 1924. Right from the outset, it compared Gandhi to Saint Francis of Assisi, describing him very picturesquely.[41] The 1930s and 1940s witnessed Gandhi's consecration. He became the incarnation of India's freedom struggle. In *Illustration*, the huge demonstrations of the 1930s were described as 'Gandhian uprisings'.[42] His trip to Europe in 1931 provided a glimpse of the mystical aura surrounding this political leader with an ascetic bearing.

Tagore and Gandhi were two very different personalities. In the shift of fame from the former to the latter, the passing of the baton from one élite class to another can be seen. Tagore was an artist and an intellectual, issuing from a long line of erudite aristocrats and social reformers who were nonetheless deeply rooted in their country's culture. The obligatory stay in

England for his higher studies was indeed a difficult time in his life. Consequently, he founded Santiniketan to help the next generation of Indian students to avoid undergoing a similar forced exile. He made use of the halo created by his artistic works to serve India's political causes. In contrast, Gandhi was a political figure, a member of the British bar, who, during his studies in England, had tried to become the perfect English gentleman. On his return from South Africa, his increasing political prominence gave him an undisputed ascendancy over others in the Congress party. He became the principal spokesman in the East–West dialogue. France found in him a figure in whom it could recognize ideals stemming from its Christian heritage. On the other hand, while Tagore's journey and activities instrumental in provoking cultural contacts with France, very little can be said in this regard as far as Gandhi was concerned. The consequences of the socio-cultural evolution of the Indian élite in the French cultural space in India were underlined by Colette Khan.[43] Tagore belonged to an educated élite that had a deep understanding of Western culture, and it cannot be disputed that a feeling of kinship drew this élite closer to French culture, in which it perceived a fundamental element of modern culture. Gandhi belonged to another cultural background and would become from the 1920's onwards as the leader of a new generation—the one some had christened the generation of 'return students'. In spite of being overtly anti-Western, it was a paradox that this generation inherited Anglo–Saxon prejudices *in toto*. In his letter to Andrée Karpelès in 1924, Rolland described Tagore and Gandhi in the following words:

> Dear friend, you ask me why I do not write like Tagore. It is indeed one of my desires. To succeed in it, I would like to go to India, stay there for a few months or a few weeks with the poet, for one cannot write Tagore as one can write Gandhi. It is a thought process that is infinitely more complex and more rich, and also more Indian.[44]

Rolland wrote his hagiography of Gandhi without ever meeting him. Gandhi's statement about the place of French culture, which Rolland had adopted as his own, is quite significant:

I paid attention to other details reputedly useful for the making of an English gentleman, but people tell me I ought to have taken lessons in dance, French and elocution.[45]

The question raised with regard to French culture in India on the eve of the country's independence was the following: would its prestige decline with the end of British rule? British rule had initially facilitated the entry of French culture, involuntarily, but once it had penetrated the cultural space of the Indian élite, the colonial masters tried to snuff it out. On the one hand, while the negative propaganda almost constantly unleashed against France and its culture did have an effect in the long-term, on the other hand, it also reinforced the conviction amidst the élite Indian nationalists that they were dealing with an anti-British and, therefore, anti-colonial culture, a brother in arms to their struggle. After 1947, this argument lost its contemporary relevance, more so as France seemed to want to delay the inevitable finality of granting independence to its own colonies, even to its trading posts in India. At the same time, the British maintained their influence through the press and through Anglo-Indian culture, with all its romantic clichés, as well as its derogatory images. On the French side too, continuity persisted *vis-à-vis* India. Caught between being an attribute of the educated Indian élite—which would diminish in size as the generations went by and against the emergence of a new élite—and a nation in search of a new raison d'être in a bipolar world that tended to relegate it to the ranks of a former power.

NOTES

1. D. Lévi, *Dans l'Inde, de Ceylan au Népal*, p. 45.
2. First resident member of the EFEO, Professor of Chinese. Professor in the Collège de France from 1911, President of the Société asiatique from 1935 until his death in 1945.
3. L'Association française des Amis de l'Orient (brochure diffusée par l'association).
4. Ibid.
5. AMAE/N – Service des Œuvres françaises à l'Étranger no. 256. N. Dé, *Madame Lévir Diary*, Kolkata: Ananda Publishers, 2000, p. 17.

6. The Institute of Indian Civilization coordinated and centralized the syllabus related to India and South-East Asia. The Institute focused particularly on the study of Sanskrit. The classes aimed at preparing to the certificate of Indian studies which is equivalent to a Licence (three-year degree in the former French system).

   See also P. Singaravélou, 'Les Indianistes français et the *Greater India*', op. cit.
7. P. Masson-Oursel, *La Philosophie comparée*, Imprimerie des Presses Universitiares de France, Paris, 1923.
8. O. Lacombe, *L'Absolu selon the Vedânta, les notions de Brahman et d'Atman dans les systèmes de Cnakara et de Râmânoudja*, Paris, Annales du musée Guimet, Geuthner, 1937.
9. P. Singaravélou, 'Les Indianistes français et the *Greater India*', op. cit.
10. Sylvain Lévi, the son of a tailor, thanks to his extraordinary academic brilliance became the youngest professor in the Collège de France. He belonged to the first generation of French Jews who were given the opportunity of benefiting from the Republican programme of social upliftment.
11. Sylvain Lévi quoted in P. Singaravélou, 'Les Indianistes français et the *Greater India*', op. cit., p. 6.
12. S. Lévi, *L'Inde et the Monde*, Paris: Honoré Champion, 1926, p. 10. On retrouvait déjà ce point de vue chez James Darmesteter.
13. 'The biggest of its sons, Buddha, she had forgotten him. While Tibet, China, Korea, Japan and Indochina piously repeated the biography of the master, India who had given him birth, did not know anymore anything about him,' p. 15, id.

   'It is pointless to add to this list. It indicates clearly enough what India owes in the awakening of its consciousness, to its contact with Europe', id., p. 18.
14. AMAE/P – AO 1918–1940, PB no. 22, CG à Stuttgart to AE, 19.05.1921 (Hommage allemand à Tagore).
15. Ibid., Ministre de France à Stockholm to AE, 1 June 1921 (Séjour en Suède du poète Rabindranath Tagore).
16. Ibid., MIP et des Beaux-Arts to AE, 20 July 1921.
17. Ibid.
18. Ibid.
19. Ibid.
20. Archives Rabindra Bhavan in Santiniketan.
21. AMAE/P – AO 1918–1940, PB no. 22, MIP et des Beaux-Arts to AE, 20 July 1921.

22. *Zeitgeist*, 'spirit of the time', philosophical school of thought in Germany which could be described as neo-romantic. It lasted through the ninteteenth century, from Goethe to Nietzsche, and experienced a revival after First World War.
23. K. Dutta and A. Robinson, *Rabindranath Tagore: The Myriad Minded Man*, pp. 247–8.
24. Ibid.
25. Ibid.
26. 'Les Appels de l'Orient', February-March 1925, quoted in R. Rolland, *Rabindranath Tagore et Romain Rolland, Lettres et autres écrits*, Cahiers Romain Rolland, no. 12, Paris: Albin Michel, 1961, pp. 132–3.

    See also: K. Nag and R. Rolland, *Correspondence: The Tower and the Sea,* C. Guha (trad., intro, notes), Calcutta: Papyrus, 1996.
27. The different references made to India by Montaigne show that it was a subject that French intellectuals precociously appropriated in the early modern period, much before the eighteenth century and long before the birth of Indology.
28. J. Julliard and M. Winock, *Dictionnaire des intellectuels français, les personnes, les lieux, les moments*, op. cit., pp. 566–7.
29. Ibid.
30. Ibid.
31. P. Morand, *La route des Indes*, Paris: Plon, 1936, carte hors texte.
32. J. Julliard and M. Winock, *Dictionnaire des intellectuels français, les personnes, les lieux, les moments*, pp. 998–9.
33. R. Tagore, 'Message de l'Inde au Japon', in R. Rolland, *Aux peuples assassinés*, 1917, Editions des jeunesses socialistes romande.
34. (S.) Liné, *Tagore Pèlerin de Lumière*, Paris: Le Rocher, 1987, pp. 245–56.
35. R. Rolland, *Inde journal (1915–1943), Tagore, Gandhi, Nehru et les problèmes indiens*, Paris, 1951.
36. R. Rolland, *Gandhi et Romain Rolland* . . ., Paris: Albin Michel, 1969, pp. 438–9.
37. 'The first topic of discussion was regarding idols. Gandhi defended them, because he thinks that the masses are unable to uplift themselves to abstract ideas. Tagore does not stand that we forever treat the people like a child. Gandhi alleged that the great achievements in Europe were obtained through the flag-idol', id., pp. 427–8.
38. A. Okada, *L'Inde, les dossiers de l'Illustration* . . ., ' L'arrestation de Gandhi'.

39. Ibid., 'Mahatma Gandhi, the messie hindou'.
40. Rolland, *Gandhi et Romain Rolland* . . ., op. cit., pp. 426–9.
41. Rolland, *Mahatma Gandhi*, 2nd edn., Paris, pp. 9–10.
42. Okada, *L'Inde, les dossiers de l'Illustration* . . ., op. cit., p. 144.
43. C. Khan, *État et développement des études françaises dans the monde indien* . . ., p. 75.
44. Rolland, *Rabindranath Tagore et Romain Rolland, Lettres et autres écrits*, Paris: Albin Michel, pp. 122–3.
45. C. Khan, *État et développement des études françaises dans the monde indien: l'exemple de la province musulmane du Bengale*, p. 75.

CHAPTER 9

Conclusion

In the modern era, relations between France and India were nurtured by direct exchanges that continued until the middle of the eighteenth century. After glimpsing the possibility of expanding its political influence, France nevertheless began to withdraw from the Indian subcontinent. Although the number of French nationals who foresaw this possibility was unknown the idea remained alive and became part of the cultural heritage. Direct contacts brought about by trade played a less and less important role in promoting Franco–Indian relations. Paradoxically, in the early nineteenth century, India occupied an increasingly important place in the French cultural and intellectual landscape, while the first English-speaking generation of Indian intellectuals incorporated French culture within its frame of reference. The years from 1870 to 1914 was a key period in Franco–Indian relations. Indian cultural dynamics and French policies played a decisive role in the evolution of the French cultural space in India. While building their national culture, the Indian élite drew on philosophical, literary, and political themes in French culture. Thus, from the last quarter of the nineteenth century, thanks to their Francophile and sometimes Francophone nature, the Bengali, Parsee, and princely élites found themselves at the forefront of the propagation of the French language in the Asian continent, thanks to their capacity for assimilation. At the end of the nineteenth century, this élite set out in search of an interlocutor capable of offering an alternative to the colonizer–colonized relationship. This quest for a dialogue with France clearly shows that the desire for independence from British rule was not founded on the rejection of Western culture. In fact, it was the representatives of the most anglicized of the Indian élite who drew closer to French culture, an assimilation that stemmed from a voluntary and dynamic process. At the same time, in France, the interest in India brought about by the Orientalist wave started to branch off towards other regions that seemed more promising in terms of the renaissance—not of humanity, as those who presided over Indology in France may have hoped for at the turn of the eighteenth century—but a more pragmatically restrained renewal: that of the French nation, for such a renewal had become imperative after Sedan's defeat by the Prussians in 1870. The lack of direct contact made France more than ever dependent on its neighbour, Britain, and soon to be an ally, in its relations with the Indian subcontinent. The directions taken by French Indology were also subject to the influence of this political development, moving towards the periphery of the British empire in India, especially in regions that fell under the direct control of France and those that were free of British influence, such as Japan and China.

From 1870 to 1914, French culture became a part of India's modern heritage, mainly due to its prestige and the efforts for the Indian élite. Without this voluntary approach and the Indian élite's astounding capacity for assimilation, French culture in India would have been relegated to a passing phase, particularly as, from the last quarter of the nineteenth century, France deliberately distanced itself from the changes taking place in Indian society. France's prestige, its richness, and its contribution to modern culture justified the interest evinced in it by the Westernized Indian élite. On the eve of First World War and during the upheaval that followed it, the question that was asked was whether French culture would remain as attractive to this élite as it had been previously.

Did First World War mark a rupture or an acceleration in Franco-Indian relations? From 1914 to 1940, the admirers of the French language in the Bombay Presidency increased, its prestige rose among the Bengali intellectual élite, and its teaching spread in southern India. However, this progress hid certain structural insufficiencies. Indeed, the rapprochement with England and the primacy of colonial interests in matters of foreign policy was strengthened even further after the war. India's exclusion from the French field of vision seemed to be confirmed. While modern means of cultural action were being set-up, the sense of colonial exclusivity was strengthened even further, to the detriment of other regions of the world. Thus, when information networks and commercial text and image distribution circuits developed, the Anglo-Saxon domination became stronger.

During this period, Indian contemporary art wrote some of the most beautiful pages in its history in France's galleries, workshops, and theatres, particularly through Tagore, Uday Shankar, and Amrita Sher-Gil. Thanks to the success of these events, traces of the continuing interest in Indian culture could be found in France. In India, at Santiniketan, French nationals took part in the educational and cultural activities of the Bengali Nobel laureate. New vocations emerged for Indian students in this pioneering educational centre where different cultures met. Other avenues were opened in France too. The careers of Andrée Karpelès, Alain Daniélou, and Christine Bossennec are examples of this. While French remained the second European language in India, it was clear that it was so on a very modest scale compared to English. The most striking feature of this period in India was the strengthening of the hold of Anglo–Saxon culture, with American influence bolstering the influence of Great Britain.

Sylvain Lévi's work gave back a certain prestige to French culture in the inter-war period. Rabindranath Tagore's cooperative ventures with Lévi once again gave birth to the hope for a cultural dialogue and friendship between the two countries—perhaps even a privileged role for France in the Indo-Western dialogue. The seeds of this intellectual cooperation were planted in the soil of Santiniketan, in the amphitheatres of the Sorbonne, and in Calcutta's historical societies. Like the relations that Tagore built across the world, several voices took part in this dialogue too. Among them were Japan, Italy, the USSR and, above all, Germany. Further, the cultural—even civilizational—dialogue in which France and India were engaged was soon caught up in the partisan politics that divided the two countries. The same divisions could also be seen among the various participants in the Franco–Indian dialogue.

Moreover, the dialogue between the two countries, both of which laid claim to being great civilizations, did not proceed smoothly, as was the case with the cooperative collaboration between Tagore and Lévi. The quest for universal humanism—the starting point from which a rapprochement and dialogue could have been established—was soon overtaken by political matters shaped by the forces of colonization and nationalism. India found itself at the confluence of France's relationships with the rest of the world, whether it was the antagonism between the East and the West, between the colonizers and the colonized, between France and Germany, or, still further, the antagonism between the communist world and the 'free' world. France's attitude towards India was summarized in the following words by a representative of the Indian political class, the great intellectual and scholar, Maulana Abul Kalam Azad:

> Europe is very wrong in believing in the hostility and resentment of Asia, and imagining that we are getting ready for some furious and vengeful assault. Our goal is very different: we aspire for liberty and peace; we dream about a world order where the East and the West, instead of being at loggerheads, would unite their forces and genius. However, who will accomplish this rapprochement and this union? The British have shown that they are incapable of doing it. Not long ago, we still counted on France, on its liberal spirit, on its generosity. The years that have passed since the Great War have made the East's great hopes crumble.[1]

The fact that Azad addressed these words to Pernot, the official representative of the Ministry of Public Instruction, responsible for the study of Islamic movements, is all the more significant. The Muslim nationalist leader, the supporter of a secular India, was already fully aware of the outrageous statements that had become stumbling blocks in achieving the rapprochement desired by the Indian élite.

The major legacy of the last quarter of the nineteenth century is the division of the world according to the colonial line. The main result of this division symbolized by the Berlin Convention in 1878 is not only the division of various regions of the world by European nations, but how this division evolved into cultural concepts and become entrenched in the general perception sustained by scientific discourse. This has been already emphasized critical analysis of the concept of Orientalism and later studies of Occidentalism. Nevertheless, it still appears necessary to corroborate the dialectical approach of Orientalism with a chronological and political one. The study of the relations between Great Britain and France, and notably the Franco–British Entente Cordiale through colonial requirements, would be more comprehensive. French admiration for British colonial achievements is obvious at least from the second half of the nineteenth century. From there onwards, France showed a conscious or unconscious solidarity with its neighbour across the Channel. France looked towards regaining an international status and a wider market for its products. In this context, British rule appears as the pillar of the colonial order on which it based its new policy. It did not consider Great Britain as a rival *per se*, contrary to what the historical popular understanding tends to assert. Its continental ambitions were focused on Germany. The British government and its various support groups such as the press used their dominant positions to discredit French power. Simultaneously, the government acted in such a way that France came to consider its interests as being closely interlinked with British interests.

The making of a fearsome image of India, and more broadly of the Orient, through a supposedly common conspiracy of nationalist movements in India and Egypt, along with Muslim communities in the French colonies, is part of this strategy. If France had been more tolerant towards the Indian nationalists, both in its metropolitan territory and in its settlements in India, the outcome of the resistance that the Raj faced in the first two decades of the twentieth century could have been different. The original perception of France regarding its interests in the world tended to be conditioned by and substituted with a vision of a world divided into two blocs. This East–West and colonizer–colonized divide provided the blueprint for further antagonistic perceptions such as democracies *versus* communist and other non-democratic countries, and Muslims *versus* non-Muslims.

Attempts to establish bridges between regions belonging to the two different blocks predictably had to take positions on this issue. At a time when contacts between the different regions of the world are increasing, the political and psychological divide seems to be widening.

In spite of this, relations between the two countries continued practically uninterrupted for more than three centuries. Was the apparently permanent nature of the Franco–Indian dialogue real or false? It is equally important to highlight the changes and ruptures in these relations as it is to emphasize their long-term nature. While India and France have nurtured cultural links at different levels in the modern era, these links have to be perceived in the light of the dynamics behind them as well as the imperatives of India's history and geography, particularly the role played by the Indian diaspora. Otherwise, there is a danger that the Franco–Indian paradox—based on a long common history and a reciprocal but superficial knowledge of each other—may become permanent, as neither are its constituent elements well known, nor have they been properly analysed. One of the distinctive elements of the cultural behaviour of the élites in both countries was certainly their tendency of claiming to be familiar with every cultural discourse of worth, even of appropriating them. In 1930, the mathematician, Weil, analysed the reasons that impelled a part of the Indian élite towards France:

> I am convinced that this country offers vast possibilities for the French, if only they would apply themselves to it. Indians are not xenophobic at all by nature—well to the contrary; it took a long and at times oppressive foreign domination to arouse in them a deep hatred for the British, as a nation. However, as for the rest, English itself, though it made some advances and seemed adaptable, received the best of welcomes in India. French is sure to be received even more warmly even now, for the Indians are thrilled to be able to compare the French and the English and to show the latter in a poor light. Highly sensitive to the prestige of European culture, suffering from having been intellectually subjected to British culture, and also being great admirers of the French Revolution and Rousseau (. . .), the road has already been paved (. . .); it is their wishful thinking that they would have got on better with the French. Above all, they appreciate the fact that the

French do not believe themselves superior, and they are thrilled that the French assimilate their culture, that they eat their food, that they are able to live in their fashion, that they learn their language: that too is part of the colonial tradition of the 18th century.[2]

This apparent familiarity was nurtured by a certain belief that the élites of both the countries had in the universality of their cultures, a belief that could lead to either a rapprochement or to a misunderstanding. The relations between Lévi–Tagore, in spite of their setbacks, still offers an excellent example of efforts seeking to find a common ground. The channels of a cultural dialogue that both nurtured and respected the specificity of either side remained to be defined. From 1870 to 1947, the beginnings, and at times even the realization, of such a dialogue could be seen in several instances of Franco–Indian episodes in both the field of the arts, as well as in the field of the sciences—in short, cultural links in the broadest sense of the term. The dream of a cosmopolitan cultural brotherhood glimpsed in the inter-war period in the dialogue between India and France, especially due to the bold explorations characteristic of the era, and which had to do with a very large geographical and semantic area, was overshadowed by political issues. The channels that were opened should certainly be explored (once again), underestimating neither the weight of the socio political motivations that conditioned their making, nor the cultural richness of the exchanges that have taken place.

The colonial dynamics and the subsequent adaptations or reactions of the colonized of the studied period (1870–1947) can hardly be understood in a univocal or even bipolar way. There are intricate relationships between the modes of representations and policies of the British Raj, the local and sometimes diverging interests within metropolitan Britain—including British living overseas—and across its borders, i.e. the neighbouring countries. In the case of France, this relationship is physical, because of the geographical proximity in Europe, accentuated by the ship–train route after the opening of the Suez canal, as well as in India, with the French enclave within the peninsula. This proximity and its ambiguous relationship are also relevant in the cultural field, with French legacy carried by England's history, as well as by its dominant position in Europe at the turn of the twentieth century. What could have turned into a *liaisons dangereuses* did not translate into a real challenge to British dominance over India as France was looking forward to challenging its continental rival, Prussia/Germany and acknowledging the power of its neighbour across the Channel. This proximity had a much weightier influence on the French perception of India and consequently in relation with the Indians. Though there were some first rank intellectuals like Sylvain Lévi, Alain Danielou, as well as Anquetil Duperron before them, who partially or entirely managed to overcome the colonial influence, as a whole France had adopted the British perception of India.

The relative failure of French diplomacy to understand, and their eagerness to draw France closer and to become a more active participant in their relationship, is due to a lack of understanding of the approach of the Indian élite to Western culture. At a time when culture was still largely based on personal initiative and relationship and not yet dictated by the rules of mass consumption and media, it would not be totally wrong to talk about a *rendezvous manqué*, or at least we can notice that the work of those intellectuals could not reverse the trend of French institutions to abandon the perception of India to British propaganda.

The Indian relationship with Western culture is also made of an intricate network of selected pieces of its various components, be it British, French, German, and later on American, and Russian. This composite appropriation of Western culture would suit alternatively the social, economic, political or cultural requirements and preoccupation of the Indian élite. In the context of Indian nationalism Greater India could be an interesting concept to draw from French indology, as well as the emphasis of Indo–European legacy celebrated by German indology, though the two schools were proposing two almost opposite patterns of interpretation of Indian civilization.

The opposition to British rule did not mean the rejection of British culture, even by those who claimed the need to repeal it, and obviously not the rejection of Western culture as a whole. The Indian élite distinguished quite acutely the differences between the various European cultures, and could be banked on their potential roles according to their needs. They were helped in that approach by the presence of their fellow countrymen settled in the concerned countries. In spite of the lack of accurate answers to the Indian élite approach, French culture played a very significant role among them as an alternate culture. The role of women into taking up the cause of French language reveals the modern aspect of French culture under the conservative and sometimes reactionary cultural stands of the Raj, as well as the deep roots it found among Bengalis and Parsees. Was French culture, as well as the Russian, the American or even the Japanese one a way to resist standardization and create rooms for alternate modes of perception, relation and expression? It was an obvious aim at the international level, but it can hardly have been a prominent feature of the approach of the Indian élite to French culture concerning the inner diversity of India. In the context of the nationalist movement they were more preoccupied by uniting than showing its diversity. So with regard to Indian composite culture, if it has played a role, and it has, it remained a really marginal one. It nevertheless tends to reinforce an acute perception of the need to counter-balance the homogenizing trend of a univocal modernization. Before 1947, there are no strong trends on the French side of banking on India to promote alternate modes of perception, relation and expression on the international scene, as well as with regards to its own diversity, perhaps because of the strong Jacobin legacy.

NOTES

1. M. Pernot, *Inquiétude de l'Orient: sur la route de l'Inde,* Paris: Hachette, 1927, p. 144.

   The author, despite the fact that he proposes to share an enlightened view in order to make the distinction between the fantastical Western vision of the Orient, describe the events, at the end of the foreword as an '*oriental drama*'.
2. AMAE/N – Service des Œuvres françaises à l'Étranger, no. 219, Indes anglaises, André Weil à Service des Œuvres françaises à l'Étranger, 18.08.1930.

Bibliography

Abeydeera, Ananda, 'Jean de Marignolli: l'envoyé du pape au jardin d'Adam', in *Purusartha*, no. 11, Paris: EHESS, 1988, pp. 57–68.

Abrioux, Cynthia, 'Macaulay and India: the power of discourse' , dans *Les Cahiers du SAHIB*, no. 2, Rennes: PUR, 1994, pp. 11–22.

Ageron, Charles, *Trois siècles de présence française en Inde*, Actes du colloque du 21 septembre, Paris: CHEAM, 1994.

Alliance Française, *Alliances 2000*, Paris: Alliance française de Paris, 2000.

Ambassade De France En Inde (ed.), *50 ans de coopération sientifique et technologique entre la France et l'Inde*, Delhi: Service Culturel Scientifique et de Coopération, 1998.

— *Former Indian Scholars and Trainees in France*, Delhi: CEDUST, 1992.

— *Malraux et l'Inde, Itinéraire d'un émerveillement*, Delhi: Thompson Press, 1996.

Annasse, Arthur, *Les Comptoirs français de l'Inde: 1664–1954, trois siècles de présence française*, Paris: La pensée Universelle, 1975.

Arokiaswami, M., 'French influence in South Indian culture', in *Journal of Indian History*, April 1962, vol. 40, no. 118, pp. 191–9.

Arputhasamy, M., *L'Eglise catholique dans l'Inde. Etude historico-juridique*, thèse de Droit de l'université de Fribourg, Pondichéry Mission catholique, 1948.

Assayag, Jackie, *L'Inde fabuleuse. Le Charme discret de l'exotisme français (XVIIe-XXe siècles)*, Paris: Kémé, 1999.

— 'L'aventurier divin et la bayadère immolée. L'Inde dans l'opéra', in *Purusartha*, no. 11, Paris: EHESS, 1988, pp. 197–228.

— 'Perfide Albion ou la France outragée, une tragédie du repli colonial sous l'Empire: Tippô-Saëb, d'Etienne de Jouy (1812)', 'Aurore et crépuscule de l'Eve indienne: l'imaginaire de la danseuse de temple entre Théophile Gautier et Pierre Loti', in Denys Lombard, *Rêver l'Asie*, Paris: EHESS, 1993, pp. 197–215 and 251–67.

Aubert, R. (dir.), *Dictionnaire d'Histoire et de Géographie Ecclésiastique*, Letouzey and Ané, v. 20.

Baneth-Nouailethas, E., 'L'infranchissable frontière: le Club dans la société anglo-indienne', dans *Frontières*, no. 3, Paris: Presses de l'Université de Paris-Sorbonne, 1992, pp. 39–51.

Baillou, Jean (dir.), *Les affaires étrangères et le corps diplomatique français*, pt. 2, Paris: Edition de la recherche scientifique, 1984.

Bagchi, Prabodh Chandra, *India and China: A Thousand Years of Cultural Relations*, Bombay: Hind Kitab, 1975.

— *Deux lexiques sanskrit-chinois. Fan Yu Tsa Ming de Li Yen et Fan Yu Ts'ien Tseu Wen de Yi-Tsing*. T. Ier, Paris: P. Geuthner, 1929 (Sino-Indica, Publications de l'université de Calcutta, pt. III).

— *Le Canon bouddhique en Chine*, coll. Les traducteurs et les traductions, pt. IIe, Paris: P. Geuthner, 1938 (Sino-Indica, Publications de l'université de Calcutta, Tome IV).

— Lévi, Sylvain, Jean Przyluski, Jules Bloch, *Pre-Aryan and Pre-Dravidian in India,* Prabodh Chandra Bagchi (trad.), Calcutta: University of Calcutta, 1975.

Baulez, M.J., *Vingt ans dans l'Inde*, Paris: Challamel aîné, 1886.

Barthold, V., *La découverte de l'Asie*, Paris: Payot, 1947.

Berard, Victor, *La révolte de l'Asie*, Paris: Armand Colin, 1905 (2nd edn.).

Berard, Victor and R. Caix, *Les questions actuelles de politique étrangère en Asie*, Paris: Plon, 1947.

Bayly, C.A., *The Raj: India and the British 1600–1947*, National Portrait Gallery Publications, London: Pearson, 1990.

— *The New Cambridge History of India: Indian Society and the Making of the British Empire*, Cambridge: Cambridge University Press, 1988.

Becker, R., *L'hindouisme face à la crise du monde moderne*, Paris, 1966.

Bernard, C., *La Politique Culturelle de la France en Chine entre les Deux Guerres Mondiales*, Mémoire de Maîtrise sous la direction de Y.H. Nouailhat, Université de Nantes Atlantique, 1991.

Berthet, S., 'L'Inde dans la presse française du milieu du XIXe siècle au début du XXe siècle', in *La Lettre du C.I.D.I.F.*, no. 21, Paris: Août, 1999.

— 'La culture française en Inde de 1870 à 1962: présences et actions. Dynamiques indiennes et politique française', thèse de doctorat dirigé par Jacques WEBER, Nantes, 2002a.

— 'Les Français, le Bengale et Shantiniketan au temps de Tagore', in J. Weber (ed.), *Les relations entre la France et l'Inde de 1673 à nos jours*, Paris: Les Indes Savantes, 2002b.

— 'Indian Diaspora in France: A Historico-Cultural Perspective', pp. 133–52, in S.D. Singh and M. Singh (eds.), *Indians Abroad*, Gurgaon: Hope India Publications, 2003.

Bies, Jean, *Littérature française et pensée hindoue*, Paris: Librairie C. Klincksieck, 1974.

Bhabha, Homi K., *The Location of Culture*, New York and London: Routledge, 1994.

Boner, A., G. Soni and L. Boner (eds.) *Alice Boner Diaries: India 1934–1967*, Delhi: Motilal Banarsidass, 1993.

Boucher, Mgr A., *Petit atlas des missions catholiques*, Paris: Hatier, 2nd edn., 1933.

Bouchon, Geneviève, 'L'image de l'Inde dans la Renaissance', in *Purusartha*, no. 11, Paris: EHESS, 1988, pp. 69–90.

Bourdieu, Pierre, *Langage et pouvoir symbolique*, Paris: Seuil, 2001.

Bromfield, Louis, *La mousson, roman sur les Indes*, in Berhte Vulliemin, (trad.), Paris: Stock, 1940 (142nd edn.).

— *Les nuits de Bombay*, CAILLÉ, François (trad), Paris: Stock, 1944 (55th edn.).

Bruézière, Maurice, *L'Alliance française 1883–1983, Histoire d'une institution*, Paris: Hachette, 1983.

Castonnet Des Fosses, Henri, *La Révolution et les Clubs dans l'Inde française*, Nantes, Revue de la Révolution, 1883, pts. 1 and 2.

Champion, Catherine, 'Du Nabab au Sahib, De l'Utopie à l'Utilitarisme. Promenade à travers les clichés de la littérature anglo-indienne' in *Purusartha*, no. 7, *Inde et Littérature*, Paris: EHESS, 1983, pp. 285–310.

— 'L'imaginaire tropical: le paysage Indien dans les romans populaires français (1880–1920)', in *Purusartha*, no. 11, Paris: EHESS, 1988, pp. 91–124.

— 'Introduction à la littérature anglo-indienne', 'L'image de l'Inde dans la fiction populaire française aux 19ème et 20ème siècle', 'L'Inde éblouie ou le rêve d'une colonie: le roman exotique au service de la mission civilisatrice', in *Rêver l'Asie*, pp. 21–37, 43–66 and 219–38.

Chanda, Rani, *Shob Hoté Apan*, Kolkata: Visva Bharati, 1995 (2nd edn.).

Chatrath, K.J.S., *Les relations diplomatiques entre la France et l'Inde depuis 1947*, Paris: Thèse Droit Université de Paris, 1988.

Chaudhury, Sukanta (ed.), *Calcutta the Living City*, vol. I, *The Past*, Calcutta: Oxford University Press, 1990.

— *Calcutta the Living City*, vol. II, *The Present and the Future*, Calcutta: Oxford University Press, 1990.

— Dé, Nandadulal, *Madamé Lévir Diary*, Kolkata: Ananda Publishers, 2000 (traduction en bengali, présentée et annotée de. Désirée LEVI *Dans l'Inde, de Ceylan au Népal*, Paris: Rieder, 1925).

Chailley, J., *L'Inde britannique. Sociétés indigènes. Politique indigène. Les idées directrices*, Paris: Colin, 1910.

Cohn, Bernard S., *Colonialism and its Forms of Knowledge: The British in India*, Delhi: Oxford University Press, 1996.

Colley, Linda, *Britons: Forging the Nation, 1707–1837*, New Haven: Yale University Press, 1992.

Combaz, G., *L'Inde et l'Orient classique*, coll 'Les Musée Guimet, documents art et archéologie', no. 1, Geuthner, 1938.

Courtillier, G., *Les anciennes civilisations de l'Inde*, Paris: Armand Colin, 1930.

Cultru, P., *Dupleix et ses plans politiques; sa disgrâce*; Etude d'histoire coloniale, Thèse de Lettre université de Paris, Paris, 1901.

Cunningham, M.S., *British India and its Rulers*, London: Allen, 1872.

Daniélou, Alain, *Le Tour du monde en 1936*, Paris: Flammarion, 1987, Saint-Amand-Montrond: Impr. Bussière.

— *Le Chemin du Labyrinthe, Souvenirs d'Orient et d'Occident*, Monaco: Le Rocher, 1993.

Darmesteter, James, *Lettres sur l'Inde, À la Frontière Afghane*, Paris: Alphonse Lemerre, 1888.

David-Néel, Alexandra, *Correspondance avec son mari, édition intégrale 1904–1941*, Paris: Plon, 2000.

— *L'Inde où j'ai vécu, avant et après l'Indépendance*, Paris: Plon, 1951.

De La Vallee Poussin, Louis, *L'Inde au temps des Mauryas et des Barbares, Grecs, Scythes, Partes et Yue-Tchi-Pan*, Histoire du monde, vol. 6 (1), Paris: De Boccard, 1930.

— *Dynasties et histoire de l'Inde depuis Kanishka jusqu'aux invasions musulmanes*. Histoire du monde, vol. 6 (2), Paris: Boccard, 1938.

De La Mazeliere, *Essai sur l'évolution de la civilisation indienne*, 2 vols., Paris: Plon, 1903.

De Saurigny, *Histoire de la Chine, du Japon, de la Perse, de l'Inde, etc. depuis les temps les plus reculés jusqu'à nos jour*, Paris: Librairie Universelle, 1846.

Degros, Maurice, 'La création de postes diplomatiques et consulaire français de 1815 à 1870', dans *La Revue d'Histoire Diplomatique*, nos. 3–4, Paris, 1986, pp. 219–20.

Delessert, A., *Souvenirs d'un voyage dans l'Inde éxécuté en 1834–1839*, Paris: Fortin Masson, 8 vues, 27 pl. gravées et coloriées et une carte, 1843.

Deleury, Guy, *Les Indes florissantes: anthologie des voyageurs français, 1750–1820*, par S.E. Idris Hassan Latif (préf.), Paris: Laffont, 1991.

Denvers, Frederic Charles, *The Portuguese in India*, 2 vols., London: Allen, 1894.

Despont, Abbé J., *Nouvel atlas des missions*, Paris et Lyon: Bureaux de l'oeuvre de la propagation de la foi, 1951.

Deveze, M., 'Les Cours de la Sorbonne', *Histoire de la colonisation française en Amérique et aux Indes au 18ème siècle*, Paris: CDU, 1949.

Droit, Roger-Pol, *L'oubli de l'Inde, une amnésie philosophique*, Paris: PUF, 1989.

— 'Victor Cousin, la Bhagavad Gita et l'ombre de Hegel', in *Purusartha*, no. 11, Paris, 1988, pp. 175–96.

Dubois, J. Abbé, *Moeurs, institutions et cérémonies des peuples de l'Inde*, postface de Alain Danielou, Métailié, Paris: PUF, 1985.

Dumont, Louis, *Hiéarchie et alliance, Notes comparatives sur la parenté dans l'Inde du Sud*, Imprimerie, Paris: SIM.

— *La civilisation indienne et nous, Esquisse de sociologie comparée.* Paris: Armand Colin, 1964.

— *Homo Hiearchicus, Essai sur le système des castes et ses implications*, Paris: Gallimard, 1967.

— *Religion, politics and history in India, colleted papers in Indian sociology*, Paris: The Hague, Mouton, 1970.

Dumont, Henri, 'Dépêches diplomatiques de Stanislas de Ostorog. L'Inde des années 1950 et les relations franco-indiennes', dans *Les Cahiers du SAHIB*, no. 1, Rennes: PUR, 1990, pp. 35–46.

— 'Au lendemain de l'indépendance des Indes et leur partage', in *Les Cahiers du SAHIB*, no. 5, Rennes: PUR, June 1997, pp. 71–85.

Dutt, T., *Le Journal de Mademoiselle d'Arvers*, Paris: Didier, 1879.

Dutta, Krishna and Andrew Robinson, *Rabindranath Tagore: The Myriad-minded Man*, Delhi: Rupa, 2000.

D'souza-Deleury, Florence, *Quand la France découvrit l'Inde, Les écrivains voyageurs en Inde (1757–1818)*, Paris: l'Harmattan.

— 'Contribution du coton à l'évolution des relations de l'Inde et la Grande-Bretagne jusqu'au milieu du 19ème siècle', in *Les Cahiers du Sahib*, no. 3, Rennes: PUR, 1995, pp. 58–64.

Eliade, Mircea, *L'Inde*, Alain Paruit (trad.), Paris: Editions de l'Herne, 1998.

— *L'Inde, 1928–1931*, Paris: Presse Pocket, 1988.

— *Journal des Indes*, Paris: Ed. de l'Herne, 1992.

— *Les promesses de l'équinoxe*, Mémoire I, *1907–1937*, Paris: Gallimard, 1980.

— *La bibliothèque du maharadjah*, suivi de *Soliloques*, Alain Paruit (trad.), Paris: Gallimard, 1996.

— *La nuit bengalie*, Paris: Gallimard, 1949–50.

— *Minuit à Serampore*, Paris: Stock, 1956.

Farrere, Claude, *L'Inde perdue*, 1933, Pondicherry-Paris: Kailash, 1990.

— *Forces spirituelles de l'Orient. Inde, Chine, Japon, Turquie*, Paris: Ernest Flammarion, 1937.

— *L'Europe en Asie*, Paris: Flammarion, 1939.

— *Le grand drame de l'Asie*, Paris: Flammarion, 1939.

Filliozat, Jean and Louis Renou, *L'Inde classique*, Paris, 1953.

Fisher, Michael H., *Counterflows to Colonialism: Indian Travellers and Settlers in Britain (1600–1857)*, Delhi: Permanent Black, 2004.

Fistie, Pierre, *Le réveil de l'Extrème-Orient, Guerres et révolutions (1834–1954)*, Paris: Les Presses Universelles, 1955.

Gandhi, M.K., *Lettres à l'ashram*, traduit par Jean Herbert, Frameries: Union des Imprimeries, 1937.

— *Gandhi à l'œuvre. Suite de sa vie écrite par lui-même*, Paris: Rieder, 1934.

Garatt, G.T. and E. Thompson, *Rise and Fulfilment of British Rule in India*, London: Macmilan & Co., 1935.

Gilbert, Etienne, *L'Inde économie et population*, P. Meile (préf.), Genêve: Droz, 1955.

— *La voie chinoise*, Paris: PUF, 1962.

— *L'agriculture indienne ou l'art du possible*, Paris: PUF, 1966.

— *Les Chances de l'Inde*, Paris: Seuil, 1969.

The Golden Book of Tagore: A homage to Rabindranath Tagore: from India and the world in celebration of his seventieth birthday, Calcutta: Ramananda Chatterjee, 1931.

Gonjo, Yasuo, *Banque coloniale ou Banque d'affaires, la Banque d'Indochine sous la Troisième République*, Paris: Comité pour l'Histoire Economique et Financière de la France, Ministère de l'économie et du budget, 1993.

Gourou, Pierre, *La terre et l'homme en Extrême-Orient*, Paris: Armand Colin, 1947.

— *L'Asie*, Paris: Hachette, 1953.

— *Manuel des études indiennes*, Paris: EFEO, 2001.

Grenard, Fernand (ministre plénipotentiaire), *Grandeur et décadence de l'Asie, L'avènement de l'Europe*, Paris: Armand Colin, 1939.

Guénon, René, *Introduction générale à l'étude des doctrines hindoues*, Etudes Traditionelles, Paris: Chacornac Frères, 1921.

— *Orient et Occident*, Paris: Les éditions Véga, 1983.

— *La crise de l'Occident moderne*, Etudes Traditionelles, Paris: Chacornac Frères, 1927, 1946.

Guimet, É. and G. Bon, *Mirages indiens, De Ceylan au Népal (1876–1886)*, Paris: Phébus, 1992.

Herbert, Jean, *Ce que Gandhi a dit vraiment*, Paris: Marabout, 1974.

— (traduction), Inano Yoga, Paul Masson-Oursel (intro) avec lettre de Romain Rolland et Paris: Albin Michel, 1948.

— *Quelques grands penseurs de l'Inde moderne* (causeries faites à Radio Genêve en juin 1937), Union des Imprimeries, Frameries, 1937.

— (traduction), *Ramakrishna (Shrî), les paroles du maître*, Union des Imprimeries, Frameries, 1937.

— *Vivekananda (Swâmi), l'homme réel et l'homme apparent*, Union des Imprimeries, Frameries, 1938 (2nd edn.).

Herrenschmidt, Clarisse, 'La forêt d'acclimatation. Inde et imaginaire chez Jules Verne', in *Purusartha*, no. 11, Paris: EHESS, 1988, pp. 125–32.

Horne, E.A., *The political system of British India with special référence to the recent constitutional changes*, Oxford: Clarendon Press, 1923.

Hulin, Jean-Paul, 'L'Inde dans les premiers écrits de Kipling: orthodoxie et déviance', in *Purusartha*, no. 11, Paris: EHESS, 1988, pp. 159–74.

Jacquemont, Victor, *Etat politique et social de l'Inde du Sud en 1832, Extrait de son journal de voyage*, vol. 1, *Avec une introduction de Alfred Martineau, Société de l'Histoire des Colonies françaises*, Paris: Ernest Leroux, 1934.

— *Etat politique et social de l'Inde du Sud en 1832, Extrait de son journal de voyage*, vol. 2, Ernest Leroux Masson et Cie, Paris, 1940.

— *Correspondance de Victor Jacquemont avec sa famille et plusieurs de ses amis, pendant son voyage dans l'Inde, 1828–1832*, Paris: Fournier, 1833, 2nd edn., 2 vols., 1835.

— Ibid., Nouvelle édition augmentée de lettres inédites, 2 vols., Paris: Garnier frères, 1841.

— *Voyage dans l'Inde*, 6 vol., Paris: Dicot, 1835–44.

Jancigny, Dubois De, A.P. (voyageur, diplomate, aide de camp du roi d'Oude, chef de service du ministère d'etat à Chandernagor), *Histoire de l'Inde ancienne et moderne et de la Confédération indo-britannique, depuis les origines jusqu'à nos jours*, Paris: Hetzel, 1858.

— *Inde*, Paris: Didot frères, 1845.

— Japon, Indo-Chine, Empire Birman (où Ava), Siam, Anam (ou Cochinchine), Péninsule Malaise, Ceylan, Paris: Didot frères, 1850.

Kaeppelin, P., *Les origines de l'Inde française: la Compagnie des Indes Orientales et François Martin; Etudes sur l'histoire du commerce des établissements français de l'Inde sous Louis 14, 1664–1719*, Thèse Lettre université de Paris 1907–1908, Paris, 1908.

Kämpchen, Martin, *Rabindranath Tagore in Germany. Four responses to a Cultural Icon*, Shimla: Indian Institute of Advanced Studies, 1999.

Kaplan, A., *Gandhi et Tolstoï, les sources d'une filiation spirituelle.* Pierre abbé (préf.), Imp. Stoquert, Nancy, 1949.

Khan, Colette, *État et développement des études françaises dans le monde indien: l'exemple de la province musulmane du Bengale*, Thèse de littérature et civilisation française de doctorat de 3ème cycle, Laurent Versini (dir.), Université de Nancy II, 1984.

Kiefer, Jean-Luc, *Anquetil-Duperron. L'Inde en France au XVIIIème siècle*, Paris: Les Belles Lettres, 1983.

Koestler, Arthur, *Le Zéro et l'Infini*, Paris: Calmann-Lévy, 1945.

— *Le Yogi et le Commissaire*, Paris: Calmann-Lévy, 1954.

— *Le Lotus et le Robot*, Paris: Calmann-Lévy, 1961.

Kripalani, K., *Rabindranath Tagore: A Biography*, Calcutta: Visva Bharati, 1980.

Labrousse, P. (ed.), *Langues'O, 1795–1995, Deux Siècles d'Histoire de l'Ecole des Langues Orientales*, INALCO, ed. Hervas, Paris, 1995.

Livre Blanc de l'orientalisme français, Communications données au Colloque 'Pour une nouvelle politique de l'Orientalisme', du 10 janvier 1992, Paris: Société Asiatique, 1993.

L'etang, Guy de (prés), *Présences de l'Inde dans le monde*, Paris: L'Harmattan, 1994.

Le Treguilly, P. and M. Moraze, *L'Inde et la France deux siècles d'histoire commune*, Paris: CNRS, 1995.

Latif, Bilkees, *L'Inde où vécut ma mère*, Eon-Frémont (trad.), J. Auboyer (préf.), Paris: Des Femmes, 1987.

Legendre, A.F., *La crise mondiale, l'Asie contre l'Europe*, Paris: Plon, 1932.

Leger, François, *Les influences occidentales dans la révolution de l'Orient, Inde-Malaisie (1850–1950)*, Paris: Plon, 1955.

Lembezat, B., 'L'Inde française', in *La France dans l'Océan Indien* (coll.), Paris: Société d'éditions géographique, maritime et coloniale, 1952.

Lévi, Sylvain, *L'Inde et le Monde*, Paris: Honoré Champion, 1926.

Levy, Roger, *Extrème-Orient et Pacifique*, Paris: Colin, 1948 (2nd edn.).

— *La révolte de l'Asie*, PUF, Que Sais-Je ?, no. 496, Paris: 1965.

— *Regards sur l'Asie*, Paris: A. Colin, 1952.

Liné, S., *Tagore Pèlerin de Lumière*, Paris: Le Rocher, 1987.

Lombard, Denys, 'La littérature exotique comme miroir nécessaire', in *Rêver l'Asie*, pp. 11–18.

Loti, Pierre, *Discours de réception de Pierre Loti à la scéance de l'Académie française du 7 avril 1892*, Paris: Calmann-Lévi, 1892.

— *Un pèlerin d'Angkor*, Paris: Calmann-Lévi, 1912.

— *La Turquie agonisante*, Paris: Calmann-Lévi, 1913.

— *Quelques aspects du vertige mondial*, Paris: Flammarion, 1917.

— *Les alliés qu'il nous faudrait*, Paris: Calmann-Lévi, 1919.

— *La mort de notre chère France en Orient*, Paris: Calmann-Lévi, 1920.

— *Suprêmes visions d'Orient*, Paris: Calmann-Lévi, 1921.

— *Cette éternelle nostalgie. Journal intime, 1878–1911*, La Table Ronde, Paris.

- *L'Inde (sans les Anglais & Mahé des Indes)*, Paris-Pondichéry: Kailash, 1992.

Malraux, A., *Le Miroir des Limbes* (I, Antimémoires, II, 5), *Œuvres complètes*, La Pleïade, NRF-Gallimard, 1996.

Lafont, Jean-Marie, *Indika: Essays on Indo-French Relations (1630–1976)*, Delhi: CSH-Manohar, 2000.

Maindron, Maurice, *Dans l'Inde du Sud: Le Carnatic et le Maduré*, vol. 1, Kailash, Pondichéry, 1992.

— *Dans l'Inde du Sud: Le Carnatic et le Maduré*, vol. 2, Pondichéry: Kailash, 1992.

— *La gardienne de l'idole noire*, Pondichéry: Kailash, 1992 (originale 1910).

Malraux, André, *Les Conquérants*, coll. Livre Moderne, J. Ferenzi et Fils, Paris, 1933.

— *La voie royale*, coul., coll. Livre Moderne, J. Ferenzi et Fils, Paris: 1944.

— *La condition humaine*, Paris: Gallimard, 1944.

Marles, M. de, *Histoire générale de l'Inde ancienne depuis l'an*

2000 avant J.-C. jusqu'à nos jours, Paris: Emler frère, 6 vols., 1826.

Masson Oursel, P., H. Stern, Willman-Grabowska, *L'Inde et la civilisation indienne*, Paris: Bibliothèque de synthèse historique, L'évolution de l'humanité no. 26, 1933.

Memmi, A., *Portrait du colonisé, Portait du Colonisateur*, Paris: Folio, 2002.

Menant, Delphine, *Les Parsis, histoire des communautés zoroastriennes de l'Inde*, Paris: Leroux, 1898, annales du Musée Guimet, Bibliothèque d'études, vol. VII.

Mende, Tibor, *L'Inde devant l'orage*, coll. Esprit 'Frontière ouverte', Paris: Seuil, 1950.

— *La révolte de l'Asie*, Paris: PUF, 1951.

— *L'Asie du sud-est entre deux mondes*, Paris: Seuil, 1954.

— *Au pays de la mousson*, Paris: Seuil, 1955.

— *Conversations avec Nehru*, Paris: Seuil, 1956.

— *La Chine et son ombre*, Paris: Seuil, 1960.

— *Réflexions sur l'histoire d'aujourd'hui, entre la peur et l'espoir*, Paris: Seuil, 1967.

— *De l'aide à la recolonisation, les leçons d'un échec.*, Paris: Seuil, 1972.

— *Soleils levants: le Japon et la Chine*, Paris: Seuil, 1975.

— *Fourmis et poissons, carnets de route*, Paris: Seuil, 1979.

Michaux, Henri, *Un barbare en Asie*, Nouv. éd. rev. et corr., Paris: Gallimard, 1994.

Misra-Besnard, Kamakshi, *Le mouvement nationaliste en Inde. Le cas de Chandernagore: le premier maillon de la décolonisation (1905–1952)*, dirigé par Weber Jacques, Université de Nantes, 1998.

Mokerjee, G.K., *Inde 1960, Anniversaire de la République Indienne*, Paris: Service d'Information du Gouvernement de l'Inde, 1960.

Montaud, Annie, 'Le Hindi en 1947: la question de la langue nationale, ses origines et ses conséquences', in *Les Cahiers du Sahib*, no. 5, Rennes: PUR, June 1997, pp. 113–21.

Morand, Paul, *Montociel, Rajah aux Grandes Indes*, Genève: Ed. du Cheval ailé, 1947.

Morrow, Ann, *The Maharajas of India*, Delhi: Shrishti Publishers & Distributors, 1998.

Mouzon, C., *Pondichéry, étude de géographie humaine*, Acte géographique no. 192, fasc. spécial consacré à l'Inde française. Cartes, plans, tables graphiques, Société de géographie, Paris, 1955.

Nag, K., *Les théories diplomatiques de l'Inde ancienne et l'Arthacâstra, Thèse Lettre Université de Paris 1922–1923*, no. 199, Paris, 1923.
Nag, K. and R. Rolland, *Correspondence, The Tower and the Sea*, Chinmoy Guha (trad., Intro, notes), Calcutta: Papyrus, 1996.
— *Memoirs*, Calcutta: Writers Workshop, 2 vols. (vol. 1: *1891–1921*; vol. 2: *1921–23*), 1991–4.
— *Discovery of Asia*: Calcutta: Institute of Asian African Relations, 1957.
— Veda Vyasa, *History of Greater India*, Lahore: Dayanand College Research Department, 1929, *1. Ancient Hindu Colony of Cambodia*.
Nehru, Jawaharlal, *Selected Works of Jawaharlal Nehru*, Editor S. Gopal, New Delhi, vol. 9, 1990, vol. 12, 1992, vol. 16, 1994, vol. 17, 1995.
Nou, Jean-Louis, Jacques Pouchepadass, *Les derniers maharajahs*, Paris: Arthaud, 1980.
Okada, Amina, *L'Inde du XIXe siècle: voyage aux sources de l'imaginaire* (avec la participation de Enrico Isacco pour l'iconographie), Marseille: Agep, 1991.
Olichin, Mgr A., *Les missions, histoire de l'expansion du catholicisme dans le monde*, Paris: Librairie Bloud et Gay, 1936.
Ostrorog, Stansilas, *Courriers d'Orient, dépêches diplomatiques*, Nancy, PUN, 1991.
Pearson, M.N., *The Portuguese in India*, Cambridge: Cambridge University Press, 1987.
Percheron, Maurice, M.-R. Percheron-Teston, *L'Inde*, Paris, 1936.
Pernot, Maurice, *Inquiétude de l'Orient: sur la route de l'Inde*, Paris: Hachette, 1927.
Petit-Dutaillis, Yves and Mani Mulla, *L'Inde dans le Monde*, de Masson-Oursel P. (préf.), Paris: Payot, 1951.
Petr, Christian, *L'Inde des romans*, collection l'Asie imaginaire, Paris: édition Kailash, 1995.
Piesse, Gabriel, *Pondichéry de 1954 à 1963, de la République française à la République indienne, histoire d'une transition*, Mémoire de Maîtrise sous la direction de Ponnou, Université de Nantes, 1999.
Piniau, Bernard, François Roche, *Histoires de diplomatie culturelle des origines à 1995*, Paris: La Documentation française, 1995.
Ponteves, S., *L'Inde à fond de train*, 9 dessins de l'auteurs, 6 phototypies et 1 carte itinéraire, Société anonyme de publication des périoddiques, Paris: Lemerre, 1884.
— *Note de voyage d'un 'hussard'. Un 'raid' en Asie* (ouvrage couronné

par l'Académie française), avec une lettre de Frederic Mistral et 1 carte de l'itinéraire, Paris: Calmann-Lévi, 1890.

Popplewell, Richard J., *Intelligence and Imperial Defence: British Intelligence and the Defence of the Indian Empire 1904–1924*, London: Frank Cass & Co., 1995.

Pouchepadass, Jacques, *L'Inde au 20ème siècle*, Paris: Presses Universitaires de France, 1975.

— *Les historiens et l'histoire de l'Inde: un regard qui change*, dans Historiens et Géographes, no. 353, pp. 37–40.

Prasad, Ishwari, *L'Inde du 7ème au 16ème siècle*, Histoire du Monde Paris: Boccard, 1930.

Racine, Jean-Luc (dir.), *Calcutta 1905–1971. Au coeur des créations et des révoltes du siècle.* Autrement, Hors-Série collection Mémoires no. 46, Paris, January 1997.

Rivet, Dominique, 'Quelques réactions de la presse française à l'accession de l'Inde à l'indépendance, 1946–1948', in Charles-Robert Ageron and Marc Michel (dir.), *L'ère des décolonisations*, actes du colloque d'Aix en Provence/1993 'Décolonisations comparées', Paris: Karthala, 1995.

Raymond, Jean-François de, *L'action culturelle extérieure de la France*, Paris: La Documentation française, 2000.

Regamey, Constantin, *Orient et Occident*, Imprimerie Centrale, Lausanne, 1946.

Renouard, Michel, 'Les Anglais en Inde', in *Historiens et Géographes*, no. 353, Paris, June-July 1996, pp. 133–50.

— 'La frontière du nord-ouest dans la mythologie anglo-indienne', in *Frontière et frontières dans le monde anglophone*, no. 3, Paris: Presses de l'Université de Paris-Sorbonne: 1992, pp. 173–80.

— 'L'odeur de l'Inde dans Kim', in *Arts, Littérature et Civilisation du Monde Anglophone*, no. 4, Pau: PUP, October 1994, pp. 197–201.

— *La littérature indienne de langue anglaise*, Que sais-je ? no. 3197, Paris: PUF, 1997.

Roberge, Gaston, 'L'invention du sous-dévellopement', in Jean-Luc Racine (dir.), *Calcutta 1905–1971. Au coeur des créations et des révoltes du siècle.* Autrement, Hors-Série collection Mémoires no. 46, Paris, January 1997, pp. 160–8.

Renouvin, Pierre, *La question d'Extrème-Orient, 1840–1940*, Paris: Hachette, 1946.

Rolland, Romain (coll.), *Hommage à Rabindranath Tagore*, Tokyo: France-Asie, 1961, pp. 2650–2780. Extr. de: 'France-Asie. Asia', no. 170, November–December 1961.

— *A la civilisation*. [Le Message de l'Inde au Japon, conférence faite à l'Université impériale à Tokyo, le 18 juin 1916, avec Rabindranath Tagore, Andrée Jouve (trad.), 1917.

— *Inde, journal 1915–1943, Tagore, Gandhi, Nehru et les problèmes indiens*, Paris: Éditions Vineta, 1951.

— (introduction) *La jeune Inde*, texte anglais de Gandhi, traduit par Hélène Hart, Paris: Stock, 1948.

— *Rabindranath Tagore et Romain Rolland: lettres et autres écrits*, Paris: Albin Michel, 1961.

— *Among the Great: Conversations with Romain Rolland, Mahatma Gandhi, Bertrand Russell, Rabindranath Tagore, Sri Aurobindo*, Bombay: Nalanda Publications, 1947.

— (préf.), *Vie de M.-K. Gandhi écrite par lui-même: histoire de mes expériences avec la vérité* (d'après le texte anglais établi par C.F. Andrews) Georgette Camille (trad.), Paris: Rieder, 1931.

— *Romain Rolland. Mahatma Gandhi.* Edition nouvelle augmentée d'une postface . . . Paris: Delamain, Boutelleau et Cie, 1924.

— *Gandhi et Romain Rolland: correspondance, extraits du Journal et textes divers*, Paris: Albin Michel, 1969.

— *Mahatma Gandhi: the man who became one with the universal being*, Catherine Groth (trad.), New York and London: Century Co., 1924.

— *Rabindranath Tagore et Romain Rolland, Lettres et autres écrits*, pp. 132–3, Cahiers Romain Rolland, no. 12, Paris: Albin Michel, 1961.

— *Gandhi et Romain Rolland, Correspondance, extraits du journal et texte divers*, Paris: Albin Michel, 1969.

— *L'indépendance de l'esprit*, André Malraux (préf.) , Paris: Albin Michel, 1969.

— *Essai sur la mystique de l'Inde vivante, la vie de Ramakrishna*, Paris: Stock, 1963.

— *Gandhi, sa vie écrite par lui-même (histoire de mes expériences avec la vérité)*, Paris: Rieder, 1931 (2nd edn.).

— *Tagore, Gandhi Nehru et le Problème de l'Inde*, Paris: Vineta, 1952.

Rouaud, S., *L'action culturelle de la France au Japon dans l'entre-deux guerres*. Mémoire de Maîtrise Jacques Weber (dir.), 2000–1, Université de Nantes.

Rousselet, Louis, Littérateur et voyageur, rédacteur en chef du 'Journal de la Jeunesse', *L'Inde des Rajahs, Voyage dans l'Inde central et dans la présidence de Bombay et du Bengale*, Paris: Hachette & Cie, 1874.

— *Tableau des races de l'Inde septentrionale*, Paris: Leroux, 1875, extrait de la *Revue d'Anthropologie*.
— *Le Charmeur de serpents*, Paris: Hachette, 1878.
— *Les royaumes de l'Inde*, Paris: Hachette & Cie, 1879.
— *La peau du Tigre*, Paris: Hachette & Cie, 1883.
Roy, K., *Rabindranath Tagore*, New Delhi: National Gallery of Modern Art, 1988.
Said, Edward W., *Orientalism: Western Conceptions of the Orient*, London: Penguin, 1995.
Salon, Albert, *L'action culturelle de la France dans le monde Analyse critique*, Université Paris I, 1981, 3 vols.
— *L'action culturelle de la France dans le monde*, Paris: Fernand Nathan, 1983.
Salvini, J., *Le Dernier gouverneur français du Bengale, Renault de Saint-Germain, 1697–1777*, Poitiers: Société française d'Imprimerie et de Librairie, 1934, extrait du Bulletin des Antiquaires de l'Ouest, 2nd edn., 1934.
Sarkar, Benoy Kumar, *French Schools of Agriculture, Manufacture and Commerce*, Calcutta: Oriental Press, 1929.
— *India in America, the diary of . . .* (Benoy Sarkar's travels and lectures in the USA), 1949. Das Tarak Nath (ed.), Ann Arbor: Craft Press, 1949.
— *Realities in the relations between East and West*, Almora: Mayavati, 1934.
— 'La Sociographie hindoue aux débuts du capitalisme moderne', in *Revue internationale de Sociologie*, vol. 44, pp. 585–601.
— *Chinese religion through Hindu eyes: A study in the tendencies of Asiatic mentality . . .*, Shanghai, 1916.
— *The Futurism of Young Asia: and other essays on the relations between the East and the West*, Leipzig: Markert & Petters, 1922.
Sarkar, Sumit, *Modern India:1885–1947*, London: Macmillan, 1983.
Sarkar, S., *Hindustan Handbook*, Calcutta: M.C. Sarkar & Son, 1955.
Schwab, R., *La renaissance orientale*, Paris: Payot, 1950.
Siegfried, A., *Voyage aux Indes*, Colin, 1951.
Sen Gupta, Padmini, *Toru Dutt (Makers of Indian Literature)*, Delhi: Sahitya Akademi, 1982.
Singaravélou, P., *L'Ecole française d'Extrême-Orient ou l'Instituti on des marges (1898–1956)*, essai d'histoire sociale et politique de la science coloniale, Paris: l'Harmattan, 1999.
Soltykoff, Prince de, *Voyage dans l'Inde*, Paris: Garnier Frères, 1858.
— *Voyage dans l'Inde et en Perse*, Paris: V. Lecou, 1853.

Sunderland, J.L., *India in bondage*, new revised edition, New York: Lewis Copeland Cy, 1932.

Tagore, Rabindranath (listes non-exhaustive), *Cygne, Poésie du temps*, Kalidas Nag et Pierre-Jean Jouve (trad.), Paris: Stock, 1923.

— *Le naufrage*, trad. de l'anglais par Miraband-Thorens, Paris: Gallimard, 1958.

— *L'offrande lyrique* (Gitanjali), André Gide (trad.), Paris: Gallimard, 1936.

— *Les Poêmes de Kabir*, Miraband-Thorens (trad.), Paris: NRF, 1922.

— *A quatre voix*, coll. 'feuilles de l'Inde', Lyon: Derain, 1955.

— *Amal et la lettre du roi*, trad. de Gide A. Coll 'Education et théâtre', Paris: Billandot, 1954.

— *Chitra et Arjuna*. Coll. 'Feuilles de l'Inde', Chitra Publication, Gap: Ophrys, 1951.

— *Lucioles*, Paris: Chitra and Hogmann, 1930.

— *La machine*, drame en un acte, Paris: Rieder, 1929.

— *Le Naufrage*, Paris: NRF, 1929.

— *Le Vagabond et Autres Nouvelles*, C. Bossennec, K. Bhattacharya (trad.), Paris: Gallimard, 1962.

— *Souvenirs d'enfance*, C. Bossennec and R. Datta (trad.), Paris: Gallimard, 1964.

Theroulde, Saint Hubert, *Voyage dans l'Inde*, notes recueillies en 1838–1839 and 1840, Paris: Duprat, 1843.

Vaïsse, Maurice, Pierreet Melandri and Frédséric Bozzo, *La France et l'O.T.A.N. 1949–1996*, Centre d'Etudes d'Histoire de la Défense, Actes du colloques du 8-10 février 1996, Paris: Ed. Complexes, 1996.

Van Woerkens, Martine, *Le voyageur étranglé: l'Inde des Thugs, le colonialisme et l'imaginaire*, Paris: Albin Michel, 1995.

— 'Procés des Thugs en 1877', 'Les confessions d'un Thug (1839) ou les trois femmes de Amir Ali', et 'Le Fleuve de Rumer Golden (1946)', in *Rêver l'Asie*, pp. 167–77, 269–76 and 443–6.

— 'Trois barbares en Asie: une énième histoire de Thugs', in *Purusartha*, no. 11, Paris, 1988, pp. 259–86.

Vasto, Lanza Del, *Le Pèlerinage aux sources*. Coll 'Le club du meilleur Livre', Paris: Le Club français du Livre, 1951.

— *Vinôba ou le nouveau pèlerinage*, Paris: Denoël, 1954.

Verne, Jules, *Découverte de la terre*, coll. Les grands voyages, Hetzel, Paris, 1878.

— *Géographie de la France et de ses colonies*, Paris: Hetzel, 1866.

— *La maison à vapeur, voyage à travers l'Inde septentrional*, coll. les voyages extraordinaires, Paris: Hetzel.

— *Les Cinq Cents millions de la Bégum. Et les révoltés du Bounty*, Paris: Hetzel.

Vincent, Rose (dir.), *L'aventure des Français en Inde (XVIIe–XXe siècles)*, Paris-Pondichéry: Kailash, 1998.

Vulda, L., *L'Inde sous Gandhi*, Aix-en-Provence: édition du Ken, 2nd edn., 1934.

Weber, Jacques, *Pondichéry et les comptoirs de l'Inde après Dupleix: la démocratie au pays des castes*, Paris: Denoël, 1996.

— *Les établissements français en Inde au 19ème siècle (1816–1914)*, Paris: Librairie de l'Inde, 1988.

— 'L'Inde française de Dupleix à Mendés France', in *Historiens et Géographes*, no. 353, Paris, June-July 1996, pp. 201–16.

— (dir.), *Compagnies et Comptoirs. L'Inde des Français, 17–20ème*, société française d'histoire d'outre-mer, Paris, 1991.

— 'Les institutions représentatives en Inde au 19ème siècle', in *Les Cahiers du Sahib*, no. 3, Rennes: PUR, pp. 135-67.

— 'La société "franco-indienne" en péril: Désordres à Pondichéry, de Georges Delamare (1938)', in *Rêver l'Asie*, pp. 381–401.

Werner, R.P.O., *Atlas des missions catholiques*, V. Groffier (trad.), Fribourg en Brisbau: Ed B. Herder.

Willerstein, I., *Impenser la science sociale, pour sortir du 19ème siècle*, trad. par A.E. Demartini and G. Papais, Paris: PUF, 1995.

PERIODICALS

Revue d'histoire des Colonies

Revue de l'histoire des colonies, 1913–1954, Tome no. 1 à 143, Paris: Société de l'histoire des colonies françaises.

Tables bibliographiques de la revue d'histoire des colonies françaises, no. 1, Paris: Société de l'histoire des colonies françaises, 1932.

— *Tables bibliographiques de la revue d'histoire des colonies*, no. 2, vol. XLV, Paris: Société de l'histoire des colonies françaises, 1961, p. 311 à 436.

India in *Les Cahiers du Cinéma* (1950–1960), *Renoir in India and the vision of India in French cinema* (1870–1962)

'Le Tigre du Bengal et le Tombeau Hindou de Fritz Lang: Der Tiger von Eschnapur (Le Tigre du Bengale), Das Indishe Grabmal (Le Tombeau hindou)', 1959, dans *l'Avant-Scène Cinéma*, no. 339, Paris, April 1985, and no. 340, May 1985.

Bazin, Jean, 'Bio-filmographie de Jean Renoir', in *Les Cahiers du Cinéma*, no. 78, Noël 1957, Paris: édition l'Etoile, 1990 (The River, 1950, p. 82).

Bertin, Célia, *Jean Renoir, cinéaste*, Découvertes Gallimard, Paris, 1994.

Hermann, J., 'Aparajito, renaissance indienne', *Les Cahiers du Cinéma*, pp. 45–7, no. 79, June 1958, Paris: édition l'Etoile, 1991.

Marcorelles, L. 'Pather Panchali', *Les Cahiers du Cinéma*, p. 19, no. 60, June 1956, Paris: édition l'Etoile, 1990.

— 'L'Inde sans mystères', *Les Cahiers du Cinéma*, pp. 7–11, no. 110, août 1960, Paris: édition l'Etoile, 1992.

Sarkar, Kobita, 'Quelques aspects du cinéma indien', *Les Cahiers du Cinéma*, pp. 12–18, no. 110, août 1960, Paris: édition l'Etoile, 1992.

Ray, Satyajit, 'Un film est né', *Les Cahiers du Cinéma*, pp. 1–6, no. 110, août 1960, Paris: édition l'Etoile, 1992.

Renoir, Jean, 'Ce bougre de monde nouveau', *Les Cahiers du Cinéma*, no. 78, Noël 1957, Paris: édition l'Etoile, 1990, pp. 4–11.

— *Ma vie et mes films*, collection Champs Contrechamps, Paris: Flammarion, 1974.

Rivette, Jacques et François Truffaut 'Nouvel entretien avec Jean Renoir', in *Les Cahiers du Cinéma*, no. 78, Noël 1957, Paris: édition l'Etoile, 1990, pp. 11–55.

Weinberg-Thomas, Catherine, 'Le Tigre mis au tombeau: l'Inde-objet de Fritz Lang', in *Purusartha*, no. 11, Paris: EHESS, 1988, pp. 229–58.

India in Le Tour du Monde (Nouveau journal des voyages), Hachette & Cie Paris: Londres, Leipzig, bi-annual created in 1860.

— 'Voyages de circumnavigation de la frégate autrichienne, La Novara, 1857–1859, îles de St Paul, Ceylan, îles Nicobar . . .', pp. 33–66, 1st semestre, 1860.

— 'Fragments d'un voyage en Orient. Eléphant de Caban à Ceylan, scènes funéraires à Calcutta', par M.G. Peppiing, pp. 87–90, 1st semestre 1860.

— 'Les îles Andaman (Océan Indien) d'après des documents inédits de Mr Ferdinand Denis', par M.O. Maillite, pp. 90–7, 1st semestre 1860.

— 'Voyage au Malabar, 1859', par le Contre-amiral Fleuriot de Langle, pp. 33–48, 1st semestre 1860.

— 'La pagode de Chillambaram', par Mr le Contre-Amiral Paris: directeur du dépôt des plans et cartes dans la marine impériale, 1838–1844; pp. 33–48, 1st semestre 1867.

— 'Le Pandjab et le Cachemire', par Mr Guillaume Lejean, 1866; pp. 177–224, 2nd semestre 1868.

— 'Voyage dans les Provinces méridionales de l'Inde', par Alfred Grandidier, 1862–1864; pp. 1–80, 1st semestre 1869.

— 'Voyage dans les Provinces méridionales de l'Inde', par Alfred Grandidier, 1862–1864; pp. 49–160, 2nd semestre 1869.

— 'Le Pandjab et le Cachemire', par Mr Guillaume Lejean, 1866; pp. 321–52, 1st semestre 1870.

— 'L'Inde des rajahs, voyage dans les royaumes de l'Inde centrale et dans la présidence du Bengale', par Mr Louis Rousselet, 1864–1868; pp. 209–88, 2nd semestre 1871.

— 'L'Inde des rajahs, voyage dans les royaumes de l'Inde centrale et dans la présidence du Bengale', par Mr Louis Rousselet, 1864–1868; pp. 177–256, 1st semestre 1872.

— 'L'Inde des rajahs, voyage dans les royaumes de l'Inde centrale et dans la présidence du Bengale', par Mr Louis Rousselet, 1864–8; pp. 145–224, 2nd semestre 1872.

— 'L'Inde des rajahs, voyage dans les royaumes de l'Inde centrale et dans la présidence du Bengale', par Mr Louis Rousselet, 1864–1868; pp. 145–92, 1st semestre 1873.

— 'L'Inde des rajahs, voyage dans les royaumes de l'Inde centrale et dans la présidence du Bengale', par Mr Louis Rousselet, 1864–1868; pp. 272–352, 2nd semestre 1873.

— 'L'Inde des rajahs, voyage dans les royaumes de l'Inde centrale et dans la présidence du Bengale', par Mr Louis Rousselet, 1864–1868; pp. 65–161, 1st semestre 1874.

— 'Voyage à Muury, Himalaya du Nord', par Mr de Bérard, 1878; pp. 113–28, 2nd semestre 1880.

— 'Voyage dans le Nord de l'Inde, excursion à Attok sur l'Indus', par Mr de Bérard, 1878; pp. 129–44, 2nd semestre 1880.

— 'Voyage au Népal', par le dr Gustave Le Bon, chargé par le ministère de l'instruction publique d'une mission archéologique dans l'Inde, pp. 225–72, 2nd semestre 1880.

— 'Voyage d'une Parisienne dans l'Himalaya occidental (Koulou, Cachemire, Balistan, Dras)', par Mmme de Ujfalvy-Bourdon, officier d'académie, 1881; pp. 209–56, 1st semestre 1883.

— 'Voyage d'une Parisienne dans l'Himalaya occidental (Koulou, Cachemire, Balistan, Dras)', par Mmme de Ujfalvy-Bourdon, officier d'académie, 1881; pp. 353–410, 2nd semestre 1883.

— 'Huit jours aux Indes', par Emile Guimet, pp. 65–96, 2nd semestre 1888.

— 'Six mois dans l'Inde, souvenirs de voyage et de danse', par M.E. Von Leipziger, pp. 129–60, 2nd semestre 1894.

India in Les Nouvelles Géographiques supplementary to Le Tour du Monde (1893–1894)

1893: *Inde (Le dernier recensementdu Bengale)*, p. 77.
1894: *Le dernier recensement de l'Inde anglaise*, pp. 39–41.

India in a Travers le Monde, supplementary to Le Tour du Monde (1896–1913)

1896: *Le Coton aux Indes*, p. 407.
1897: *Soulèvement à la frontière Indo-afghane*, pp. 329–31.
1900: *Une visite aux affamés de l'Inde*, pp. 262–3, et *Relations entre Anglais et Indiens.*
1901: *Pourquoi Edouard 3 est-il populaire aux Indes*, p. 197, et *Le mariage et la femme aux Indes*, p. 199.
1905: *Le développement de la puissance anglaise dans le bassin de l'Océan Indien*, pp. 21–2, *Les fondements de la domination anglaise aux Indes*, pp. 150–1, *L'assainissement dans les villes de l'Inde*, pp. 331–2.
1906: *La lutte contre la famine aux Indes*, p. 47, *La plus courte voie ferrée vers les Indes*, p. 54, *Les Rapports des grands feudataires de l'Inde avec l'Angleterre*, pp. 110–11, *Les travaux d'irrigation dans l'Inde*, pp. 237–8, *Le réveil national de* l'Inde, pp. 350–1, *La Rénovation des Indes anglaises*, pp. 387–8.
1908: *L'agitation aux Indes se généralise*, p. 158, *L'Inde anglaise réclame ses libertés*, pp. 169–72, *La crise de l'Inde anglaise*, p. 244.
1909: *Femmes hindoues à la conférence de Madras*, pp. 310–11.
1910: *Assam*, p. 173.
1911: *Femmes et veuves de l'Inde*, p. 246.
1913: *La bombe de la nouvelle Delhi et le nationalisme aux Indes*, p. 350.

Index